The Civilization of the American Indian Series

Colonial Yucatan

The
Indian Background
of
Colonial Yucatan

By

RALPH L. ROYS

With an Introductory Note by

J. Eric S. Thompson

University of Oklahoma Press

Norman

By Ralph L. Roys

The Ethno-Botany of the Maya (New Orleans, 1931)

The Titles of Ebtun (Washington, D.C., 1939)

The Indian Background of Colonial Yucatan (Washington, D.C., 1943; new edition, Norman, 1972)

The Maya Chontal Indians of Acalan-Tixchel; A Contribution to the History and Ethnography of the Yucatan Peninsula (with France V. Scholes) (Washington, D.C., 1948; Norman, 1968)

The Political Geography of the Yucatan Maya (Washington, D.C., 1957)

Ritual of the Bacabs: A Book of Maya Incantations (translator and editor) (Norman, 1965)

The Book of Chilam Balam of Chumayel (translator and editor) (Washington, D.C., 1933; new edition, Norman, 1967)

International Standard Book Number: 0–8061–0996–3

Library of Congress Catalog Card Number: 70–177344

New edition copyright 1972 by the University of Oklahoma Press, Publishing Division of the University, reproduced from the first edition published by the Carnegie Institution of Washington in 1943. Manufactured in the U.S.A. First printing of the new edition, 1972.

The Indian Background of Colonial Yucatan is Volume 118 in *The Civilization of the American Indian Series.*

Preface

THE STUDIES contained in this volume have been made with the purpose of providing a background for the history of the conquest of Yucatan and of the colonial period which followed. The events of the conquest can be explained only by taking into account the part played by the native population; and the same is true of the subsequent political and social development. The latter resulted in the gradual evolution of a Hispano-Indian civilization, in which not only the Indians but also the great majority of people of mixed blood speak Maya, not Spanish, in their homes at the present time.

An attempt is made here to draw a very general picture of Yucatecan Maya civilization as the Spaniards found it at the time of the conquest, since the archaeological remains indicate that this aspect of their culture differed somewhat from their earlier civilization. This survey is accompanied by a short bibliographical sketch of the principal sources for the ethnology and history of the Maya of Yucatan and their neighbors. A complete bibliography of the authorities which have been consulted in the preparation of this study will be found in the list of references.

The cacique system discussed in these pages represented a policy in which the local government of the Indian pueblos by the natives themselves, although under Spanish supervision, was given a certain stability by maintaining the prestige, and thus securing the loyalty and cooperation, of certain families which had already governed the people in pre-Spanish times.

The Mani land treaty of 1557 presented in the appendix furnishes an illustration of the manner in which the colonial government solved the problem of transforming a collection of warring independent states into a single peaceful administrative unit.

I wish to acknowledge the cooperation of the Middle American Research Institute of Tulane University and of Mr. Frans Blom in supplying photographs of the Tulane manuscript of the Mani land treaty presented here. The study of the cacique system in Yucatan has been made possible through the aid and collaboration of Dr. A. M. Tozzer and the Peabody Museum of Harvard University in furnishing photostats of the Xiu Chronicle, the original of which belongs to the museum. Comparisons of the cacique system in Yucatan with that in Mexico have been made from a large number of documents in the Archivo General de la Nación, Mexico, selected by Dr. France V. Scholes, who obtained copies of them for the Carnegie Institution of Washington. In making the

ethnographic studies contained in this work I received much assistance and
generous hospitality from the schoolteachers of Tekax, Peto, Mama, Tixmeuac,
and Tahdziu. Finally, I wish to acknowledge the aid and advice of Dr. A. V.
Kidder, Chairman of the Division of Historical Research, who has given freely
of his time during the preparation of these studies.

March, 1943   RALPH L. ROYS

An Introductory Note

by

J. Eric S. Thompson

"OH ... that my adversary had written a book," Job bellicosely declaimed, and having myself written too many, I see his point; a book may tell you a lot about its author—too much sometimes for his good. How one comes to be written can also inform as to the character of the author; the way in which *The Indian Background of Colonial Yucatan* reached its final form does that and at the same time the story lifts a corner of the curtain on an act in which two old friends held the stage.

That lovable but at times rather vexatious character Sylvanus G. Morley, colleague and friend of both Ralph Roys and myself, was an incurable romantic, above all when it came to the Maya. Just about everything the ancient Egyptians did, the Maya, he was certain, had done as well or better. The most obvious exception to his creed was supplied by the pharaohs; the Maya had nothing to equal that succession of dynasties ruling Egypt for more than three thousand years. It wasn't only the pharaohs; the Maya could not hold a candle to the Capets or even the Normans and Plantagenets.

Vay, as Morley was always called, had an abiding interest in the Xiu, one of the chief ruling families in Yucatan at the time of the Spanish conquest and who, to strengthen their position as comparative newcomers to Yucatan, claimed that their ancestors had founded the great archaeological site of Uxmal about A.D. 1000 (in a katun which ran from A.D. 987 to A.D. 1007). Unfortunately, Uxmal had been abandoned before the date at which the first Xiu was supposed to have established himself there.

In the Peabody Museum of Archaeology and Ethnology, Harvard University, is a portfolio of documents known as the Xiu papers, since they were the private archives of that family during the colonial period. Among them is a family tree which depicts a line of descent from a certain Hun Uitzil Chac Tutul Xiu who, according to the picture (the tree grows from his loins), was head of the Tutul Xiu about a century before the arrival of the Spaniards. It covers eight generations.

About 1934, Morley began to toy with the idea that an examination of the other papers in the portfolio might extend the family tree, if not to rival Old World dynasties, at least to give a respectable antiquity to the one Maya ruling family about which a fair amount was known. Ralph Roys was the obvious choice for the job, for he was the only scholar north of the Río Grande with a sufficient knowledge of Maya to translate the documents, most of which were in that language.

Yielding to Vay's notoriously persuasive tongue, Ralph agreed to the proposal. That involved him not only in the difficult task of translating and co-ordinating the papers, but much collateral work to set them in the context of relations between the new Spanish rulers of the land and the descendants of the former Maya nobility. Moreover, the research meant abandoning for long spells his own studies—something no scholar relishes—but Ralph never turned a deaf ear to a cry for help from a colleague, and cheerfully and selflessly set to work on the new investigation. The historian France Scholes, also then on the staff of Carnegie Institution of Washington, came to his aid with more documents bearing on the problem, found in the national archives of Mexico.

In the end Roys was able to bridge the gap of about two and one-half centuries separating the last Xiu painted on the tree and the last Xiu mentioned in the papers, an entry for the year 1821.

Unfortunately, Vay, who would never use a paragraph if he could say the same in a chapter, had written his part at enormous length. Every last irrelevant detail of each one of the Xiu with their sisters and their cousins and their aunts was there with long discursive speculation about who exactly was some second cousin once removed, although such flowers blooming on the remotest twig of the family tree had nothing to do with the case.

Ralph's part of the manuscript extended far beyond the Xiu family to embrace a full investigation of the problem of the position, rights, and powers of the old Maya nobility both in pre-Columbian and colonial times as well as such matters as the highly important land treaty of 1557 with its accompanying map (see pages 175–94 of this book).

A. V. Kidder, then chairman of our division of the Carnegie Institution of Washington, realized that the manuscript as it stood was unpublishable—Vay's verbosity made that clear. He decided that the manuscript should be deposited in the library of the Peabody Museum, which already held the Xiu papers, but suggested to Ralph that he should present his material in a book covering a wider field. The result of that suggestion was the present book. The whole of the second part of *The Indian Background of Colonial Yucatan* is the material on the old nobility and the cacique system which Ralph had amassed in his researches, lifted with minor changes and compression from the stillborn collaboration. Other sections from the original manuscript are incorporated in the first part of the book.

Morley, on his part, published in his book *The Ancient Maya* (Stanford University Press, 1946) the painting of the Xiu tree and a bit about those forty generations together with photographs of the palm-thatched hut of the present Xiu and the imposing building at Uxmal traditionally called the House of the Governors, in the near-marble halls of which Vay fondly dreamed the Xiu had once dwelt. I myself in *Maya Archaeologist* added a last melancholy postscript to the Xiu saga, a letter from Gerardo Xiu's father to Morley telling of how his wife had left him and how he was ordered to pay four pesos weekly for maintenance of Gerardo and his sister. As four pesos are about thirty-five cents United States currency, the royal family had certainly fallen low.

Kind hearts are more than coronets, as we are told and Alec Guinness has demonstrated. Had it not been for Ralph's kind heart in collaborating on the (to me somewhat unpleasant) uncrowned Xiu, you, gentle reader, would not now be able to enjoy this brilliant book.

Meanwhile, Morley was busy interviewing surviving members of the family living at Oxkutzcab and nearby Mani, seat of the dynasty after the fall of Mayapan about A.D. 1450. The family had certainly come down in the world; its members were now living in simple palm-thatched huts and were almost indistinguishable from the ordinary Maya peasant. Morley succeeded in tracing the pedigree of Gerardo Xiu, born in 1943, back to the last Xiu of 1821 mentioned in the family papers. Skating on exceedingly thin ice, he boldly assumed that eighteen generations had been omitted between the founder at the bottom of the family tree and the next name written on the trunk. Thereby he carried the line back to the first Xiu supposed to have established himself at Uxmal at A.D. 1000, but as I have already noted, there is every reason to believe Uxmal had been abandoned before that date. Just conceivably the final abandonment of the site fell a decade or two later.

Thus Vay managed to raise his bid to forty generations of the royal house of Tutul Xiu, just equal to the number of rulers of England from William the Conqueror to Elizabeth II and spanning just about the same period, but Vay's cards were a very dubious full house, more like a busted royal flush.

The manuscript on the Tutul Xiu, the joint product of both investigators, was completed in 1941.

Contents

PART II. THE CACIQUE SYSTEM IN YUCATAN

Illustrations

Note: The omission of accents in this book, save in direct quotations and bibliographical references, follows the practice of the Division of Historical Research of the Carnegie Institution of Washington in its archaeological and ethnological publications. This procedure was adopted because of difficulties arising from the accenting of Maya and Hispanicized Maya place names.

PART I.
What the Spaniards Found in Yucatan

Chapter 1. The Country

THE SPANISH explorers and early settlers formed a poor opinion of the natives of the Antilles. It is hardly surprising that they should have regarded the man-eating Caribs as degraded savages; but they saw little merit in any of the islanders, although many of them were not without a considerable degree of culture. Cassava, sweet potatoes, maize, and other products were cultivated, cotton cloth was woven, and there was a little metal work in gold, but the Spaniards probably took these achievements for granted. These people had no permanent architecture, and many of them, particularly the men, went about shamelessly unclothed. In every way they fell so far short of the civilization of the Far East, as described in Toscanelli's letter to Columbus, that they puzzled the Spaniards, who at that time seem to have known little, if anything, of the more primitive peoples who comprised no small portion of the population of the East Indies.

The early voyages to the mainland were also disappointing in this respect. It was only during Columbus' fourth voyage in 1502 that more encouraging signs were noted. When he stopped at Guanaja, one of the Bay Islands off the northern coast of Honduras, he came upon a large native trading craft, by which he was deeply impressed. This was "an Indian canoe, as long as a galley, and eight foot in breadth, laden with western commodities, which it is likely belong'd to the Province of Yucatan."[1] Over the center was a canopy of mats, which sheltered the cargo and some women and children. The merchandise consisted of cacao, copper plates, hatchets and bells, flint-edged wooden swords, and a considerable quantity of colored cotton garments. The occupants were decently clothed, and it was evident that this encounter represented a contact with a civilization superior to anything the Spaniards had previously observed.

Fifteen years were to pass before a Spanish expedition landed in Yucatan, and it was still another decade later that the first attempt was made to explore the country. To the Spaniards it was indeed a strange land. Quite apart from the people and their unfamiliar culture, the country itself was unlike anything ever seen before. Here the rivers flowed underground; and although it was a well-populated agricultural area, four-fifths of the land was covered with brush or forest. The corn was often seen to grow more luxuriantly on a bare rocky knoll than on loamy soil.

[1] Herrera y Tordesillas, 1725-26 (Eng. ed.), 1: 259-60.

3

Northern Yucatan is a great rocky plain and, where not in cultivation, covered mostly by a dry forest growth. Except for a few important settlements on the southwestern and southeastern coasts, this was the most thickly inhabited part of the peninsula, and here the principal towns were found. A range of high hills divides the peninsula, and northeast of this range is the greater part of the large plain. The actual ground is mostly rough; between low limestone ridges are thin pockets of soil, much of it a reddish loam.

The northern plain has no surface streams, since the rain water seeps rapidly through the limestone rock to the water table beneath. In a few localities a deposit of some sort would appear to have prevented this infiltration, and we find a few shallow surface ponds or small lakes; but in the inhabited part of the north the water is not considered potable. Since this plain, generally speaking, rises from the northern coast at the rate of about a foot to the mile, in much of this area the ground water lies at a considerable depth and wells were difficult to dig for a people depending upon stone tools. There are, however, many cenotes, or natural wells formed by erosion, which vary somewhat in appearance. One type is a subterranean cavern, in the roof of which is a small opening above the water. In many instances, however, the entire roof has fallen in, leaving a pool of water at the bottom between perpendicular walls. Frequently one side of the surrounding wall has disintegrated and the talus slopes down to a pool of water on the opposite side; but in other cases the wall has fallen in on all sides, covering the water completely. In such depressions and in regions near the coast it was possible to dig to water. These supplies were supplemented by natural rock tanks, which are numerous, and they probably also had artificial cisterns, although few, if indeed any, have been reported from the ruined sites on the northern plain.

Beyond the sierra, as the low range of hills is called, a V-shaped plateau projects from the south into the western half of the large northern plain. Here are detached hills, and the level ground is high above the water table. Artificial wells were quite impossible to dig without iron or steel tools, and there were no cenotes. Water could be obtained by considerable effort from a few deep caves; but the main dependence was on natural and artificial reservoirs, and here fortunately the water of the surface ponds could be drunk. Although the soil is deeper and more fertile and the archaeological remains show plainly that the region had once been densely inhabited, at the time of the conquest the settlements here were few and very small. Nevertheless much of this land was cultivated by people, many of them probably the descendants of its former occupants, who came across the range and remained on their farms during the growing season but who did not reside there permanently.

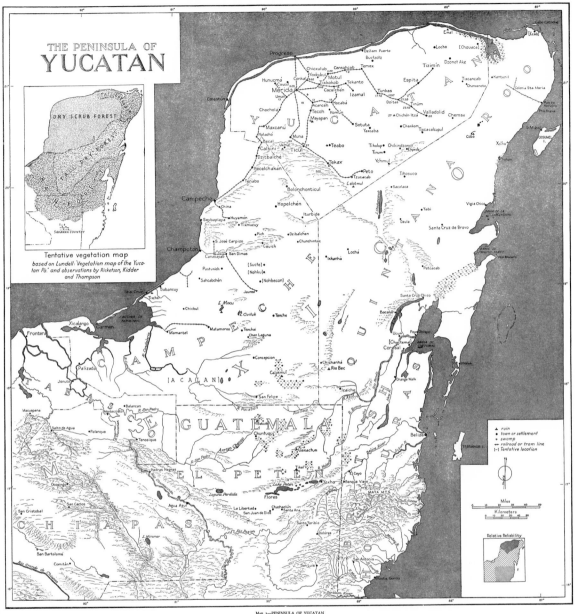

Map 1—PENINSULA OF YUCATAN
Based on Shattuck, "The Peninsula of Yucatan" (1933) and Tulane-Carnegie map of "Archaeological Sites in the Maya Area" (1940).

Figure 1—SACRED CENOTE, CHICHEN ITZA

Figure 2—AGUADA DE PANCALIENTE, CAMPECHE (AFTER ANDREWS)

FIGURE 3—SHORE ON EAST COAST LOOKING NORTH FROM TULUM
(AFTER LOTHROP)

FIGURE 4—SHORE ON NORTH COAST AT YALAHAU (AFTER STEPHENS)

On the western side of this triangular plateau another low range separated it from a coastal plain extending along the Gulf of Mexico as far south as Campeche. Here, as at the present time, were a number of towns and a prosperous farming area.

The coast of the Yucatan Peninsula was not easy for European ships to navigate, but it probably offered less difficulty to the large native trading canoes, which had a shallow draught and could easily be beached when a storm was seen approaching. Harbors are few; the low shores are lined with shoals on the west and north coasts, and fringed with dangerous reefs on the east. Along the northwestern and northern littoral extends a narrow swampy lagoon separated from the gulf by the banks and dunes of a barrier beach. Bordering the lagoon is a margin of mangrove swamp, behind which a level limestone floor slowly rises. It is covered at first by savannas or a low brushy growth, and on the dry northwestern coast are thickets of various cacti. Farther inland the vegetation increases in height, and the smooth rocky floor gradually becomes more rolling, until it turns into the succession of stony ridges and knolls so characteristic of northern Yucatan. Frequent in the coastal area and especially in the northeast are grassy savannas or other large open stretches covered by a low and rather sparse scrub. Similar tracts of open country occur, although more rarely, in the interior of northern Yucatan; but farther south, in what is known as the Chenes country of northeastern Campeche, large savannas covered with tall grass spread over hundreds of miles. The remains of many ancient cities, already long deserted at the time of the conquest, are found in the region, and Lundell suggests the possibility that these savannas are, in part at least, the result of soil exhaustion from excessive cultivation.

In spite of the flatness of the northern plain, it is so broken by limestone reefs and depressions that it can be described only as choppy, and there are great quantities of loose stone lying everywhere. The Spaniards complained of the narrow Indian trails, which were rough under foot and cut through the thick scrub high enough for only a pedestrian to pass, making travel difficult for horsemen and dangerously exposed to enemy attack. The following extract from an early report is typical of their comments: "The roads . . . are rough and stony, although the country is flat, since most of it is all living rock. It is thickly wooded, and the roads are crooked and badly cleared, while the rocks are like very bad reefs on a seacoast."[2]

Here we find the scrubby and often thorny forest growth which abounds between the tropics, where a fairly high annual rainfall is mostly restricted to a comparatively short period in the year. Since the land has been burned for

[2] Relaciones de Yucatán (hereinafter cited as RY), 2: 16.

cultivation for centuries, this scrub brush is second growth. As one travels along the roads, several species of Acacia, a mimosa, and the gumbo limbo are especially noticeable, as is an occasional great ceiba in the villages and hamlets. The breadnut, zapote, Honduras walnut, and large Spanish cedars formerly used to make canoes seem to have been more frequent in the northeast and east. Since a milpa, or cornfield, is rarely cultivated more than two or three years before it is abandoned and left to revert to forest, the overgrown fields in various stages of reforestation are now, as they always have been, a prominent feature of the landscape in any populated region. For more than a year weeds and grasses spring up luxuriantly and are followed by almost impenetrable brambly thickets, from which the scrubby secondary forest gradually emerges. Standley notes that many of the trees and plant products were already familiar to the first Spanish explorers from their previous residence in the West Indies.

South of the northern plain and north of Lake Peten, the land rises to a maximum height of 300 m. Lundell tells us that through the central and basal sections of the peninsula extend ranges of forested hills intersected by valleys, many of the latter forming extensive areas of wooded swamp, called *akalches*. These silted lakes are characteristic of the region and are difficult to cross. One of them near the large ruined site of Calakmul in southern Campeche is described as approximately 57 km. long and 19 km. wide. They are inundated during the rainy season and covered largely with thorny wiry trees rarely over 8 m. high; often there is much logwood. In the center sometimes are sawtoothed sedges. In the dry season the soil bakes and cracks, and frequently only a small pool remains in the center. Father Avendaño gives us a harrowing account of his sufferings in crossing these swamps on his return from Lake Peten in 1696. At a higher level than the akalches are surface ponds known as *aguadas* in Spanish and *akal* or *kaxek* in Maya. Many of them dry out only during unusually dry seasons, and they form the chief water supply in the central part of the peninsula. Large savannas are also reported from many parts of the country. The only actual mountains are the rugged Maya Mountains in southern British Honduras.

Short streams run into the Gulf of Mexico near Campeche and Champoton; and farther south the more extensive Candelaria system and the Rio San Pedro Martyr penetrate southwestern Campeche and northern Peten. On the Caribbean slope south of Chetumal Bay are many rivers. The three most important are the Rio Hondo, known to the Maya as the Nohukum, or "great river"; the New River, formerly called the Dzuluinic, or "river of the foreigner"; and the Belize River. These were navigable for canoes a long distance inland. A series of small lakes extends from Lake Chichankanab on the southern edge of the populated northern area to Lake Bacalar near Chetumal Bay; and similar bodies of water are reported from various parts of southern Campeche. Travel in these regions has always been difficult during the rainy season.

The scrubby vegetation of northern Yucatan extends north and west of a line roughly estimated as running east some distance from Champoton and curving toward the northeast, until it reaches a crescent-shaped area covered by a taller greener forest lying east, north, and northwest of Valladolid. Ricketson's and Kidder's aerial observations indicate that the southeastern limit of this high green forest is a short distance south of the ruins of Coba.

Southwestern Campeche is a rolling country covered by tropical rain forest. On the slopes of the hills along the new railway line running south from Campeche are zapote, mahogany, and Spanish cedar. Northeast from this rain forest extends a broad belt of dry forest; in its western part the two dominant trees are the zapote and gumbo limbo. Lundell tells of a great plain in southern Campeche, bounded on the south, east, and west by low hills and covering more than 7000 sq. km. It is locally known as the Dzequelar, a name which recalls the northern Maya *dzekel,* or *tzekel,* which means "a place abounding with loose rock." Bartlett, however, reports a habitat name from British Honduras as sequelar and derives it from the Spanish *sequeral,* "a place with dry unwatered soil." No description of the northeastern portion of the great dry forest is available, but it is bordered on the north by the scrubby area already mentioned and by the green forested area around Coba surveyed by Ricketson and Kidder from the air. Thompson has noted the gradualness of the change from the scrubby country to the taller dry forest, and he observed a marked change to rain forest a few kilometers west of Rio Bec, where he first encountered allspice and mahogany. In his journey across southern Campeche and Quintana Roo he saw no savanna country and remarked the absence of cohune palms until within 25 or 30 km. from the Rio Hondo.

South and southeast of the dry forest are the rain forests of northern Peten and southeastern Quintana Roo. Ricketson and Kidder fix the northern border of the latter at two points. One, a short distance northeast of the point noted by Thompson, is about 123 km. north of Uaxactun near the line between Campeche and Quintana Roo, and the other is approximately 40 km. north of Lake Bacalar.

Northern Peten, with its undulating uplands covered with high forests, its swampy bottoms, and its streams and lakes, has been amply described by Lundell, who gives a detailed account of the vegetation of the country. Here are dense groves of breadnut, and the zapote is especially prominent. The Maya prized the latter for its fruit and wood, and today it is still important for the chicle gum, which it produces. Other useful trees, of the several hundred species represented, are the allspice, mamey, cohune palm, copal, Spanish cedar, and mahogany.

For more than a century after the Spanish conquest of Yucatan a considerable population lived on or near Lake Peten, and there were scattered settlements to the east and south; but the rain forest immediately to the north was very sparsely inhabited. Father Avendaño wandered for more than two weeks in this region without meeting a single person. This is of interest in view of the many large ruined sites which have been found in the area. C. Wythe Cooke, of the United States Geological Survey, believes that at the time when these cities were occupied the swampy thickets were open lakes, which facilitated communication by canoe, instead of being an almost impenetrable barrier. His theory is that they later became silted. We have as yet, however, no evidence of an earlier method of cultivation more intensive than the present milpa system, which, he suggests, would have caused more rapid erosion and hastened the silting process. Morley doubts that the silting of these swamps occurred as late as the period of human occupation of the region.

South of Lake Peten is the savanna country of central Peten, which is characterized by the many flat clay grasslands lying between low forested limestone hills. In southern Quintana Roo a large area of zapote and mahogany forest is reported; and in British Honduras the Cuban pine grows on the sandy tongues of land between the rivers.

In a report by the corporation of the city of Merida written in 1581 we find an account of the climate of northern Yucatan from the standpoint of the sixteenth-century Spanish settler:

Generally this land is hot and dry, and the waters which give nourishment to the soil are those which fall from the heavens. God provides that they begin each year in May and the most efficacious of them last until the end of August. During these four months they raise their principal products which are maize, chile, beans and cotton. The crops depend on whether the rains are scanty or plentiful and come in or out of season. If water is lacking the soil immediately dries up, as it does not retain moisture. The prevailing wind is from the northeast, we call it the *brisa,* and it is the healthiest which sweeps the land, though the same is true of the east and southeast winds. But when it comes toward the south or is from the northwest or north, it has a very different effect on the native people and the Spaniards. The reason is that these are cold winds which come from the sea. Coming unexpectedly and finding the pores open from the usual heat, they cause sickness and death; and ordinarily more people die after the northers commence, which is from September until February. Some years they are so violent that they blow down the Indians' houses and uproot great trees; and if they happen to blow at the end of July and in August, they beat down and break the maize in the fields, bringing great famines in some years.[3]

Agriculture is still in many respects what it was at the time of the conquest, and a modern Yucatecan farmer's almanac offers a useful description of the seasons.[4] In January and February there are only a few light rains and the season is a pleasant one. Timber is cut for construction, granaries are built, and houses are thatched with palm leaves. March, April, and May are hot and dry, but many forest trees blossom during the first part of this period. Later the cut fields are burned and ready for planting when the rains come. June, July, and August are hot wet months and constitute the growing season. September is somewhat cooler, but the rains continue, often accompanied by wind storms. October and November are still cooler with steadily diminishing precipitation. In December there is not much rain, and the people of the country consider the weather uncomfortably cool.

Mean monthly temperatures range only from about 72° to 80° Fahrenheit on the northwest coast and from 71° to 82° at Chichen Itza, but there is a much greater difference between the lowest and highest temperatures. At Merida we find a minimum of 45° in January and February and a maximum of about 105° in March and May. At Valladolid the range in these months is from 46° to a little over 100°. Especially pronounced are the sudden variations during the winter and spring, when ranges of 40° or 50° have been recorded during a single month. According to the old report which we have quoted, however, it would appear that a rapid change in temperature affected the health of the people most seriously, when it was accompanied by a north wind and little warmth could be retained in the cage-like homes of the poorer people. The plastered wall dividing the houses of the more prosperous would furnish somewhat more protection. The tropical hurricanes and northers mentioned in the report are important climatic features; and along the flat northern coast the latter, especially when accompanied by an exceptionally heavy rainfall, sometimes flood the country for miles inland. At Chicxulub, 16 km. from the coastal lagoon, people tell of northers which have inundated the town to a depth of a meter or more.

Page shows a very considerable geographical variation in the rainfall of the peninsula. Except for a narrow very dry strip along the northwest coast, a wider coastal belt extending from Campeche nearly to Chetumal Bay has a range of 30–40 inches. Farther inland is a large area with 40–60 inches, increasing toward

---

[3] RY, 1: 45. Cf. Roys, 1931, pp. 345–46.
[4] Espinosa E. and Espinosa H., 1928; Roys, 1931, pp. 345–46.

the south, until in northern Peten an average of 65 inches is reported by Lundell. In northern Yucatan the annual rainfall increases from west to east. Computed for various periods of years during the first third of the present century, it is 34.33 inches in Merida, 39.80 inches at Izamal, 46.69 inches at Chichen Itza, and 47.50 inches at Valladolid. Farther east we have no records, but Thompson states that in the rain forest around the ruins of Coba it is obviously still greater. The dry coastal belt on the west coast ends south of Campeche, and at Champoton the annual rainfall is 51 inches.

This, of course, by no means covers the situation, for there have always been cycles of wet and dry years, which meant the difference between plenty and famine to an agricultural population. Between 1895 and 1928 the annual rainfall at Merida has ranged from 16 inches in 1902 to 64 inches in 1916, and in northern Peten from 35 inches to 93 inches during 1928 and 1929.

Another important factor, especially from the farmer's standpoint, is the distribution of the rainfall during the year. In the well-populated western portion of northern Yucatan 80–90 per cent of the annual precipitation occurs during the farmer's growing season from May to October. This compensates for the lighter annual rainfall in this region, since it comes when it is most needed, but it is not generally good for the forests. Farther east it is 70–80 per cent, and in the rain forests of the south and east it is 60–70 per cent, which is more favorable to the forest growth. It would seem probable that these factors have had an important influence on the shifting of centers of population which occurred during the centuries preceding the Spanish conquest.

Drought and its disastrous consequences play an important role in the native Maya literature. At such times people deserted the towns, leaving the aged and infirm to starve, and scattered in the forests, where they lived on the fruit and roots of wild trees and plants. In this connection we find especial mention of the breadnut, ear tree, *cup* (apparently a vine with a fleshy root identified as *Calopogonium coeruleum* Benth.), *baatun* (a name applied in Peten to *Anthurium tetragonum* Hook.), and the zapote, or sapodilla.[5] Lundell and Bartlett note a high correlation of the breadnut and *A. tetragonum* with the presence of ancient ruins in Peten; and Bartlett has suggested that the abundance of the zapote over a very large area may be due to its being spared by the ancient Maya farmers, when they cleared their milpas. Ciudad Real, a famous sixteenth-century Maya scholar who spent most of his life in Yucatan, observed during a journey through Chiapas that the *pich,* or ear tree, was especially fruitful in years when the maize crop failed.

[5] Roys, 1931, pp. 226, 272, 275; 1933, pp. 103, 120, 122, 133; 1939, pp. 54, 291; Lundell, 1937, p. 162.

At the time of the conquest the Maya-speaking portion of the peninsula was divided into approximately eighteen territorial divisions, most of which might be designated as independent states. Certainly each of these subdivisions was independent of its neighbors. Some of them possessed a well-organized political system headed by a single ruler; others were more or less closely knit confederacies of towns or groups of towns; still others seem to have been merely collections of towns in a given area, whose relations with one another are largely a matter of conjecture. The Spanish conquerors and early settlers called these territorial divisions provinces (*provincias*), and I shall continue to give them this designation. In Maya we sometimes find the word *cuchcabal* employed, but the word really means jurisdiction and seems to be applied to the district subject to a single town or ruler. I offer tentatively the following list of "provinces," but it will probably be subject to some correction, when we learn more about the ethnography of the country.

Cozumel, or Cuzamil	Chakan
Ecab, or Ekab	Sotuta
Chetumal, or Chactemal	Hocaba and Homun
Chikincheel, or Chauaca	Tutul Xiu, or Mani
Tazes	Ah Canul
Cupul	Canpech
Cochuah ,	Champoton
Ah Kin Chel	Cehaches
Ceh Pech	Tayasal, or Tah Itza

Some of these so-called provinces were named for the leading family or lineage of the district, such as Cupul, Cochuah, Ah Kin Chel, Ceh Pech, Tutul Xiu, and Ah Canul; others like Chactemal, Chauaca, Sotuta, Hocaba and Homun, Canpech, and Champoton took the names of their principal towns; a few names like Cozumel ("place of the swallows"), Chikincheel ("west woods"), and Chakan ("savanna") appear to be descriptive. In the list, it will be noted, some of them have more than one name. Chikincheel was also called Chauaca, or Chauacha, and Tutul Xiu, Mani after their principal towns. Cozumel, Chetumal, and Tayasal were Spanish adaptations of the actual Maya names, which follow in each case.[6]

From the Maya records of various land agreements which were made in colonial times it has been possible to map the Provinces of Sotuta and Mani and trace the western and southern boundaries of Cupul. Much of this material has

[6] Molina Solis (1896, pp. 212–13) tells of a Province of Zipatan in northwestern Yucatan, but I have been unable to find confirmation of this statement. I do, however, find the expression, "here in the district of Zipatan Yucatan Merida" (*uai tu petenil Sipatan Yucatan ti ho lae*), but I doubt that it refers to the area described by Molina Solis (Doc. de tierras de Chicxulub, p. 25).

already been published, and the remainder is presented elsewhere in this volume.[7] We also know from the published sixteenth-century reports the names and locations of many of the principal towns of the other provinces; and much information regarding their boundaries exists in the Crónica de Calkini and the documents discovered and photographed by France V. Scholes in the Spanish archives at Seville. The boundaries, which have already been traced, and the general location of the other native states of the peninsula are shown in Map 4.

Our knowledge of the historical antecedents of these territorial divisions is fragmentary and extremely vague for the period prior to the middle of the fifteenth century. According to some of the native accounts, Chichen Itza had formerly governed the entire country for about 200 years, and it does seem probable that this was more or less true of most of northern Yucatan, although we also find a statement that Uxmal, Chichen Itza, and Mayapan ruled the area during this length of time. A similar claim was made for Mayapan during a later period, and although we have some evidence that northern Yucatan from the Gulf of Mexico east to Cupul was, for a time at least, subject to a joint government located at this city, it is doubtful that its hegemony included Campeche and Champoton. Indeed, it appears possible that it did not extend to the east coast of the peninsula.[8]

We do know, however, that when the joint government existing at Mayapan was disrupted and the city destroyed about a century before the final Spanish conquest, certain important families who had lived there established a number of independent states: the Canul in Ah Canul, the Chel in Ah Kin Chel, the Cocom in Sotuta, and the Xiu in Mani. Evidence also exists that the Euan family of Caucel, the principal town of Chakan, and the Pech of Ceh Pech had already been governing their towns from Mayapan before its fall, since the various "lords" who were the members of the joint government resided at the capital.

[7] Roys, 1939, pp. 6–21; appendix below.
[8] RY, 1: 242; Brinton, 1882, p. 102.

Chapter 2. First Impressions

WHEN FRANCISCO HERNANDEZ DE CORDOBA discovered Yucatan in 1517, he found evidence of a new culture definitely superior to anything with which the Spaniards had previously met in the New World. His expedition appears to have landed first at Mujeres Island just off the northeast coast of the peninsula.[1] Here were some salt beds and several stepped pyramids on which were found a number of idols believed to represent women. The latter circumstance was the reason they gave the place its name. No settlement of any importance seems to have been noted here, but the discoverers are said to have been much astonished at the temples. The pyramids and temple walls were of stone, but the roofs are reported to have been thatched.

At Cape Cotoche, a short distance farther north, they came to a town larger than any they had seen in the West Indies and which they named "Gran Cayro." There can be little doubt that it was the town of Ecab, which was very close to Cape Cotoche and where, according to native tradition, the Spaniards first landed in Yucatan.[2] Out to the ships paddled a number of large dugout canoes, some of them holding as many as forty Indians, who were dressed in sleeveless jackets and loincloths. Their chief, making signs to the Spaniards to come ashore and visit his town, is said to have called to them, *"conex cotoche,"* which means "Come to our houses." The newcomers took this to be the name of the site and called the cape Cotoche.

The invitation was accepted, although not without some misgivings, and the Spaniards even availed themselves of some of the native craft to go ashore. They went well provided with firearms and crossbows as well as swords and lances or pikes, but seem to have stopped and hesitated from time to time as they proceeded toward the town. The chief continued to press his invitation. Suddenly, as they approached a wooded spot, the chief gave a signal, and a body of warriors sprang from ambush and vigorously attacked them. This force was armed with bows and arrows, spears, slings, and the flint-edged wooden swords Columbus had already seen at Guanaja fifteen years before. They were protected with shields and quilted cotton armor. A number of the Spaniards

---

[1] Saville casts doubt on Cordoba's visit at Mujeres Island, but he notes that a Point "Magieles" already appears in Apianus' 1520 map. Juan Diaz' account of the Grijalva expedition, although it did not land there, associates the site with "women who live without men," and since the latter was also published in 1520, it is difficult to see how the association with women at the place could have originated if Cordoba had not already visited it (Saville, 1918, p. 448; Juan Diaz, 1939, p. 24).

[2] RY, 2: 173–74; Roys, 1933, p. 81.

were wounded and two of them afterward died; but the attacking party apparently was not a large one and was soon defeated with a loss of fifteen killed and two prisoners, whom the visitors carried off to serve as interpreters for a future occasion.

As this was the first time the Spaniards encountered the Maya on their own soil and the latter could have known little of the efficacy of European arms, it would be of considerable interest to know whether deliberate treachery had been planned from the first. The Spaniards were naturally convinced that such was the case. Ecab, however, was evidently a large commercial town, whose people could hardly have been unaccustomed to dealing with peoples of strange languages and cultures. There was an extensive canoe trade between the east coast of Yucatan and the population of the Caribbean coast for a long distance to the southeast; and the settlements of the Nahuatl-speaking Desaguadero and Sigua of Nicaragua and Panama were probably outposts of Mexican and Yucatecan commerce.[3] Furthermore, gifts had been accepted by the natives and friendly relations established with the chief and others who had come aboard the ships. Although it is possible that repercussions of the Spanish invasion of Veragua or those of a more recent slave-raiding expedition to the Bay Islands had already aroused the implacable hostility of the coast towns of Yucatan, it would seem more in keeping with their previous conduct elsewhere if some of the Spaniards, careless, arrogant, and ignorant of native conventions, had done something which provoked the attack. It is obvious that the Spanish leaders had no desire to antagonize the Indians on this particular occasion.

Near the scene of the fight was a small square with three stone temples. Here were found clay idols, some of them thought to resemble devils and others apparently effigies of women. In small wooden chests were other idols and a number of small articles made of a mixture of gold and copper, among them thin disks, crowns, fish, and ducks. Evidently these temples outside the town and near the seashore were frequented by fishermen and hunters.

Cordoba then sailed westward around the peninsula to Campeche, where the natives inquired by signs whether the Spaniards had come from the east and, to the astonishment of the latter, pronounced the words "Castilan, Castilan." Bernal Diaz, who was present at the time, later associated this with the fact that two shipwrecked Spaniards had long been held captive on the east coast; but it seems equally probable that the name of the Spaniards had been carried, directly or indirectly, by native traders along the coast from Veragua, or perhaps from the Bay Islands. Whether, as Fiske has suggested, news of the

[3] Lothrop, 1940, p. 427.

Spaniards had traveled to Yucatan from the West Indies is difficult to determine. There is no record of commercial relations between these two regions; but we know that Grijalva the following year encountered a Jamaican woman who had been cast away on the shore of Cozumel. All the men of her party had been promptly sacrificed. Chilam Balam's revival of an old prophecy that strange men would come from the east may well have been inspired by Columbus' voyage to the Guanajas and the northern coast of Honduras, as it was supposed to have been delivered soon after the turn of the century.[4]

The impressions received by the Spaniards at Cotoche were further confirmed at Campeche. They were invited to come to the town and were conducted to some large temples of lime and stone, set on pyramids. Here an altar stained with blood showed signs of a recent human sacrifice; and they saw idols, figures of serpents, and fierce animals, and what appeared to be painted representations of crosses. The serpent was a well-known religious symbol found everywhere in the Maya and Mexican areas. The cross was a conventionalized tree, probably personified, and associated with rain ceremonies; in every wayside shrine today it is still painted green. The fierce animals may have been gods, but more likely they represented the Mexican military orders, which had been introduced into Yucatan. We find frequent reference to them in the Maya prophecies.

At first the chief seemed cordial, and some trading with the Indians ensued, during which the Spaniards are said to have acquired cotton mantles, featherwork, and objects of tortoise shell and gold. Later the attitude of the natives changed. Men dressed in shabby mantles, perhaps slaves, brought a quantity of dry reeds, and two companies of armed warriors stationed themselves near by. Then ten priests robed in long white mantles and carrying clay braziers of burning incense came out of a temple and indicated by signs that the reeds would be burned and the Spaniards must depart before they were consumed. The fire was lighted and the priests silently withdrew. The warriors began to sound their whistles, trumpets, and drums, and the Spaniards prudently left the scene and promptly embarked.

The next stop was at Champoton, where they landed to fill their water casks. Here armed natives quietly approached and by signs asked the same question as at Campeche. The Spaniards spent the night on shore, but by morning a large army of Indian warriors had assembled and began to attack them. The visitors stood their ground for a time, but the Indian forces were too great for them. Two were captured (and no doubt later sacrificed), fifty

[4] Roys, 1933, p. 187. Chilam Balam was a Maya prophet, who lived a short time before the Spanish conquest.

were killed, and almost all the remainder wounded, some of them mortally. The Spaniards retreated and embarked with difficulty, leaving their water casks behind them.

These events of Cordoba's voyage will be familiar to most readers, but a brief summary of them seems relevant here, since in our study of the Maya religion some attempt will be made to discuss the problem of the effect of the Kukulcan prophecies on the native attitude toward the Spaniards. As we shall see, the facts are confusing. Some of the Maya were evidently opportunists who hoped to turn the invasion to their own advantage; others were reluctant appeasers who temporized with the invaders; but there were many who, in spite of a certain supernatural awe in which the Spaniards were held, bitterly resisted them from first to last.

Chapter 3. Towns and Buildings

ANY ATTEMPT to reconstruct a picture of the Yucatecan Maya towns at the time of the conquest is destined to prove unsatisfactory. Nevertheless we are able to form some idea of their appearance from the rather scanty descriptions which have come down to us from the conquerors and early Spanish settlers.

It is difficult to escape the conclusion that many of the coast towns presented a very different appearance from those of the interior. We find many references to stone houses on the coast, but in the interior, except for the few contemporary temples of which we have any description, there is little indication that many buildings with stone walls were in actual use at the time, although abandoned vaulted structures were everywhere in evidence. To the Spaniards the culture of the coast in general seemed superior to that of the interior. In a report from Valladolid we are told that "these Indian men and women of Chauaca have keener minds than those of the other provinces; and the people of Chikincheel, both men and women, are more precise in what they say and more polished in their language, although the latter is everywhere the same in Yucatan." These people called the Cupuls and Cochuahs of the interior "Ah Mayas, despising them as mean and base people of low minds and propensities."[1]

Neither on the coast nor in the interior do the towns appear to have been regularly laid out in streets. This is specifically stated of the village of Zama and of such larger towns as Chauaca and Campeche. It is probable, however, that certain paved avenues in some towns led from the center to the outskirts, presumably to the ceremonial entrances of the town at the four cardinal points. Juan Diaz, the chaplain of Grijalva's expedition, tells us that one of the towns on Cozumel Island had paved concave streets raised on either side. Remesal notes that the houses of Campeche were widely separated from one another, and Oviedo states that Chauaca occupied a very large area, so it is probable that this was true of the coast towns generally. A large market square was reported at Cachi and beside it was a building which housed a court where disputes were settled. Champoton was enclosed with walls of dry stone and a ditch. Chamberlain and I noted the remains of a similar ditch and rampart at Ake.[2]

[1] RY, 2: 14, 22.
[2] Oviedo y Valdes, 1851–55, bk. 33, ch. 5; Roys, 1937.

There were many stone houses in the Cozumel towns; some had stone-and-mud masonry halfway up the walls, but all seem to have been thatched with straw. Oviedo, referring probably to the central part of the town, tells us that at Chauaca most of the houses were of hewn stone and the greater part of the inhabitants were "lords," burghers *(ciudadanos)*, and merchants. Another description of this town states that their houses were "of stone masonry thatched with straw, where they had their assemblies and markets . . . , the inhabitants *(vecinos)* of that town having their large houses of wood, very strong, thatched with palm leaves."[3] This suggests that the stone structures were public buildings and perhaps also homes of persons holding official positions. Both Juan and Bernal Diaz tell of stone houses at Champoton. Oviedo describes the town as having a very large number of thatched stone houses and some flat roofs *(azoteas)*. This is the only mention of the use of the azotea in Yucatan at the time of the conquest that has come down to us, but such roofs have been found in the ruins of Tulum on the east coast.

We have no detailed description of the stone dwellings. They may well have resembled those which had once existed in an earlier period at Chichen Itza, where we find them pictured in the frescoes. Those excavated by Wauchope are rectangular, with a single room or several side by side opening on a porch in front. Even on the coast, however, most of the dwellings, with the stockade or wattle walls often daubed with mud, were no doubt of the perishable materials we find in Yucatan today. Remesal is probably describing houses with stockade walls when he tells us that at Campeche they were constructed of cane and resembled cages. Walls of horizontal wattle are still common at Dzilam on the north coast.

The temples of the coast towns seem to have aroused more interest in the Spaniards than did those which they found in actual use in the interior. They were stepped pyramids, sometimes large, which were ascended by stone stairways and surmounted by small superstructures which the Spaniards called chapels. Many of these edifices had thatched roofs, but some, especially at Cozumel, are said to have been roofed with slabs of stone and were probably vaulted. Possibly others had flat, beamed roofs like those found in the ruins of Tulum. On Mujeres Island only thatched temples were reported, although a ruined vaulted structure is still to be seen there. One temple on Cozumel is described as rectangular, with a door on each side and a corridor extending around the central chamber, and roofed with thatch. At the foot of the pyramid was a court enclosed by a battlemented stone wall, and "in the midst of it

[3] RY, 2: 13–14.

a cross of white lime three yards high, which they held to be the god of rain."[4] Besides the larger temples, Juan Diaz counted on the shore of the island a number of small "towers," one of which was only eight spans long and about the height of a man. These were probably shrines of fishermen, for similar structures have been found on the east coast of Yucatan. Large white temple pyramids were observed at Campeche and Champoton, both in the towns and on the shore, and one at the latter town was built on a reef some distance out in the water. Besides the masonry platform at Campeche, with its sculptured figures of serpents and fierce animals, one chronicler also tells of an arrangement of beams for punishing criminals, but we may well surmise that it was something like the Mexican *tzompantli,* or skull rack, on which the skulls of sacrificed captives were preserved and displayed.

The Spaniards were evidently less impressed by the contemporary architecture in the interior of Yucatan. Montejo, in an early letter to the Crown, has little to say of the temples and other buildings, but he writes: "The land is well populated with large cities and towns, very fresh [with verdure]; every town is an orchard of fruit trees."[5] The newcomers were struck with the magnificence of the ancient monuments, few of which appear to have been in use at the time of the conquest. Uxmal was deserted, and I can find no record of any town still existing on the ground of the great ruined city of Izamal until the founding of the monastery there in 1552. The handsome remains at Merida were covered by a dense growth of forest, and Montejo found only a miserable village of thatched huts near the site. Although it is true that pilgrims still made sacrifices at the Sacred Cenote of Chichen Itza, the settlement there was small and the large edifices had greatly deteriorated.[6]

A Maya town described by Landa is no doubt typical of the interior of the country, where he had traveled extensively before the Spaniards had time to effect many changes in the manner of living:

Before the Spaniards had conquered that country, the natives lived together in towns in a very civilized fashion. They kept the land well cleared and free from weeds, and planted very good trees. Their dwelling place was as follows:— in the middle of the town were their temples with beautiful plazas, and all around the temples stood the houses of the lords and the priests, and then (those of) the most important people. Thus came the houses of the richest and

---

[4] Herrera y Tordesillas, 1725–26, 2: 121.

[5] Documentos inéditos del archivo de las Indias (hereinafter cited as DII), 13: 87.

[6] Brinton, 1882, p. 243. According to Brinton (*ibid.,* pp. 195, 218) the words *te xebna* in the Chronicle of Chac Xulub Chen are translated "rest in these houses"; but an unpublished version of the same narrative (Doc. de Tierras de Chicxulub, p. 23) renders the text as *te xelebna,* which could be translated as "those are broken or cracked houses there." Cf. "Xelbil, a pedazos. Grieta" (Pio Perez, 1866–67, p. 392).

of those who were held in the highest estimation nearest to these, and at the outskirts of the town were the houses of the lower class. And the wells, if there were but few of them, were near the houses of the lords; and they had their improved lands planted with wine trees and they sowed cotton, pepper and maize, and they lived thus close together for fear of their enemies, who took them captive, and it was owing to the wars of the Spaniards that they scattered in the woods.[7]

Although the fear of enemies may have caused a concentration of the population in some places, we have evidence that many people were scattered in small hamlets in pre-Spanish times.

As on the coast, the towns were not laid out in regular streets. Nevertheless every town had four ceremonial entrances at the cardinal points marked by a stone mound on either side, and a road led from each of these to the center, where the more important inhabitants resided. The larger towns were composed of subdivisions, of which we know little.[8] They were widely spread out, as each house had a large yard, and we find that on order of Lopez Medel clumps of trees (arboledas) should be cut down unless they were fruit trees. Dwellings are said to have been set on high places where possible. These were doubtless in some cases artificial house mounds but perhaps more often natural rocky hummocks. The latter are still favorite house sites in the smaller hamlets of eastern Yucatan. This custom and the fact that houses rarely faced the west, whence came the unhealthy winds, would contribute to the irregular appearance of the town.

We find no mention of the stone fences which enclose the yards of most native homes today, but we do read of fences of gumbo limbo posts, which take root when set in the ground.[9] It is difficult, however, to believe that stone fences did not exist in a country abounding with loose stone.

Dwellings in the interior of Yucatan were thatched, and few had stone walls. In reports written in 1581 we read that only caciques now had stone houses and that this was in imitation or on account of the Spaniards. Wooden houses were considered cooler and healthier. The most complete description of a Maya dwelling is by Landa, who writes:

[7] Landa, 1941, pp. 62–64.

[8] One of the parcialidades, or subdivisions, of Tekax was named Petcah, which means "round town." The names of several at Ppencuyut were not unlike ordinary place names. Archivo General de Indias (hereinafter cited as AGI), Tekax trial, 1609–10, Escribanía de Cámara 319C; Archivo General de la Nación, Mexico (hereinafter cited as AGM), Cuenta e visita del pueblo de Ppencuyut, 1584, Tierras 2809, no. 20.

[9] RY, 1: 167. The sixteenth-century Motul dictionary mentions a wooden fence (cololche), a wattle fence (tulum che), and a wall or fence of dry stone (cot, ticin cot), but the last may have been introduced by the Spaniards. Wauchope does not mention finding any pre-Spanish stone fences in the course of his investigations of dwellings at Chichen Itza.

The way that they built their houses was to cover them with straw which they have of very good quality and in great abundance, or with palm leaves, which is very well fitted for this, and they have steep slopes, so that rain water may not penetrate. And then they build a wall in the middle dividing the house lengthwise, leaving several doors in the wall into the half which they call the back of the house, where they have their beds; and the other half they whitened very nicely with lime. And the lords have their walls painted with great elegance; and this half is for the reception and lodging of their guests. And this room has no doors, but is open the whole length of the house; and the slope of the roof comes down very low in front on account . . . of sun and rain. And they say that this is also for another object, to control their enemies from within in time of need.[10]

The kitchen may have been in a small separate building, as it is today.

House walls are described as being of poles lashed in place with vines. These were probably the stockade walls so familiar in Yucatan today, where vertical poles are bound to horizontal stringers on the outside; but there can be no doubt that there were many wattled walls as well. Walls were often daubed with mud on the outside. The ground plan of the pole-and-thatch house at the time of the conquest is difficult to determine. Both rectangular and oval (or apsidal) houses are in use today, and the latter form is by far the most general; but we find no mention of it by any of the explorers or the Spanish colonial writers.[11]

Multiple-family houses were evidently numerous. Bienvenida, writing in 1548, states that, "there is hardly a house which has only one citizen *(vecino)*. On the contrary every house has two, three, four, six, and some still more; and among them is a paterfamilias who is the head of the house."[12] Although this manner of living was forbidden by the Ordinances of Lopez Medel in 1552, we still find such houses in Cozumel in 1570. It is probable, however, that this was not everywhere the custom, for Landa tells us that during the first years of marriage young men lived in small houses near those of their fathers or fathers-in-law.

Although we have many early descriptions of the ancient temples at Merida, Uxmal, Izamal, and Chichen Itza, we find little in the early Spanish reports

[10] Landa, 1941, pp. 85–86. In eastern Yucatan we are told that the eaves came down to the ground except on the east side where the door was (RY, 2: 191).

[11] Wauchope (1940, pp. 233–34) notes that the apsidal form is very early at Uaxactun in the Peten but believes that "sixteenth-century houses in Yucatan were probably rectangular." He admits that "Yucatecan dwellings have been prevailingly apsidal since at least 1843 and probably earlier"; but it should also be noted that Scholes and I found the remains of a stone apsidal structure at the deserted Xiu town of Calotmul south of Tzuccacab, which disappears from history after the middle of the seventeenth century (Scholes, 1939, p. 253). Apsidal stone houses are frequent in Yucatan today, but the question of their existence in the sixteenth century lies beyond the scope of this study.

[12] Cartas de Indias, 1877, pp. 77–82.

about those which were found in current use in the interior of the country. Landa refers to a number of temple ceremonies and to a temple patio or enclosure, but descriptions of the structure itself are brief and rare. At Valladolid we read of a very high rounded stone pyramid surmounted by a white apartment, which could be seen from a great distance. At Cacalchen also the temple is described as a small stone building set on a substructure, but in neither case is anything said about the roof. Landa's reference to the occasional rebuilding or renovation of the temples suggests the use of perishable materials in their construction.

The contrast between the contemporary architecture of the interior and the imposing monuments of the past represents only one aspect of a change which had evidently been going on for some time. We shall note other evidences of it in the course of this study, as it formed an important part of the social and political background of the Yucatecan Maya. The ancient structures naturally aroused the curiosity of the Spaniards. Some of the Indians told them that they were the work of their own ancestors, while others ascribed them to foreigners whom the natives of the country had killed. A great revolution had occurred about the middle of the fifteenth century, resulting in the end of a centralized government and the destruction of its capital at Mayapan, "the last notable city which the natives had." The country now broke up into a number of small independent states, which were constantly at war with one another. Mayapan was indeed a large fortified stone city, but its remains are so much less impressive than those of Uxmal, Chichen Itza, and other ancient centers of population, that one is tempted to believe that an architectural decline had already set in before its fall. It would appear, however, that if the coast towns also suffered from this decline, it was less marked than in the interior.

Chapter 4. Physical Appearance and Costume

LANDA DESCRIBES the Yucatecan Maya as a people of pleasing appearance and tall stature, robust and very strong. The present Indians, however, are not tall. Steggerda finds that the average stature for the adult male is only 5 ft. 1 in. and that they are shorter than most other Indians, even when they are born. They have large chests and wide shoulders, and their arms are long in relation to their height. The head is broad, and it is common to see a prognathous upper jaw, a retreating chin, and a prominent curved nose. The beard is sparse and coarse.

At the time of the conquest the head was flattened in infancy by pressure between two slightly concave pieces of wood. A squint was much admired, and this was achieved by hanging a small disk of pitch from the child's hair, so that it would dangle in front of the eyes. We are told that women filed their teeth to a point, and the archaeologists show that men also mutilated their teeth in various ways.

The one indispensable article of male attire was the loincloth *(ex)*, a long narrow cotton band dyed various colors. It passed between the legs and three or four times around the waist, and the ends, which hung down in front and behind, were frequently ornamented with embroidery or featherwork. Every man, even a slave, wore or carried a mantle. This was a large square of cloth, which passed under the right arm and was knotted over the left shoulder. It could be either white or colored, and was sometimes decorated with feathers. Generally speaking, the commoners dressed much more plainly than the nobles.

Another garment, worn only by the upper class, was the *xicul,* a short sleeveless jacket, which was brightly colored, often striped or interwoven with feathers. It was probably introduced from Mexico in preconquest times, for its name is evidently a variation of the Aztec *xicolli.* Sandals *(xanab)* were sometimes, but not always, worn. They were made of henequen or stiff dry-tanned deerskin and attached to the foot with a cord, which passed between the toes and fastened behind the heel.

Men cut or scorched the hair from the crown of the head but left over the forehead a fringe, which was pushed up to form a crest and bound by a thin colored band of the bark of a wild fig tree. The hair grew long behind. It was braided, fastened with colored yarn or feathers, and coiled at the back of the head, with a tassel-like end left hanging down. Sometimes a cloth was wound about the head like a turban.

The face and body were painted and tattooed. The paint was usually a mixture of red earth or soot with resin. Unmarried youths painted themselves black, as did everybody during fasts and penances, but their elders generally chose red and black. Young men tattooed themselves but little until marriage or even until the age of twenty-five. Only valiant warriors might tattoo their hands. The designs are said to have consisted largely of eagles, snakes, and other birds and animals. The pattern was first painted on the flesh and then cut in, after which the colors were rubbed on—a process that amounted practically to scarification. The wounds were apt to fester, and the method was altogether a very painful one.

Much jewelry was worn by the members of the upper class. Collars and bracelets were of red shell or green stone beads, sometimes jade. One highly prized ornament was a carved shell or jade pendant, which was hung over the breast. Earplugs were made of jade, a certain cheap blue or green stone, and of small sticks covered with gold leaf. We surmise that, as in Tabasco, they were also made of obsidian. The septum of the nose was pierced, and a long bead of the yellow topaz called amber was inserted. We also find representations of a bead button worn in the nostril. Men carried mirrors, probably of obsidian or iron pyrites, on the back or shoulder.

Women frequently went nude to the waist, wearing only a short skirt which hung just below the knees. Many, however, also wore a light, loosely woven scarf, which passed under one armpit, covered the breast, and was thrown over the other shoulder, sometimes covering the head. A short sleeveless garment like a chemisette is also described; and in Bacalar and Campeche a folded cloth was tied over the breast, passing beneath the arms. A large mantle, used as a bed cover, was sometimes worn but more often carried folded or rolled. Women usually went barefoot but wore sandals when on the road. The hair was coiled on either side of the head in a handsome coiffure.

Women are said to have painted and tattooed themselves, but only on the arms, back, and shoulders. Those who could afford it mixed the paint with a resin of sweetgum, now found only in British Honduras. Like the men, they wore earplugs and nose beads.

Chapter 5. Manners and Customs

MAYA WOMEN were prolific and children were much desired. Childless women prayed and made offerings to the deities for offspring, especially to the goddess Ix Chel, whose image was placed under the bed during childbirth. Soon after the child was born, an augury was made by the priests, and a childhood name was bestowed.[1] Children went naked until the age of four or five, when the boys were given a loincloth and the girls, a skirt. As a mark of childhood the former wore a stone bead fastened to the hair and the latter, a red shell or shell bead suspended in front from a cord around the loins as a token of virginity.

Later came the important ceremony of baptism. Authorities disagree as to the age at which it was performed, but we may surmise that it was a puberty ceremony, since the mark of childhood and virginity was removed and it was considered a license to marry. The feast was given by one of the principal men of the town in his yard or compound. Aided by four temple assistants, the priest administered the rite to the assembled children. The place was ceremonially purified and the evil spirits driven out. A burnt offering of ground maize and incense was made, and with elaborate ceremonies the children were sprinkled and anointed with holy water. After the children were dismissed, the parents made gifts to the priest, assistants, and guests, and there was much feasting and deep drinking.

It seems very possible that this elaborate ritual, perhaps even any baptism at all, was a prerogative of the ruling class, which, as we shall see, believed itself to be of foreign origin. Lopez Medel tells us that baptism was not obligatory or general. An initiation ceremony, however, was also performed at the temple, where all the boys and girls of the town were assembled. Here an old woman, known as "the conductress" and clad in a feather dress, struck each of them nine light blows on the back of the hand. This was to make them skillful in the crafts and other occupations of their fathers and mothers.[2]

---

[1] The modern domestic ceremony called *hetzmek* and performed at the age of three or four months, when a child is first carried astride its mother's hip, probably dates from pre-Spanish times (Redfield and Villa, 1934, p. 189).

[2] Lopez Medel, 1941, p. 226; ch. 9, *infra;* Landa, 1941, p. 15 and note. Lizana states that an unbaptized person would be possessed of the devil, and Gaspar Antonio Chi, that he could neither marry nor become a priest and would suffer more in hell than one who had been baptized (Lopez de Cogolludo, 1867–68, bk. 4, ch. 6; RY, 1: 51). The latter was a noble and the son of a priest, and I believe that these statements represented the views of the ruling caste, whose religious beliefs and methods of burial differed in some respects from those of the common people. Lopez Medel was a careful observer, and his statements can usually be relied upon.

At puberty, and probably even earlier, the sexes were separated until marriage, and, except for their parents, the unmarried had little to do with the married. The youths slept in a large open public building, where they also gathered for games and other diversions. This institution was also found among the Chol, in Tabasco, and in the highlands of Mexico. In Yucatan, where the youths were accustomed to bring prostitutes to this building, the discipline was evidently not so strict as in the Aztec men's house, although among the latter the young men were permitted to go out at night and visit their mistresses. By day the Maya boys and youths spent most of the time with their fathers, aiding them in their farming and other work. The girls lived at home, where they were trained in household tasks and strictly brought up by their mothers, who punished them severely for laziness or unseemly behavior.

Marriage is said to have been usual at the age of twenty, but we find indications that it often took place several years earlier. This event was preceded by many formalities and performed with much ceremony. With rare exceptions, no one could marry a person bearing the same patronymic as himself; but, apart from close relatives, kinship on the mother's side was no bar to matrimony. Sometimes the betrothal took place in childhood. The initiative was taken by the youth's father, who sought for his son a wife of his own social rank but he dealt through a matchmaker. He paid to the bride's father a small purchase price of cloth and other commodities, which, however, had to be returned if the young woman bore no children. Otherwise the husband might sell her. The groom's mother provided the couple with clothing for the event.

The marriage ceremony was performed at the bride's home by the priest, who perfumed the house, admonished the couple, and recited a ritual blessing. The bride's father provided a banquet, on which most of the purchase price was spent. All this ceremony was for first marriages only; widows and widowers were united with little formality. The man simply came to the woman's home and she gave him a meal, whereupon they were considered married.

After the wedding the young couple lived with the bride's father for five or six years, and the husband worked for his father-in-law. His refusal to do this, however, did not necessarily disrupt the marriage. There are indications that often, though not always, he eventually brought his wife to his father's home for permanent residence.

Among the common people monogamy seems to have been the rule, but separation and an informal remarriage to another mate often occurred. Either partner was free to leave the other, although in the case of a serious quarrel the relatives attempted to reconcile them. Young children remained with the mother, but if they were older, the father took the sons and the mother, the daughters.

Poligyny was frequent in the upper class, especially among the wealthy, some of whom are said to have had five or six wives. The principal wife was of the same social rank as her husband, but the others were apt to be slave concubines. It is plain that such relations were legitimate and did not constitute marital infidelity; nor were they mentioned in the formal confession before death. All the children bore the patronymic of the father. Those of the principal wife inherited the social status of the father, but the position of the others is uncertain. Their fate was somewhat precarious, especially if the father died. Such are the children evidently referred to in the account that "in the district of Chichen Itza, when the lord died, they sold his sons and daughters and all those of his house as slaves."[3] Wealthy men sold or donated for sacrifice orphans whom they were bringing up in their homes, some of them the children of deceased brothers or of other male relatives by slave concubines. We know of two young orphan boys purchased for sacrifice, for whom their guardians received five red shell beads each. We also read of pious men who gave their own children for this purpose, but it may be surmised that they were the offspring of slave women.

Death was much feared and believed to be a penalty for wrongdoing, especially offenses against religion. When a person became very ill, he usually confessed his past sins, to the priest if possible, otherwise to the wife or a close relative. When the sick person did not die, a confession of infidelity often resulted in serious quarrels between husband and wife, in which the corespondent was apt to become involved. In eastern Yucatan, when a person was on the point of death, the attendants are reported to have broken his back (lomos), "that he might not suffer."[4] Avendaño tells us that the Cehaches and the Itza of Lake Peten were accustomed to behead the older men at the age of fifty, "so that they shall not learn to be wizards and to kill, except the priests of their idols, for whom they have great respect." This was not the case with the people of northern Yucatan, in whose prophecies the Itza are repeatedly accused of unfilial conduct.[5]

Beside the body of the deceased, wrapped in a shroud, newly killed birds were placed. Maize paste and beads, which were used for money, were put in the mouth to provide for food and expenses on the journey to the other world.

Commoners were buried beneath or behind their homes and some of their

[3] RY, 2: 38.
[4] Ibid., 2: 24.
[5] Means, 1917, pp. 131–32; Codex Perez, p. 161.

idols were placed in the graves. If the departed was a sorcerer, his divining stones and other paraphernalia accompanied the remains; if a priest, some of his books. The spirits of the dead were dreaded, and unless it was one of the larger multiple-family dwellings, the house was usually abandoned after the funeral.

With the upper class, or, as Landa puts it, "nobles and persons of high esteem," cremation was practiced. The ashes with elaborate grave offerings were placed in large clay urns or effigy jars and buried in the substructure of a temple. In other cases the body was only partly burned, and the ashes were put into a hollow wooden statue representing the head of the deceased. Of the Cocom rulers it is said that the skull was cleaned and the back removed by sawing; then the face was reconstructed of bitumen or some other plastic material. These statues were kept in the family oratory, and on certain festivals offerings of food were made to them. The archaeologists have uncovered interments of uncremated remains, presumably of the upper class, in urns, stone cists, shafts, and vaults, some of them secondary burials; but it is uncertain to what extent such methods were still in use at the time of the conquest. Stephens reports a grave in a mound in northeastern Yucatan, where several skeletons were found accompanied by clay vases containing beads, stones, carved shells, obsidian projectile points, and a steel penknife with a horn handle, so it is evident that in some parts of the country this manner of burial among the upper class survived down to the period of European contact.

The relatives mourned the dead for a considerable time, in silence during the day and with loud wailing by night. Their demonstrations of sorrow were accompanied by fasting and abstinence, especially on the part of the husband or wife. The last were expected to remain continent and not to remarry for a year; disregard of this rule was believed to bring on some calamity.

The estate of the deceased was divided among the sons, the one who had aided most in accumulating the property receiving the largest share. The daughters were given little, and that only as a favor. If there were no sons, a brother or cousin on the father's side inherited the estate, which consisted of personal effects, beehives, and improvements to the land, such as houses, fruit trees, and cacao groves. For minor heirs a guardian was appointed, usually a close relative, who turned the property over to them when they came of age, but he was not obliged to account for any products from the trees or hives which had accumulated during this tutelage.

Feasts and banquets played an important part in the life of the Maya. Some of these were public and religious, the entire town contributing to them. An intoxicating drink of fermented honey and water seasoned with certain bark or with roots was consumed in large quantities, and a saturnalia ensued. Drunkenness was general and was accompanied by brawling, destruction of property, and wild sexual excesses. Toward the end of the year one of the richest men of the town also gave a series of feasts at his home. These were apparently for the local nobility and were characterized by similar uproar and intoxication. We find this account of the festivals confirmed in the native prophecies, which suggest that the extravagant behavior was part of a religious pattern and not merely incidental to the general inebriation. One Maya narrative seems to ascribe the erotic features of these festivals to the introduction of the Kukulcan cult from Mexico.

Besides the wedding feasts and others connected with the ancestral or lineage cult, certain elaborate banquets were given by members of the ruling class. At these each guest was served with maize cakes, much cacao, and an entire roasted fowl, after which he was presented with a mantle, a stool, and a handsomely decorated cup or bowl. It was compulsory for the guest to reciprocate with a similar feast, and if he died, his family or other relatives fell heir to the obligation. We are not told the occasion for such a banquet, but it might well have been connected with some honor conferred on the guest, adding prestige also to his kin. In colonial times such celebrations were given for the new incumbents by the Indian alcaldes leaving office.

At feasts the guests were seated by twos or fours, and drink was served by young women, who turned away their heads until the cup was emptied. There was dancing and music, and comedians gave entertainment.

The kinds of dances were manifold; to one early Spanish observer it seemed as though there must be more than a thousand. Many, possibly most, had some religious significance. On one occasion all of 800 men were so engaged at a time. Landa tells of a dance in which a man in the center of a large circle of dancers carried a bundle of reeds and cast them like darts at the others, who cleverly caught them. In another the dancers carried on their shoulders a litter, on which was a high painted stand like a pulpit. In this was a handsomely dressed man holding a rattle in one hand and a feather fan in the other; and he swayed, twisted his body, and whistled, keeping time to the beat of a drum. At one of the New Year ceremonies dancers performed on high stilts. In the Maya dictionaries compiled by the missionaries we read of a "bad old dance" called the "cloud dance" and other forbidden patterns, the names of which might be translated as "shield dance" or "monkey dance," "grandfather's song," and "shadow of the tree."[6] A dance of the "lords" was called *tankinam,* meaning "valor" or "great power."

[6] Ciudad Real, 1873, 2: 411; Vienna dictionary, f. 25r; San Francisco dictionary, Spanish-Maya, p. 62.

Music was produced by various percussion and wind instruments. Among the former were a kettledrum played by the hand, a hollow log with two carved tongues forming sounding boards beaten with rubber-tipped sticks, a tortoise shell struck with the hand or beaten with a deer antler, and a gourd rattle. The wind instruments included a wooden trumpet with a flaring mouth made of a twisted gourd, a reed flute, a bone whistle, and a conch shell. The old prophecies were sung or chanted to the accompaniment of the drum and rattle.

Dramatic representations, especially those given by professional performers, were mostly comedies. Sometimes they took place indoors and sometimes on open-air stages. Besides their usual entertainments at feasts and banquets, the comedians played an important part at the annual festival of Kukulcan, when they went about the town, performing at the principal houses and collecting offerings. They were graceful and witty and were very elegantly costumed. Often they wore masks and impersonated birds, making fun of the town magnates to their faces, but with old proverbs and veiled allusions. Indeed, they enjoyed the license of the European court jester.

We are told little of the comedies they enacted, but the names of a few, in one of the old dictionaries, give us some idea of their character: "the parasite," "the pot vendor," "the chile vendor," "the cacao grower."[7] Landa describes two stages for such comedies at Chichen Itza and they can be identified today. One of them is ornamented with cones, which were familiar symbols of Kukulcan, or Quetzalcoatl. The Mexican relief carvings on these structures and the association of the comedies with the worship of Kukulcan suggest that the institution, at least such as we find it at the time of the conquest, had been imported from Mexico.

Landa draws a pleasant picture of the daily life of the people generally. Large groups of men aided one another in producing crops or building houses and also performed communal labor for the municipality. Women did the same with their spinning and weaving, and the work was enlivened with banter, stories, and pleasant gossip. This was true when women gathered at the town cenote to draw water, as they do in these days; and the Maya equivalent of "a little bird told me" is still "I heard it at the rim of the cenote."[8]

Among men, visits were conducted with much formality. The caller brought a gift and received one in return. The humbler of the two constantly repeated the title-name and rank of the other in the course of the conversation, while the listener encouraged the speaker, as he does today, by exclaiming in a low voice from time to time, "true, true," or "so it is, indeed."

[7] Motul dictionary, 1929, pp. 80, 101.   [8] Redfield and Villa, 1934, p. 70.

People were very hospitable. Every visitor was offered food or drink, according to the time of day, and the traveler received lodging gratis. Only the itinerant merchant paid for his entertainment, since this was considered a regular business expense. If one merely sat down to eat by the roadside, he must offer food to anyone who joined him, no matter how little he had.

Women were very modest in their demeanor. When they met men on the road, they stepped aside and turned away to let them pass, and it was most improper to look up or smile. At festivals they also drank, but by themselves, and they were usually careful not to become very drunk. Upon them devolved the responsibility of seeing that an intoxicated husband got safely home. Industrious housewives, they worked early and late, attending to their children, preparing food, raising turkeys, spinning and weaving, going to market to barter, and sometimes cultivating the garden. Gentle as they were, they could be very jealous and ready to tear the hair of a rival or of an unfaithful husband.

Justice was usually administered by the *batab,* or local chief, of the town, but cases in which people of different towns were involved seem to have been referred to the *halach uinic,* or territorial ruler, where such existed.

In civil suits the batab received the litigants and listened to the complaint and the defense. His *ah ḳulels,* or deputies, served as advocates, and witnesses gave their evidence. The batab decided the case, but he carefully considered the opinions of the ah kulels. We read that officers like constables were always in attendance. All the proceedings were oral, and there appears to have been no appeal. They had a sort of oath, which consisted in calling down misfortunes on one's own head if a statement were false, and we find this in Maya legal documents long after the Spanish conquest.

Damages were sought in court for injuries committed without malice. Among the latter were accidental homicide and innocently causing a conflagration of a house, crops, a granary, or beehives. A rather strange misdeed, for which the kin might bring suit, was the provocation by a husband or wife resulting in the suicide of the other spouse. People often committed suicide because of grief, low spirits, trouble or sickness, and those who hanged themselves were sure of going to heaven. If the compensation awarded for an accidental killing was not paid, the kin of the dead man lay in wait for the defendant and killed him from ambush. Usually, however, his own kin helped him, if he was unable to satisfy the judgment.

In criminal cases the penalties were death or enslavement. Flogging was not practiced, and although victims awaiting sacrifice were confined in painted wooden cages, such imprisonment does not seem to have been employed as a punishment for crime. A prisoner was secured, however, by binding his wrists and fastening a wooden collar or yoke about his neck. To this was attached a cord, by which his guard could lead him.[9] At Campeche the first discoverers observed a stone platform or dais, on which were sculptured figures of a man attacked by animals and a large serpent swallowing a cougar. Here evildoers were punished, and Oviedo tells of an erect pole or mast, in the square at Cachi in northeastern Yucatan, which served as a place of execution.

The penalty for murder was usually death at the hands of the kin of the dead man, but a youth who killed an older man might be enslaved. A wealthy or powerful man, however, sometimes was allowed to give a slave or make other reparation. Arson and sex offenses were usually punished by death. For adultery, Chi tells us that both the man and the woman were slain with arrows. Landa says that the man was bound to a post, and the injured husband might either drop a heavy stone on his head or pardon him, whereas the disgrace was considered sufficient chastisement for the woman. As Chi was a member of the nobility it is possible that he refers to the custom only of his own social caste, among whom this transgression was especially abhorred. A man could be convicted of adultery only when taken *flagrante delicto,* but if he was caught under very compromising circumstances, he could be stripped, bound, and shorn—a grave dishonor.

Like the adulterer, a thief could be convicted only if found in the act. The penalty for stealing was enslavement, no matter how small the theft. He was held in slavery as long as he was unable to pay for what he had stolen; and Chi states that he remained a slave all his life unless he was redeemed, presumably by his family or kin. If a member of the upper class was caught stealing, a special sentence was imposed. He was publicly tattooed on both sides, from chin to forehead, which was indeed a great disgrace.

[9] Chi, 1941, pp. 231–32; Roys, 1933, p. 92, fig. 21.

Chapter 6. Social Organization

YUCATECAN MAYA society was definitely divided into three classes: nobles, commoners, and slaves. The Maya word for noble is *almehen*— derived from *al,* a woman's offspring, and *mehen,* a man's progeny— and thus the term implies known descent in both the male and female line. The nobles constituted the ruling class, filled the more important political offices, and were not only the most valiant warriors and members of the military orders but also the wealthiest farmers and merchants. Their economic advantage might well be ascribed partly to a certain preferred position in the use of the land and partly to their opportunities to exploit the labor of others, especially slaves, who were mostly captives taken in war. We know that many priests belonged to the nobility, as did probably the entire profession, so as holders of political office, military leaders, principal merchants, and clergy, the ruling class was able to control most fields of human activity. Nevertheless, except possibly for certain persons whose condition may have resembled serfdom, we have little evidence that the free plebeians generally had much reason to complain of oppression on the part of the nobles at the time of the conquest.[1]

The ruling class believed itself to be descended, in the male line at least, from certain foreigners who had come from Mexico. The origin of this caste will be discussed when we come to examine the historical background of the political organization of the country. They paid much attention to their genealogy, and Landa tells us, "They are very particular about knowing the origin of their families, especially if they are the descendants of some family of Mayapan, and they find this out from the priests, since it is one of their sciences, and they are very proud of the men who have been distinguished in their families."[2] Although Mayapan was destroyed about the middle of the fifteenth century, the descendants of the noble families, who had once lived within the walls of the capital, still knew the sites of their former houses. All these things were public information, but the upper class also had a secret lore handed down from father to son, a sort of ritual in which many words had a concealed meaning not understood by any except the initiates. The knowledge of this code was an important evidence of noble descent.[3]

[1] Motul dictionary, 1929, pp. 116, 119, 623. "Noble by lineage or reputation: *ah chibal, almehenil"* (Vienna dictionary, f. 151r). Lopez de Cogolludo, 1867–68, bk. 4, ch. 4; Roys, 1933, App. E, F.
[2] Landa, 1941, p. 98.
[3] Roys, 1933, pp. 88–96.

The commoners made up the vast majority of the population. They comprised the free workers of the country, including the artisans, fishermen, and small farmers and merchants generally.[4] This class, however, seems to have had an upper and a lower fringe, of which we have little information. The former consisted of the wealthier people who were not members of the nobility; but unfortunately the sixteenth-century Spanish writers do not make any very definite distinction between them and the hereditary upper class. Landa, describing a typical Maya town, tells us that in the center, around the temples with their plazas, were the homes of the "lords" and priests, and next to them were those of the most important people, whom we take to be the nobles. Then came the houses of the richest and most esteemed, and it seems possible that these were the more prosperous commoners. In the Province of Ah Canul we find the term *ayikal,* or rich man, employed as a title.[5] Sometimes commoners, apparently men of wealth or influence, insinuated themselves into political positions considered to be above their station. We read, however, of a sort of civil service examination, and the official hierarchy was purged from time to time of the pretenders and upstarts, who were not versed in the occult knowledge of the upper class.

There is some indication that below the ordinary commoners was a stratum of society, the members of which might be considered serfs, like the *mayeques* of Mexico.[6] Tomas Lopez Medel, writing only a decade after the conquest, refers to certain persons who work for the caciques and principal men in their houses and on their farms and plantations but who do not seem to be slaves. It is possible that this is the class meant by Cogolludo, when he states that, "the children of slaves remained slaves, until they were redeemed or were made tributaries."[7]

There were many slaves, most of them belonging to the nobles or wealthy commoners. The majority of them were men, women, and children of the plebeian class, who were captured in war. Noble prisoners were usually sacrificed, although they were sometimes ransomed. As we shall see, one of the principal causes of war was the desire to capture slaves. Others were seized for theft, especially in time of famine, and for unpaid damages at law, but their kin could always redeem them. Also a person who impregnated or married a slave was enslaved by the owner of the latter. A person could be born in servi-

---

[4] "*Yalba uinic en:* I am small or low in stature or I am a common and plebeian man" (Motul dictionary, 1929, pp. 440–41).
[5] Crónica de Calkini, pp. 20–21. Cf. Motul dictionary, 1929, p. 69: "*Açmen uinic:* a man between a principal and a plebeian, of middling status."
[6] Zurita, 1891, pp. 156–57.
[7] Lopez Medel *apud* Lopez de Cogolludo, 1867–68, bk. 5, ch. 16; Lopez de Cogolludo, 1867–68, bk. 4, ch. 4.

tude, but even then redemption was possible, and we find no evidence of breeding slaves for profit.

A large slave traffic existed, both for export and for domestic labor. Slaves were employed for heavy manual labor, working on the farms and in the fishing industry, as carriers on the road and as paddlers in 'the trading canoes. They were also useful in domestic service, the women grinding maize and cooking, the men carrying wood. Drawing water and carrying it to the house is women's work today; we do not know whether or not the task was assigned to male slaves. We should expect some slaves to be employed as skilled artisans, but no mention of this is found. If a newly purchased slave died or escaped and was not recaptured, the seller was obligated to refund a part of the price paid.[8]

The hair of a male slave was cut short, but he otherwise dressed like the poorer freemen in a loincloth and ragged mantle; he wore sandals when on the road. These people were made to carry weighty burdens; Aguilar, who was long a slave on the east coast of Yucatan, was loaded so heavily that he fell ill on a short journey of only 4 leagues. They were subjected to severity and harshness, and frequently sacrificed at the religious festivals. Hooton's examination of several skeletons of sacrificial victims recovered from the Sacred Cenote at Chichen Itza revealed some indications of malnutrition and definite evidence of abuse for a considerable period prior to death.

Yucatecan society was also divided vertically into lineage groups. Many of these included nobles and commoners alike, a circumstance which must have contributed greatly to social solidarity. People of the same patronymic considered themselves to be of the same kin and treated one another as such. If a stranger needed help, he had only to find someone of his own name, and he would be kindly received and assisted. Only under exceptional conditions did a man marry a woman of the same patronymic. The lineage had its own patron deity, sometimes a deified ancestor, and such matters were discussed in their hieroglyphic books.

There can be little doubt that the lineage group was felt bound by a genuine kinship, but just how this manifested itself between the noble and plebeian members of the same group still remains something of a problem. We read of banquets to which the entire pedigree of the town was invited. In Ceh Pech, however, where a very considerable proportion of the population of the province bore the name of Pech, certain Pech nobles write of themselves as being of the "first lineage" (*yax chibal*) of their towns. Although this may mean simply that they belonged to the Naum Pech line, the ruler of the province, the Pech

[8] Crónica de Calkini, p. 38; Anghiera *apud* Landa, 1941, p. 35; Cervantes de Salazar, 1941, p. 237; Chi, 1941, p. 232.

family was so numerous that this could hardly have been much of a distinction; and I suspect that it refers rather to their own high rank among members
of this name.

Parallel to the more important patrilineal system is a matrilineal reckoning
of descent. Just as a person inherited the father's patronymic, like our own surname, so the mother's first name was also handed down to her children. In the
case of a son it was preceded by the syllable *na-,* which means mother, and this
name was called the *naal,* or "mother name." Thus the son of a woman named
Ix Chan Pan, the wife of a certain Namay Canche, was named Nachan Canche.[9]

At birth, as we have seen, a boy was given a childhood name. After baptism,
Landa tells us, he could bear the name of his father. Apparently he now prefixed his childhood name to his patronymic. After marriage, Landa continues,
"they were called by the names of their father and mother," that is, the childhood name gave place to the naal that now preceded the patronymic. Later in
life, if he achieved distinction, the name of his office preceded his patronymic as
a title. Applying Landa's explanation to the various names of a certain member
of the Canul family found in the Crónica de Calkini, the batab of Tepakam
was named Ah Man at birth. After baptism he would begin to use his father's
patronymic and be called Ah Man Canul, but at marriage he would drop
Ah Man, use his mother's first name, and be known as Nabatun Canul. After
he became batab, he would also be called Batab Canul. As a matter of practice,
however, we know that many men were called by their childhood name and
patronymic throughout their lives. Besides these names we find a sobriquet,
which the Maya called a "jesting name," or *coco kaba.* The few slaves' names
which have come down to us correspond to the childhood and naal names of
free persons.

The Yucatecan Maya system of land tenure is not clear. Various authorities
write of communal ownership, and they seem to have got their information
from Gaspar Antonio Chi, whose own report reads: "The lands were in common and so between the towns there were no boundaries or landmarks to
divide them except between one province and another because of wars, and
in the case of certain hollows and caves, plantations of fruit trees and cacao
trees, and certain lands which had been purchased for the purpose of improv-
ing them in some respect."[10] It is difficult to tell just what he means when he
says, "in common." He asserts that "salt beds were also held in common," but
we know that the people who worked them were obliged to pay a royalty to

---

[9] Crónica de Calkini, p. 15; Roys, 1940, pp. 37–38.
[10] Chi, 1941, p. 230.

the local "lord." Chi no doubt intends to convey the idea that there was no private ownership of land in the Spanish sense of the term. In the Mani land treaty of 1557 is a statement which suggests that the ruling class had in some way a preferred position in regard to the land. We read: "Herewith we declare our true testimony that the land is not slave which we leave to them, in order that the nobles may sustain themselves, in order that they may farm it in time to come."[11] Landa, writing about 1566, declares that, "The lands today are common property, and so he who first occupies them becomes the possessor of them."[12] This suggests that such had not always been the case, and the documents of the Pech family point out that in the time of Tomas Lopez Medel, who effected a number of reforms in 1552, there was a royal cedula giving the lands to the people who were settled upon them.

The Titles of Ebtun give some indication of the existence of landholding organizations. In an acknowledgment of sale dated 1638 the vendor, Diego Chay, affirms that he was an "Ah Kin Chan Tacu" of the town of Ebtun and that he, together with an "Ah Balam Chay" of Cuncunul, placed the landmarks on the property. Litigation followed, and in later documents we read that the landmarks were set by the Ah Kin Chan Tacus and the Ah Balam Chays, and that some Indians called Ah Kin Chan Tacu sold the property.

Very early in the colonial period there is evidence of both individual and municipal ownership of land. In a document of 1561 and another on the reverse of the same sheet, written probably about the same time, is recorded an individual title to a tract of land and its conveyance "to the principal men of the town here at Ebtun." The vendor states that it is the "title of the forest of my ancestors." In this connection it might be noted that among the Aztec, although certain lands were held by groups called *calpullis,* they were actually occupied by individual families, among whom the right of occupancy was handed down from father to son. Such land, however, could not be alienated from the calpulli.

In colonial times in Yucatan we also find a group of three towns exercising joint ownership over their lands, a practice which still survives among the Indians of Quintana Roo and which, as Redfield notes, may go back to old traditions. Town lots were often owned by the municipality during this period, but fruit trees remained private property. In pre-Spanish times, when orchards and gardens within the town were larger and more common, we might expect the home sites to be treated as private property by virtue of the improvements.

---

[11] Appendix *infra.* It is uncertain what is meant by "slave" land. The term employed, *ppentac,* is defined as "male slave purchased or sold, captive or servant" (Motul dictionary, 1929, p. 794).

[12] Landa, 1941, pp. 96–97.

Chapter 7. Agriculture and Food

THE AGRICULTURAL system of Yucatan offers a startling contrast to the architectural remains everywhere in evidence. Farming methods are, and always have been, so primitive that it is difficult at first sight to believe that they could ever have supported a civilization like that of the Yucatecan Maya. This manner of farming is generally known as the milpa system, a term derived from the Aztec word for cornfield.

When the dry season commences, usually in December or January, a tract of forest is cut, and the trees and brush are allowed to dry thoroughly. Late in March or in April the field is burned. Toward the latter part of May or early in June the rains come, and the seed is planted with a sharp stick among the charred stumps and partly burned trunks of the larger trees, both in the pockets of thin soil and even in the cracks and fissures of the bare rocky knolls. This is mostly corn, mixed however with a few black or Lima beans and squash seeds, all in the same hole. During the rainy summer season the weeds are cleared once or twice, but that is all the attention the crop receives until it ripens in October or November, although some green corn is gathered in September. When the grain ripens, the stalks are bent over to keep the moisture from the kernels and the corn is left to harden. More or less of it is taken and used as needed, and the remainder is stored, closely packed, in granaries in the field. The second year, the land is cleared of cornstalks and new brush, burned, and planted again; but the yield is smaller, owing perhaps to the repeated burning of the soil as well as to the increased weed competition. Especially good land may be planted again a third or even a fourth year, but this is rare, and it is more usual to cut a new tract of forest the third year. The old field is left to grow up to bush for at least seven years and often more; the longer it remains fallow, the more abundant the next harvest will be.

This, it is generally agreed, has always been the agricultural system of Yucatan. It is a little difficult to understand how they formerly managed to fell with stone axes the dense scrubby growths of hardwoods that usually predominate. They had a few copper axes, but it seems doubtful that there were enough for agricultural purposes; and even these were not possessed in earlier times, when milpa cutting was as extensive as later. Redfield and Villa note that sometimes the land cleared one year is not fired until the next. This may have been a more frequent practice in pre-Spanish times; and many trees, now cut down, could have been girdled, killed, and left to dry for a year before firing. The process is, of course, wasteful and bad for the soil. The burning destroys the humus, and although the ash acts as a fertilizer, many of its valuable constituents are dissolved and washed away by the heavy rains. In defense of the system, however, it may be said that it has supported a very considerable population for many centuries and produced a civilization of no little worth. Also, it is difficult to conceive of any other practicable method of farming the rocky soil of northern Yucatan.

Dr. Kempton has estimated that the present Yucatecan Maya farmer can satisfy nearly 80 per cent of his family's food requirements on 250 hours' work per year. Even if we add the time for other necessary activities, this would still allow a considerable margin for the disadvantage of stone tools. The same authority also believes it possible, even with the forest being cut only once every twenty years, for the land to support a population, at its present level of subsistence, of approximately 50 persons per square mile employed in agriculture and 10 others engaged in nonagricultural activities.

The principal root and tuber crops were sweet potatoes, jicamas (*Pachyrhizus erosus* Urban), cassava including both the bitter and sweet varieties, and a plant called *macal*. Today the yam, an importation from Africa, is usually known by this name, but the description of the pre-Spanish macal suggests one of the Araceae, possibly the *malanga* (*Xanthosoma violaceum* Schott), a well-known food plant of Central America. Sweet cassava, a plant of western South American origin, was evidently a pre-Spanish importation from the southern neighbors of the Maya; and the Maya name of the jicama, *chicam,* suggests that it was introduced by the Mexicans. Sweet potatoes and jicamas are sometimes planted between the corn but more often grown separately in the fields. All these, as well as a certain early variety of corn, seem to have been grown both in town gardens and in the fields at the time of the conquest. Also raised in gardens or in separate patches of the field were chile peppers, chaya (*Jatropha aconitifolia* Mill.), a small tree or shrub the leaves of which are boiled as a pot herb, a small variety of tomato, *annatto,* and possibly the chayote (*Sechium edule* Sw.). The last may have been a postconquest importation from Mexico; it is called "spiny rind squash" by the Maya.

Although home sites are by no means small today, there are indications that they were still larger at the time of the conquest; and it seems likely that many vegetables now usually grown in patches in the fields were formerly cultivated in town gardens adjoining the houses. Intentional fertilization is not known to have been practiced, but between the dogs, turkeys, and the fact that pit latrines were unknown among the Indians, the soil of the town gardens was unquestionably enriched.

Cacao was an important food, although something of a luxury. In northern Yucatan it was imported mostly from Tabasco, Honduras, and the Province of Chetumal. A certain amount, however, was grown locally in hollows, where the soil is moist and not far above the water table. Depressions suitable for this purpose occur more frequently in eastern Yucatan, but some are to be seen in the Xiu area.

Many fruits were, and still are, cultivated; but except for the papaya, the wild variety of which is not edible, the domesticated fruits differ little, if at all, from those found growing in the forest. Some, however, like the custard apple and aguacate, may not be native to northern Yucatan. The zapote and breadnut occur in large numbers around the ruins farther south. The latter also grows around almost every home in the north; like the mamey, it ripens in the latter part of the dry season, when the corn supply was often low and sometimes exhausted. Other fruit trees said to have been cultivated in the sixteenth century, and frequent in the forests as well, were various annonas, hog plums, the guava, *guayo* (*Talisia olivaeformis* Radlk.), *kanizte* (*Lucuma campechiana* HBK.), *nancen* (*Byrsonima crassifolia* DC.), *bec* (*Ehretia tinifolia* L.), *kopte* (*Cordia dodecandra* DC.), cow okra (*Parmentiera edulis* DC.), *kunche,* (*Pileus mexicanus* Standl.), and a palm called *cocoyol* or *tuk* (*Acrocomia mexicana* Karw.). Some of these trees may have been planted as much for shade as for their fruit, but the last two, like the breadnut, were of especial value in time of famine.

The pulp of the breadnut is edible, but more frequently its seeds are boiled, roasted, or ground into a meal from which a gruel and a sort of bread are made. Even the milky latex from the trunk has a food value. A kind of custard is prepared from the pulp of the kunche, a preserve is formed from the rind, and a food and drink are said to have been made of the spongy interior of the trunk. The flesh of the cocoyol nut is edible, and the very palatable kernel of the pit is ground to make a drink like maize gruel. Other foods in times of scarcity were the root of a vine called *cup,* or *jicama cimarrona* (*Calopogonium coeruleum* Benth.), some part of the *baatun,* which in Peten is the name of a large coarse plant identified as *Anthurium tetragonum* Hook., and the boiled leaves of a wild variety of chaya. Some of the wild fruits and roots eaten in time of famine were thought by the Spaniards to be unwholesome and said to have caused the deaths of many persons, but it seems equally possible that the cause was simply malnutrition.

Practically the only fowl or domestic animals raised for food were turkeys and certain small hairless dogs. Of the latter, we are told, the males were castrated and fattened for eating; evidently the females were kept for breeding. A few coatis, curassows, and native ducks were domesticated; the last are said to have been kept chiefly for their feathers, which were woven into certain garments. Dogs and turkeys were especially acceptable as sacrifices and were little eaten except on ceremonial occasions, although it should be remembered that religious festivals came fairly often. Game has always been plentiful in Yucatan, and although there could hardly have been sufficient to furnish a large proportion of the regular diet of the population, when we consider that about 80 per cent of the land was always growing up to thicket and forest, it seems probable that a considerable amount was consumed. The wild animals which were hunted or trapped for food were the deer, brocket, armadillo, peccary, rabbit, agouti, coati, opossum, and pocket gopher. Game birds were wild turkeys, partridges, various wild pigeons or doves, curassows, guan, quail, and wild ducks.

Deer, brockets, and probably peccaries were hunted by large groups of fifty to a hundred men, and twenty or thirty deer would be killed in such a hunt. We are told that they were all archers, but some no doubt acted as beaters. The native dogs were useful, as they were good both at following a scent and at flushing birds. To keep venison from spoiling, it was dried or partly roasted on a wooden rack or grate over a fire. When the hunters returned, a share was given to the batab, to the priest, and probably also to the heads of the subdivisions of the town to which the hunters belonged. If the hunt was successful, the hunters smeared the faces of their idols with blood, but otherwise they beat them. Although guns are used today, the technique of such a hunt is still much the same. If possible, a grassy place like the site of a deserted village is surrounded. Boys or men who have no guns are accompanied by dogs and drive the game toward the armed hunters, who wait on the side away from the wind. The man who shoots a deer or peccary receives one leg, the head, hide, belly, and liver, and the remainder of the carcass is divided among the other members of the party. Game, even including deer, was also trapped with snares, deadfalls, and probably pitfalls. Birds were shot with the blowgun, evidently imported from the southern neighbors of the Maya, as it is of South American origin. Instead of the poisoned dart, however, the missile was a clay pellet, often armed with a bone point. A bone is usually mentioned in connection with the blowgun in the native literature.[1]

The many large iguanas were a favorite food, although they are rarely eaten

[1] Redfield and Villa, 1934, p. 48; Vienna dictionary, f. 196v; Codex Tro-Cortesianus apud Tozzer and Allen, 1910, pls. 29, 30, 33; Book of Chilam Balam of Tizimin, p. 22.

today. They were snared on trees and at their holes. After the conquest the
Church classed them with fish, and Landa states that they were so plentiful
that they were a great help in keeping the Lenten fasts. Fish have always been
good and abundant in Yucatecan waters, and the people of the coast devoted
much of their energy to fishing, both for their own consumption and for sale
to the inhabitants of the interior. Among the latter, however, there was more
or less illness from eating badly preserved fish. In the interior they also caught
cenote fish, particularly small catfish and others which the Spaniards called
mojarras, apparently a very small broad fish. There was probably no great
quantity of these taken, but they added somewhat to the protein content of the
native diet.

Much honey was produced in Yucatan. Besides the wild honey gathered in
the woods, most families had hives of the small stingless native bees, which had
evidently been domesticated for centuries. The hives consisted of hollowed
sections of tree trunks, the bees entering from a small hole in the side. The ends
were closed with a flat piece of wood or stone and plastered in place with mud,
so they could easily be opened to remove the honey. The hives were set on
sloping racks like an A-frame, beneath a thatched shelter. Apiculture is still
the same in Yucatan, except that we are told that no use was made of wax
in pre-Spanish times. This may simply mean that wax candles for lighting
were unknown, as J. E. S. Thompson has shown that in all probability wax
had a ceremonial function. From the early Spanish writers one might infer
that honey was mostly an ingredient of the intoxicating drink called *balche;*
but since it appears to have been the only concentrated sweet produced in any
considerable quantity, it must have been an important food article. It was probably strained, as it is today, and was an essential in preparing the various con-
serves of which we find mention. A sweet made of toasted squash seeds and
honey is still popular, and one of parched corn and honey is mentioned in
the Chumayel manuscript.

Balche, drunk only on ceremonial occasions, was concocted of fermented
honey and water, in which was soaked the pounded bark of the tree (*Loncho-
carpus longistylus* Pittier) for which the beverage was named. It has been
described as a mild intoxicant, but great vats of it were made for nearly every
religious festival and everybody drank it in sufficient quantities to become
very drunk. It is reported to have acted also as a purge and was considered
very healthful.

From some of the sixteenth-century sources we gather that there were other
intoxicating beverages as well, although honey seems to have been the base of
all of them. One of these "they made of water, honey, maize, and other roots,

which made it strong."[2] Of another it is said that honey and the root of an agave were the principal ingredients, although "other roots of trees were added." Possibly we have here two descriptions of the same drink. In this connection it is of interest to note that *ci,* the Maya name for several species of agave, meant wine in general, and that *cii* was one of the two words designating something sweet.[3]

The main food staple was maize, which was prepared in much the same way that it is today. The grain is soaked overnight in limewater, after which it is rinsed and freed of the husk. It is then ground to a paste between two stones. The lower of these, called a *metate,* is a small sloping stone table with a curved surface and supported by three short legs. The other is a slightly tapering, cylindrical, hand stone. The paste is then shaped into round maize cakes, or tortillas, and baked on a flat clay griddle, called a *comal* (Maya, *xamach*), which is set on three stones over a small fire. We know that this method of baking the tortillas goes back to the sixteenth century, since the xamach, or comal, is mentioned in the Motul dictionary. Archaeological evidence of the use of the comal in Yucatan before the conquest is doubtful, but an older technique is suggested by certain ceremonial breadstuffs still in use today. These are larger and thicker cakes containing a considerable quantity of squash seeds, which are cooked in a pit oven.[4] Today squash seeds are much favored, but before the introduction of European swine contributed lard to the native diet, their high fat content probably made them an even more important food. Root crops, maize meal mixed with beans, and meat are also cooked in these pit ovens, which are put to service mostly, though not always, at religious festivals. Next to maize, Landa mentions beans as the most important article of diet.

The morning meal, which was taken at dawn or even earlier, is said to have consisted only of a hot gruel called atole (Maya, *za*). This was made of the maize paste described above and flavored with chile pepper. In the Province of Ah Kin Chel and probably other regions not far from the coast, chocolate, probably mixed with atole, was drunk in the morning, but in most parts of the country it seems to have been reserved for banquets and religious festivals. Sometimes the breakfast was varied by drinking pinole, made of toasted maize paste. A man carried to his milpa a large gourd of drinking water and a calabash dish containing a lump of dough. Whenever he was hungry during the day, he dissolved some of this in water and drank it. It is called *pozole.*

---

[2] RY, 1: 97.
[3] *Ibid.,* 1: 57; Motul dictionary, 1929, p. 181. This association of the agave with wine or something sweet recalls the sweet juice of certain agaves in the highlands of Mexico and the pulque made from it.
[4] Vienna dictionary, f. 41r; Landa, 1941, pp. 89–90.

The principal meal of the day was eaten about an hour before sunset, after the worker returned from the field. It consisted of tortillas seasoned with ground chile and salt water, boiled beans, and a vegetable stew. Squash seeds prepared in various forms were an ingredient of most of these foods. The stew contained game or fish often in the homes of the upper class but rarely in those of commoners, who are said to have eaten little meat except at festivals. There is no doubt that the nobility ate more meat than did the plebeians. Not only did the batab receive a share of the game taken by every hunting party, but the beaters were no doubt all commoners; and although some plebeians would be archers, in the long run the upper class would receive a larger average share of the kill. On the other hand, we know there was much individual hunting, and, as we have seen, quantities of game were trapped, so the common man probably had frequent opportunities to take meat. The average inhabitant of Chan Kom today eats venison, peccary, or agouti about once a week.

Morris Steggerda has made an extensive study of the food of the modern Maya and finds that on a basis of fresh weight, cooked maize averages 73 per cent of the diet examined. This, of course, represents a high proportion of carbohydrates. Dry white maize, however, contains 4.6 per cent fat; squash seeds, 39.1 per cent. The daily protein intake is low, averaging only 74 grams per individual. As compared with 3500 calories for the average North American laborer, a man's daily energy intake is only 2565 calories, 70 per cent derived from carbohydrates, 13 per cent from fat, and 17 per cent from protein, the last supplied largely from beans and meat. This, of course, is not very different from the European diet, which is given as 67, 17, and 16 per cent respectively; and Steggerda finds it adequate so far as energy and protein needs are concerned.[5] The diet studied by this authority is probably not very different, on the whole, from that of the pre-Spanish Maya, but it should be noted that it contains a certain amount of lard and hens' eggs. European fowl and pigs represent an important addition to the former Maya diet. The Maya had turkeys, it is true, but their eggs were not an important food, if, indeed, they were eaten at all. We can only surmise that this deficiency in fats was made up by higher consumption of squash seeds.

On the other side of the ledger, it seems probable that formerly more fruit was eaten than today. Steggerda finds that in spite of the abundance of fruit during the greater part of the year, the modern Indians eat little compared with white people in the northern United States. It is difficult to account for this. We find many accounts of the food of the Maya in the reports of the

<hr/>

[5] Benedict and Steggerda, 1936, pp. 168, 188. Since these writers cite Voit, a German authority, they probably refer to the diet of continental Europe.

sixteenth-century Spanish settlers and missionaries; here we are certainly given the impression that the Indians ate large quantities of fresh fruit. This would, of course, add considerably to the vitamins and salts in their diet.

We have seen that the agricultural system of the Yucatecan Maya could hardly have been a matter of choice, but was rather imposed upon them by the character of the soil and climate. Linton has shown that this system may well account for the territorial form of government, which appears to have existed over a large part of the peninsula. The shifting character of Yucatecan agriculture necessitated the spread of a considerable portion of the population to outlying areas, some distance from the towns, where they lived in scattered hamlets. Only through the protection of a fairly strong territorial government could such people be reasonably safe from constant raids by outsiders. Even so, as we shall see farther on, settlements near the borders of a province were often raided; but the threat of retaliation by a powerful enemy restrained such attacks sufficiently to make it possible to cultivate these areas.

The custom of keeping the corn in field granaries until needed at home was a certain advantage during the usual attack. The raiders generally plundered a captured town and quickly retired, and there was not time to search the surrounding farming area for food, although a good deal was often found in the houses of the town. The agricultural system was, however, a serious disadvantage in the case of a foreign invasion. There was more or less latitude in the time for clearing, burning, or harvesting, whereas planting had to be done precisely when the rains came. Among the Yucatecan states this affected one side as much as the other; but with foreign invaders like the Spaniards, who lived on plunder and had no farms of their own, it was a different matter. When the rains came, the defending forces melted away, each man returning to his milpa to plant his crop. This was what checked the initially successful native uprising of 1847, and it seems probable that it was an important factor during the Spanish invasion.

To the Maya mind from time immemorial there has been something peculiarly sacred about the growing corn. The growing maize plant was personified by the beautiful young corn god, who is often portrayed on the monuments and in the codices. As we shall see farther on, people did not go to war during the growing season; and it seems likely that they were influenced in this by religious as well as by practical considerations. From what we know of the Maya, it is difficult to imagine that they ever devastated the growing corn in the fields of their enemies, at least in pre-Spanish times.

Chapter 8. Industry and Commerce

ACCORDING TO the early Spanish writers the most important articles of commerce were salt, textiles, fish, and copal incense. To these we might add pottery, flint implements, and certain objects of wood. There was also more or less sale or barter of other goods, but we gather from the various reports that they were largely produced by the consumer as needed. Except in some localities on or near the coast, like Chauacha and Zama, where little maize was grown, nearly everybody seems to have done some farming; and the producers of merchantable goods followed their callings at such times as work in the fields and necessary tasks about the home did not require their attention. A man might make many things for his own use but manufacture for sale only the one thing for the production of which he was specially trained or naturally adept. In the Motul dictionary a certain term is defined as "he who knows many crafts and he who is very proficient in some particular one." Here too we find the Maya names of a number of crafts or other occupations, such as carrier, charcoal-burner, dyer, farmer, fisherman, flint-worker, mason, painter or writer, potter, salt-gatherer, sandal-maker, stone-cutter, tanner, and weaver.[1] We suspect, indeed, that certain skilled craftsmen, whose products were much in demand, cultivated smaller milpas than the average person.

The textile industry was probably the most important. Everyone wore cotton clothing, practically every housewife spun and wove cotton, and the plant is said to have been cultivated almost everywhere. Two varieties are mentioned, an annual and a perennial, which bore for five or six years; and a strong cloth is still sometimes made from the silky fiber of a species of ceiba. Cotton was probably spun as it is today at Chan Kom, where the spindle is weighted with a wooden whorl and spun in a shallow gourd dish. Little weaving is now done in northern Yucatan, but the loom was no doubt similar to that still used in British Honduras and among the Lacandons. The rod at one end of the warp is attached to a tree or post and that at the other, to a backstrap. Alternate warp threads are connected with another rod, which is raised to form the shed beneath which the shuttle passes. The last is simply a thin stick on which the weft is wound obliquely. The designs are applied, as in tapestry, while the cloth is being woven. One kind of cloth was about 62 cm. wide, and another, only 30 cm. or less. The various grades ranged from thick or coarse to thin

[1] Motul dictionary, 1929, pp. 74–111.

and delicate. Some very elaborate weaves of textiles have been recovered from the Sacred Cenote at Chichen Itza. Often the cloth was dyed, or else designs were woven with dyed cotton thread or an imported colored yarn of rabbit hair. Duck feathers, and probably other plumage, were sometimes woven into the fabric.[2]

The mats on which people sat and slept were woven from bulrushes called *poop,* probably *Scirpus validus* Vahl, and *Typha angustifolia* L. Four types of baskets are described. The smallest sometimes had a support of some sort, another was a large storage basket, a third is said to have resembled a long chest, and the fourth was a high narrow basket for carrying or holding cotton, chile, or salt. Like the modern Maya baskets, they were probably made from vine stems and ribs or strips of palm fronds.[3]

Henequen fiber was much used for cordage. A pack net was woven of this material, but we find little mention of the agave fabrics so common and even worn for clothing in Mexico and other parts of Middle America.

Salt was taken from the beds found along the coast from near Campeche to Mujeres Island. By the long salt lagoons were shallow ponds, which filled up during the rains. In the dry season the water retreated leaving a deposit of salt, which was heaped up on the shore. It was believed that the rain water caused the salt to coagulate in lumps, and the workers sometimes gathered these from the bottom of the pool. A fire, built around the mound of salt, formed a hard crust which the rain did not penetrate. The "lords" of the coast provinces are said to have possessed riparian rights to certain sections of the water front, where they permitted the people of their towns to gather salt but exacted a royalty for the privilege. As we shall see, people from the interior provinces sometimes attempted to gather salt but were driven away; this monopoly of the coast dwellers caused much ill feeling and occasional wars.

The fish in the lagoon were not large but plentiful and good; people who did not have boats and nets shot them with arrows in the shallows. On the east coast Juan Diaz observed that the mouth of one of the small openings was surrounded by piling, which he believed to be a weir; and the wickerwork fish-pots adapted to the cenotes no doubt also saw service in the lagoons of the coast. Deep-sea fishing was an important industry; sweep nets and dragnets, hooks and lines yielded to the coast dwellers the fish for which Yucatecan waters are still famous.[4] The fish, if not immediately eaten, were salted, dried, or roasted over a fire or simply sun-dried for shipment. Other sea foods were

[2] Vienna dictionary, f. 191*v*; Motul dictionary, 1929, p. 155; RY, 1: 67, 87; Molina, 1880, f. 148*r*.
[3] RY, 2: 43; Vienna dictionary, ff. 58*r*, 127*r*; Standley, 1930, p. 216; Roys, 1931, p. 279.
[4] Vienna dictionary, ff. 58*r*, 177*r*.

turtles and their eggs, oysters, cuttlefish eggs, crabs, and lobsters, but we do not know that these were transported to the interior. The manatee, which was especially prized for its fat, was harpooned all along the coast, particularly in the region north of Campeche.[5]

Pottery making was a major occupation, but the sixteenth-century writers tell us little about it; nor do we know which towns specialized in this trade. Many water jars are now produced at Ticul, and that town may well have been a center of the industry in pre-Spanish times. Pottery was probably made by women, although men also are engaged in this craft today. We know that the clay was first ground in a stone mortar. The modern technique of modeling is probably not very different from what it was in the conquest period. The wheel is not employed, but the mass of wet clay is placed on a square block of wood; this is turned by the feet of the potter, who sits on a low stool and models the jar by hand. Gann states that the larger pots were made by coiling strips of wet clay and smoothing the surface with a flat spoon-shaped instrument of pottery or wood, and that the pottery was fired under glowing charcoal. This is borne out by the old Maya terms for a potter's kiln, which are *cumku*, "nest of pots," and *mucab*, which could mean something covered up. It is believed that the potter's art had declined greatly at the time of the conquest. The early Spanish writers say little of the decoration; one mentions a bowl "painted with small white pebbles" and called *choo lac*. Much of the pottery was red, being colored with certain varieties of red earth called *cab* and *choben*.[6]

In the older dictionaries we find the names of various clay vessels; there was a cooking pot called *cum*, and a somewhat similar pot seems to have been used for storage. Jars for liquids were known as *ppul*. Two of the codices illustrate kettles with a somewhat flattened globular body and a low, slightly constricted neck almost as wide as the pot. Jars apparently used for storage or holding liquids are taller and have higher flaring necks. Shallow bowls and plates were called *lac*; those with feet are called *ocliz lac* today. A small jar or pot was used for making atole; some of these had handles.[7] None of the clay griddles already in use in the sixteenth century have been found complete. Thompson doubts that they were used before this time and, indeed, we know that certain things were baked on heated flat stones.[8] Large quantities of incense burners and idols were made. The earthen drums, which were beaten by hand, are not mentioned in the early reports; but they are still in use among the

---

[5] Vienna dictionary, f. 34r; Beltran de Santa Rosa, 1859, p. 230.

[6] Vienna dictionary, f. 126v; Motul dictionary, 1929, pp. 162, 212, 334, 635.

[7] *Ibid.*, pp. 212, 533, 804; Vienna dictionary, ff. 33r, 34v; Codex Troano, pp. 8, 13, 20, 23, 27; Codex Cortesianus, p. 31.

[8] Thompson, 1939, p. 126; Vienna dictionary, f. 162v; cf. RY, 1: 198.

Lacandons and we see them in a fresco at Santa Rita and in the Maya codices.

Pottery was supplemented by the use of calabash cups, bowls, and other dishes. These were often handsomely carved and painted, an artistry that must have been of some prominence. The earlier sixteenth-century reports have much to say of the usefulness of the tree gourd, but, strangely enough, until about the end of that century there is little mention of the genuine gourd, which grows much larger and plays so important a part in the native domestic economy to-day. The one exception that we have found is a small wild gourd called *bux,* probably a native species of Lagenaria, which the Indians used for keeping powdered tobacco. Standley states that the large gourds now used are an Old World plant, *Lagenaria siceraria* Standl.[9]

Cortez found native masons at Cozumel, and even in areas where most buildings were of pole and thatch there was some stone construction; but aside from this, stone working seems to have been confined largely to the making of metates, hand stones, stone troughs or tanks, and flint implements.

Most of the metates are crudely fashioned of hard limestone, although a few are finely carved from lava. These must, of course, have been imported, as there are no volcanic rocks in Yucatan. Many are of the three-legged type, but more are simply a solid block of stone, the sides and bottom roughly shaped, the top fairly well finished. At Chichen Itza have come to light some very small metates with legs, in which chile or other condiments may have been ground; they seem rather small for cacao or even squash seeds. We do not know, how-ever, whether they were still in use at the time of the conquest. They appear to have been hewn by the pecking process, which the Maya called *thoh tunich.* There are also many old, rudely fashioned water troughs. Besides the potter's stone mortars, smaller ones apparently did service in the home.

Landa tells us that since the Maya lacked metals, ". . . God provided them with a ridge of flint near the range of hills, which . . . crosses the land, from which they got stones from which they made the heads of their lances for war and the knives for the sacrifices (of which the priests kept a good supply). They made the heads for their arrows and they still make them, and so flint served them for metal."[10] Small flint knives and drills are also mentioned. The technique of working flint is suggested by one of the early dictionaries, where we read: "To make lancets and knives of flints and points for arrows, getting them from some thick [piece of] flint, which is set upright: *bah tok*."[11] A more literal translation of the Maya term would be, "to drive something like

9 Motul dictionary, 1929, p. 160; Vienna dictionary, f. 32v.
10 Landa, 1941, p. 186.
11 Vienna dictionary, ff. 7v, 134r, 150r; Motul dictionary, 1929, p. 128.

a punch or chisel into the flint." Evidently indirect rest percussion was employed. The piece of flint was no doubt held upright between the feet of the worker; and the implement was probably finished by a pressure process, such as the Lacandons still use. Certain finely executed, eccentrically shaped flints have been found in British Honduras, roughly resembling crosses, reptiles, animals, and human figures. Apparently they were still being made at the time of the conquest, for Gann reports a find of this sort accompanied by a vessel of Spanish origin. Axe heads, which had been bound to a wooden haft, and the adzes used for hollowing out beehives and other wooden objects were made of both local flint and certain hard stone which was imported.

Flint deposits are reported from Peten and the mountains of British Honduras as well as from the Yucatecan sierra. There were two kinds, the "good" white flint and a red variety. We find the Maya expression meaning "to dig for flint,"[12] and it is obvious that the weathered material on the surface would not be suitable for making implements. When a stratum of flint was encountered in digging a well, a fire was built over it to "soften" it. We should expect water to be thrown on the heated stone to shatter it, and it seems probable that a similar procedure was followed in mining the material.

As in any forested country, wooden objects too numerous to mention were made and used in great quantities. The local trees, mostly hardwoods, furnished the material for most of these, but the soft straight-grained Spanish cedar was especially desirable for many purposes. Although it grows only in the high forests, much of it was used everywhere. We know that the town of Buctzotz in Ah Kin Chel made a special business of getting out cedar lumber.

A most important specialist was the woodcarver. Secluded in a specially built hut and accompanied by much ceremony, fasting, and penance, he carved the wooden idols, a dangerous and awesome task. These images were always of cedar, carved with small chisels of imported copper. The same material and technique doubtless went into the making of the wooden masks which played an important part in certain religious ceremonies. Sometimes the masks were covered with gold leaf or mosaic of precious stones, but we do not know that these were of local manufacture. Masks were also made of calabash shells.

The people of Mazanaho near Lake Bacalar made a specialty of boat building, supplying the people of the entire region; this was likewise true of the inhabitants of some parts of the northeast coast, where Bernal Diaz tells of canoes holding as many as forty men. These were evidently cedar dugouts, but we also read of the ear tree, or conacaste, being used for the same purpose in spite of its hard wood. This grows in the more thickly populated part of the

[12] Vienna dictionary, f. 159r.

country farther west. Ceiba and cedar are still used for canoes in British Honduras.

Many wooden articles were made by the consumer himself; but it seems likely that the blowgun, which was bored with a special copper tool, and the rather complicated hollow wooden drum were the work of the professional. So, doubtless, were the finely carved chests, stools, and other furniture in the temples or in the homes of persons of rank and wealth.

Some other industries might be mentioned. Paints and dyes were made·of certain red and yellow earth, annatto, cochineal, logwood, indigo, brazil, *Duranta plumieri* Jacq., and other unidentified trees or plants. The production of copal gum for incense was an important industry in the Province of Chikincheel. Here copal trees were both native and cultivated. This tree, *Protium copal* Engl., was said to have thrived only in this region, although it grows in British Honduras and is a common forest tree in the Peten. Oviedo tells of well-tended groves of incense trees at Sinsimato. Some metal work in copper and probably in gold was done, for we read of the importation of copper plates and sheets.

There was much commerce, both domestic and foreign, and trade was, as in Mexico, a highly honorable calling, especially when conducted on a large scale. The son of the last Cocom ruler at Mayapan was in Honduras on a trading expedition at the time of the fall of that city. Merchants ranged from the wealthy and noble wholesalers, who had their own factors, trading canoes, and slave carriers, to the petty itinerant who carried his own pack.[13] Once there had been wide causeways across the country, leading to certain centers of pilgrimage, but at the time of the conquest they were completely a thing of the past and had probably not been used for centuries. The highways of commerce were then rough narrow trails through the thick bush, the overhanging branches cut high enough just to clear a man's head and pack. Needless to say, the mounted Spaniards found them difficult to travel.

Large market places were established at Cachi and Chauacha, important commercial centers in northeastern Yucatan. At the former, as we have already noted, there was a market-court at one corner of the square, where disputes were settled by certain officials. In the latter town a part of the market was housed in stone buildings with thatched roofs. It would seem probable that they were open in front like the houses of certain chiefs. Similar markets were likely organized at other large towns on the coast. In the interior of the country none of the markets seem to have impressed the Spaniards sufficiently to elicit a description, but they are mentioned and they evidently existed in the more

[13] Vienna dictionary, f. 145*v*; Motul dictionary, 1929, p. 92.

populous communities. Whether the smaller groups had them is more doubtful, for one of the Lopez ordinances prescribes the establishment of a market in every town and forbids the sale of anything elsewhere. In the Motul dictionary we read of hawkers, who went about buying and selling, and it seems probable that Lopez was attempting to abolish this practice. Ordinary travelers were usually entertained gratis by the chiefs, but merchants paid for their food and lodging as part of their business expenses. Contracts were oral, but "they gave credit and made loans, for which payment was made courteously and without interest." Nevertheless, as we shall see, war was sometimes caused by too drastic an attempt to collect a debt.

The principal media of exchange were cacao beans, beads of red shell, jade, and other green stones, small copper hatchets, and bells like sleigh bells. Cacao and shell beads came the nearest to taking the place of money. There can be little doubt, as Boekelman has shown, that the shell beads were made from a red spiny or rock oyster shell *(Spondylus princeps)* found on the Pacific coast from California to Colombia. Colima paid a tribute of these shells to Montezuma, but those brought to Yucatan seem to have come from southwestern Nicaragua. A string of these beads 18 cm. long was worth half a peso. As the shell is found in deep water and is difficult to detach from the rock, there was little danger of an overproduction and depreciation of this currency.

We find many accounts of the domestic commerce of Yucatan. Salt and preserved fish were carried from the coast to various parts of the interior; copal gum was shipped inland from Sinsimato and cacao from Chetumal, the only province of Yucatan where it was produced on any considerable scale. From a Maya document at Tulane University we learn of a regular route on which cacao was packed overland from Ucum on the lower Rio Hondo to the Xiu towns at the base of the sierra, a distance of 235 km. by air and much farther by the winding trail.[14] Salt, which was heavier, seems to have been transported by water wherever possible. To send it to the Cehaches in central southern Yucatan, it was shipped down the west coast, past Champoton to Laguna de Terminos, across the lagoon and up the Candelaria River, in spite of its rapids and portages, to Acalan. From there it was packed overland to its destination. Northern Yucatan, however, has no rivers, and all goods from the coast could be transported to the towns of the interior only on the backs of carriers.

In return, the inland towns supplied the coast with flint, game, fruit, various manufactured goods and some maize for local consumption, and cotton cloth for export. Maize did not grow well at Ecab or around Chauacha, where there were many savannas; at Zama people preferred fishing to farming; and in the northwestern corner of the peninsula the rainfall is light and the maize crop

[14] Documentos de Tabi.

often fails. Also fishing, salt-gathering, and commerce were the chief occupations along the coast. As we shall see farther on, however, the constant warfare between certain states interfered more or less with this trade, especially the enmity between Ah Kin Chel and its Sotuta and Cupul neighbors, and that between Chikincheel and the Cupuls. The Chels would not sell salt and fish to the people of Sotuta, and in retaliation the latter refused to sell fruit and game to Ah Kin Chel.

Beyond Chetumal and a short distance south of Champoton merchandise could be shipped only by water, and the foreign commerce with Tabasco and Honduras is of especial interest. The main exports to both of these countries were salt, cloth, honey, and slaves; indeed, one of the principal purposes of the wars between the various Yucatecan Maya states was to capture slaves for sale. Also the exports were heavier and bulkier than the goods brought home in exchange. More hands were needed on the outward journey, either to carry the produce or to paddle and beach the canoes and their loads in rough weather; so it was obviously profitable to sell some of them at the point of destination before returning home. There was an excellent market for slaves in Tabasco, where they were also brought from the highlands of Mexico. Among the Aztec the slave dealers were among the most highly honored members of the merchants' guild.

The commercial prosperity of northern Yucatan was based largely on its exports of cloth and salt. The country was famous for its decorated cotton mantles, which are said to have been carried even to the highlands of Mexico; and the Yucatecans enjoyed what was virtually a monopoly of the salt business on the Atlantic seaboard. Its importance as an article of diet among agricultural peoples who eat comparatively little meat can scarcely be exaggerated. There were many saline springs in the interior of southern Mexico, a few of them not very far distant from the coast. Here salt was manufactured by boiling the water in kettles, and the same thing could of course be done with seawater anywhere. It is obvious, however, that such sources could hardly compete with the Yucatecan salt, which needed only to be shoveled from the beds at the proper season and could be transported for much, if not all, of the distance to its foreign market by canoe. Similar salt beds existed in the lagoons of the Pacific coast, but these were far away. In any case, we know that nearly all the salt in Tabasco was brought from Yucatan.[15]

Little honey was produced in Tabasco, for we are told that the early Spanish settlers were obliged to obtain all their wax for candles from Yucatan. Less was probably exported to Honduras, where, although bees were not domes-

[15] De Mendizabal, 1930, pp. 93–100 and map. A few small natural salt beds existed near Laguna de Terminos, but these were of little importance.

ticated, as in Yucatan, a considerable amount of wild honey was gathered in the forests. There must have been some exportation of flint, which was abundant in Yucatan. It could hardly have been obtained on the alluvial plain of Tabasco; and although obsidian from the interior was available on the coast of Honduras, the tougher flint axes used for clearing the fields are known to have been scarce, and many people did not have them.

The cacao plantations in the river bottoms of Chetumal and the small groves in the hollows farther north did not begin to supply the demand in Yucatan, and large quantities of cacao were brought from both Tabasco and Honduras. Other imports were small copper bells and axes as well as plates and thin sheets of the same metal, to be made into similar ornaments and tools. Copper was brought from Tabasco and probably originated in Oaxaca. Yucatan produced neither copper nor gold, both of which had been introduced in any considerable quantity into northern Middle America only comparatively few centuries before the conquest. Considering the purchasing power and commercial contacts of the Yucatecan Maya, remarkably little gold was found there, and much of that contained a heavy copper alloy. As we have seen, a certain amount was found by the Spanish at the coast towns, such as small disks, crowns, votive offerings, and wooden masks plated with thin gold leaf. Only at the town of Chetumal was any considerable quantity taken; here, Oviedo tells us, the Spaniards seized manufactured gold articles with a bullion value of 2000 pesos. Most of the gold recovered from the Sacred Cenote at Chichen Itza is believed to have come from Costa Rica or Panama; but at the time of the conquest there were other possible sources nearer home. Placer gold was mined near the coast of Veracruz and probably in northern Honduras, where we find such mines reported as early as 1544.

Another import was the skeins of dyed rabbit hair called *tuchumite,* used for woven cloth designs. It was brought to Tabasco by Aztec merchants and is said to have originated in the Mixteca country of Oaxaca. This was the well-known *tochomitl,* which was an important article of commerce in the highlands of Mexico.[16] We have already described the red shell beads, which came from the Pacific coast of Nicaragua by way of Honduras. Besides the beads, some of the actual shell was also imported and apparently manufactured locally.

Precious stones were not mined in Yucatan but wholly imported, probably by way of Tabasco and Hibueras, although the original sources of some of them are still unknown. These were mostly the jade and allied green stones called *tun,* which were made into beads and other ornaments. One "very precious stone" was called *kantixal* and is elsewhere described as a jewel worn on the

16 Sahagun, 1938, 2: 355; RY, 1: 304.

breast. It was no doubt a carved pendant of jade or some other stone, which hung from the neck. At Chetumal the Spaniards found masks encrusted with turquoises and the crystalline green stones they called "emeralds" (Maya, *potzil tun*). It is difficult to tell where they were mined; merchants brought them from Tabasco to the Valley of Mexico. From the highlands of Chiapas and via Tabasco came the yellow topaz nose beads, which the Spaniards called "amber" and the Maya, *maat, matun*, or *zuli mat*. Landa states that the Maya pierced the septum of the nose and inserted "a stone of amber" in the hole. This apparently was the *apozonalli* of the Aztec markets, appraised in three grades, one not very costly. It was probably not very common in Yucatan, where little, if indeed any, has been found by archaeologists.[17]

The tail feathers of the quetzal and macaw were especially valued. Both were imported, for the macaw was scarce in Yucatan and the precious quetzal plumage came from the mountains of Verapaz in Guatemala. The parrots of Honduras were said to be the finest in the Indies. Quetzal feathers, which were also transported directly to Tenochtitlan, could have reached Yucatan by way of either Honduras or Tabasco. The former is more likely, for not only was Honduras nearer to Verapaz, but the quetzal is also found there. Honduras, indeed, was known far and wide as "the land of gold, feathers, and cacao."[18]

Obsidian is not found in Yucatan, but points, knives, and other implements of this material have been recovered from many ancient sites. It was still being imported at the time of the conquest, for a European penknife has been found associated with obsidian blades in a burial at Kantunil. Obsidian was probably brought from both Honduras and Tabasco. There were mines up the Motagua River near Zacapa, and Aztec merchants are known to have brought obsidian knives and earplugs to Xicalango.

From the archaeological finds we know that at various times in the past there had been a foreign trade in pottery. Long before the conquest, a carved slate ware, probably from northwestern Yucatan, was apparently exported to some extent. Later, vessels with a natural glaze known as plumbate were imported from some region as yet undetermined, perhaps from southwestern Guatemala or Chiapas; and a fine orange ware was brought from Veracruz. At the time of the conquest we hear nothing of any foreign trade in pottery, nor has there been discovered in Yucatan any fine earthenware which appears to have been manufactured after the fall of Mayapan.

In spite of the intervening distance, there was much commerce between Tabasco and northern Honduras. When Cortez made his famous journey

[17] Oviedo y Valdes, 1851–55, bk. 33, ch. 6; Vienna dictionary, ff. 13r, 98r, 162v. Sahagun, 1938, 2: 355, 3: 280.
[18] Paxbolon relación, Chontal text, AGI, Mexico 138, photo, p. 160.

overland to the latter country, the merchants of Tabasco and Xicalango gave him a map painted on cotton cloth showing a route across the base of the Yucatan Peninsula to Nito on the Rio Dulce and the coast towns beyond. From here further routes branched, one apparently along the Caribbean coast to Panama, and the other to the Pacific coast of Nicaragua. The thickly populated part of Yucatan, however, lay to the north of this route.

Alfaro's report describes the inland water route, which wound its way along the network of rivers in Tabasco, across Laguna de Terminos, and up the Estero de Sabancuy. From the end of this estuary there is little doubt that goods were carried along the shore of the Gulf of Mexico to Champoton and Campeche, and thence to various parts of Yucatan. Here we find little, if any, mention of large seagoing canoes like those seen on the east coast. It does, however, seem likely that the long swampy lagoon, which parallels the entire north coast, was utilized for water transportation, at least during certain seasons of the year. The large consumption of cacao in Ah Kin Chel suggests that this imported commodity was cheaper and more abundant in the northern coast provinces than farther inland. We have already mentioned the overland route from the neighborhood of Ticul to Chetumal Bay, and the water traffic from there to Honduras is well known. When Chichen Itza flourished, the embarking point for Honduras was on Ascencion Bay, but in early colonial times the port was at Zama. When Cortez came to Cozumel, he was told of merchants there who had recently seen the Spanish captives, Aguilar and Guerrero, the latter of whom was at Chetumal at this time. From Cozumel it was not far to the towns of Chikincheel, whose people were called "the lords of the sea." In view of the large markets and commercial importance of these towns, it seems probable that salt was shipped directly by water from northeastern Yucatan to Honduras. Indeed, in spite of the lack of direct evidence, we could cite various circumstances strongly suggesting that canoes made the entire voyage around the Yucatan Peninsula from Tabasco to Honduras. Among the pilgrims who came to Cozumel some are said to have been from Tabasco and Xicalango, which could be more easily understood if the island lay on a water route connecting Tabasco with Honduras.

We have dwelt on the commerce of Yucatan at some length because of its historical and geographical implications. It represents the last phase of an exchange of merchandise and ideas which had been going on for centuries. It also shows that Yucatan, Tabasco, and northern Honduras were commercially dependent on one another and constituted an economic bloc, in which the production and marketing of cacao, salt, and cotton cloth played an important part. In view of Montejo's activities in both Tabasco and Honduras as well as in Yucatan, it would appear that he was well aware of this economic situation.

Chapter 9. Political Institutions

IT IS DIFFICULT to appraise the political organization of the Yucatecan Maya without taking into account something of its historical background. Although our knowledge of Maya history in pre-Spanish times is sketchy, it seems sufficient to furnish an explanation of at least some of the features of the political system which we find operating in Yucatan at the time of the conquest.

Although we may modify this opinion as additional material comes to light, it would now appear that all the historical information that we have treats only of the actions of certain Mexican intruders and their alleged descendants. This is to imply that such history as we know concerns itself little, if at all, with the Yucatecan Maya before they came under Mexican influence.

By Mexican we mean the bearers of a Nahua culture. They all appear to have come from Tabasco, although some of them may have actually entered the country from its eastern side. It is possible that a Mexican occupation of the north coast of Honduras even preceded that of Yucatan. Some of these intruders spoke Nahuatl, for we find a number of Nahuatl words and names in Yucatan. Although we have less positive grounds for the belief, there is evidence that many, perhaps most, of them also spoke Chontal, the language of the Tabasco Maya and closely related to that of Yucatan.[1] Within the Chontal area were a number of Mexican-speaking towns in central and northern Tabasco, among them Cimatan and Xicalango, which were two of the most important commercial centers of the region. Farther west were larger Nahuatl-speaking areas in southern Veracruz and western Tabasco, which included much of the land of the Olmeca, or "rubber people." To the Aztec, Cimatan and Xicalango, as well as Coatzacoalcos which lies a considerable distance west of the Chontal country, were all a part of a region which they called the "Province of Anahuac Xicalanco."

Our historical sources for Yucatan are partly the accounts which the Indians related to the sixteenth-century Spanish settlers. The best of these came from Gaspar Antonio Chi, a native court interpreter related to the ruling family of Mani. He grew to adolescence under the old regime and afterward became an excellent Spanish and Latin scholar. Fray Diego de Landa, afterward bishop

---

[1] Torquemada, 1723, bk. 3, chs. 7, 13. The existence in both Honduras and Mexico of a legend that the Mexican people had originally come from the former country, in spite of a general belief to the contrary, argues strongly for an early occupation of the Honduras coast by people of a Nahua culture (RY, 1 409–10).

of Yucatan, received much of the information contained in his famous report on the Maya from both Gaspar Antonio Chi and Nachi Cocom, the last halach uinic, or territorial ruler, of Sotuta. The other most important sources are found in the native literature written in Maya but in European script: the five so-called Maya chronicles, several isolated historical narratives, and many prophecies containing historical allusions. Besides these we have a number of land documents, in which certain historical material was introduced in order to show that the ownership of the lands in question was legitimate, especially when they were town lands.

Maya history begins with a vague account of certain foreigners who occupied the east coast and Chichen Itza for a time but were driven out. These seem to be a people called the Itza, who probably came originally from Tabasco. Later they returned, this time apparently from the southwest, and occupied Chichen Itza again. In one of the early Spanish reports we read: "At one time all this land was under the rule of a single lord, when the ancient city of Chichen Itza was still unimpaired. To him all the lords of this province were tributary; and even from without the province, from Mexico, Guatemala, Chiapas, and other provinces they sent them presents in token of peace and friendship."[2] Of the lords of Chichen Itza another similar report states that "their rule lasted more than two hundred years." The Maya chronicles tell of the conquest of Chichen Itza by the halach uinic of Mayapan, who was aided by a number of warriors with Mexican names, and we are elsewhere told that the Canul figured prominently in this episode. Subsequently we find the hegemony transferred to Mayapan, where there was a centralized joint government under the leadership of three prominent families, the Cocom, Xiu, and Canul. The Xiu had come from Uxmal, but the Cocom and Canul may have been older allies and longer resident at Mayapan. The other prominent chiefs of the country resided at the capital and each ruled his own towns from there. Finally about the middle of the fifteenth century the Xiu headed a successful conspiracy against the Cocom, Mayapan was destroyed, and the joint government dissolved into a number of independent states. Of these, the Xiu founded the so-called Province of Mani; the Cocom, that of Sotuta; and the Canul, Ah Canul. We hear little of the Itza of Chichen Itza after the establishment of the hegemony of Mayapan. The Spaniards found them living around Lake Peten in northern Guatemala, where they are believed to have migrated after the fall of Chichen Itza. They remained unconquered until the close of the seventeenth century.

Mexican architectural and sculptural features are conspicuous in the ruins

[2] RY, I: 120.

of Chichen Itza, and some are to be seen at Mayapan. There are a few at Uxmal, but they are much less evident, and it is difficult to know whether to ascribe them to the Xiu, who had come from Mexico, or to some earlier contact with the latter country.

The descendants of the Mexican intruders continued to be characterized by their mobility. If forced out of one region, they sought another where they could dominate the autochthonous inhabitants, exact a moderate tribute, raid their neighbors for slaves, and, if possible, control commerce. Besides the shifts already noted, we find one such group in the late fourteenth century moving from Cozumel to the Usumacinta valley. Here they collected the local Chontal-speaking inhabitants into a town at Tenosique, where they apparently attempted to control the commerce of the great river, which formed part of an important trade route between Tabasco and the rich coast of northern Honduras. Later they settled at Tixchel on the main water route from Tabasco to Yucatan. Driven from that strategic site, they finally established a large commercial center farther inland in the Candelaria basin.[3]

From their own point of view they were local benefactors. One of the descendants of the Ah Canuls, telling of his ancestors who settled in western Yucatan after the fall of Mayapan, writes in his own language: "They were not greedy for chieftainship, nor were they provokers of discord. . . . They began to love the towns and the batabs, and they were also loved by the towns."[4]

Among the Yucatecan Maya, government was in the hands of the ruling caste already described, whose members prided themselves on their Mexican ancestry. The word Zuiua, a legendary Nahuatl place name, was the symbol of their Mexican origin. In a chapter of the Book of Chilam Balam of Chumayel we are told that only persons of illustrious lineage, apparently the descendants of the Zuiua people, should hold political offices of any importance. Here is a questionnaire, the language of which has a hidden meaning. Officeholders who did not know the answers, which are called the language of Zuiua, were thus shown to be impostors and suffered an unpleasant death, described in considerable detail.

Many of the independent states were governed by a single ruler, and this dignitary was called the halach uinic, literally the "real man." We know that the Provinces of Mani, Sotuta, Ceh Pech, Hocaba, Cochuah, Champoton, and Cozumel had this form of government, and probably Ah Kin Chel, Tazes, and Tayasal also.

The halach uinic seems to have been primarily a war chief, like the head of the Mexican confederacy; and if we compare the peaceful character of the

---

[3] Paxbolon relación, AGI, Mexico 138.   [4] Crónica de Calkini, pp. 13–14.

majority of the earlier Maya sculptures with the warlike representations found
on the monuments of the Mexican invaders, especially at Chichen Itza, it is
difficult to escape the conclusion that the change was brought about by the
newcomers. Reports, evidently inspired by Gaspar Antonio Chi, tell of the
peaceful character of the Xiu penetration of Yucatan; but the same reports
carry the information that it was a Xiu leader who founded the military orders
(*caballería*) so characteristic of the Nahua of the highlands of Mexico and
bitterly hated by the Maya.

The office of halach uinic was confined to a certain family in each province
where it existed: to the Xiu in Mani, the Cocom in Sotuta, the Pech in Ceh
Pech, the Cochuah in the state that bore their name, and probably the Chel
in Ah Kin Chel. Landa tells us that the office descended from father to son if
the latter was of age, otherwise to a brother, who held the office for life but
who was succeeded by the son of the older brother. If there was no brother,
a capable person was chosen, probably a relative of the same patronymic. We
find the same system of succession among the Chontal of Itzamkanac and in
the Valley of Mexico.

Besides acting as the local executive of the town which was his capital, the
halach uinic formulated foreign policy and directed the government of his
province through the local town heads, or batabs, many of whom were related
to him. Although the batab usually acted as magistrate, serious cases (probably
where more than one town was involved) were referred to the territorial ruler.
The latter took it upon himself to keep track of the boundaries of his province,
guard against encroachments by the people of the neighboring states, and see
that his own towns did not trespass on one another's lands. In 1545 Nachi
Cocom of Sotuta personally made a survey of his entire frontier and conferred
with various Cochuah and Cupul chiefs who lived close to his borders, evidently discussing local differences of opinion in regard to the frontiers. Again
in 1557 there was a boundary conference at Mani presided over by the halach
uinic, Francisco de Montejo Xiu (Kukum Xiu), and attended by his own
batabs and those of the adjoining states. Here were determined not only the
limits of the Province of Mani but also those of the lands belonging to the
various towns within the area.

In addition to his political and judicial activities, the halach uinic evidently
had certain definite religious functions as well. In the Motul dictionary we find
the term halach uinic defined as "bishop, *oidor* [a certain superior judge],
governor, provincial, or *comisario* [the traveling inspector of a religious order];
it is the name of these and other similar dignities."[5] This is confirmed by the

---

[5] Motul dictionary, 1929, p. 369.

records of Landa's inquisition of 1562, which state not only that a certain human sacrifice was performed at Yaxcaba at the written order of the halach uinic of Sotuta, but also that on another occasion the latter aided personally in excising the heart of the victim.

The halach uinic had a number of sources of income. Besides the produce of the cacao groves and farms worked by his own slaves, he would, as the local head of his capital, enjoy the usual compensation and service given to the batab of a town. Acting in his judicial capacity, he would receive the customary gifts which litigants and petitioners presented to the judge as court fees. Finally, as territorial ruler he exacted certain tribute from the towns of his province. This levy is said to have been very light everywhere. Each town contributed moderate quantities of maize, beans, chile, poultry, honey, cotton cloth, and game. Salt and fish were also collected, if any of his towns lay on the coast. Nacahun Cochuah received certain precious green stones, probably jade beads; and slaves were included from Tekit in the Xiu area. Strangely enough only rarely are cacao beans mentioned as a part of the tribute given to the halach uinic. Although the tithe was considered light, which it no doubt was, compared to that exacted later by the Spaniards, the small town of Tahdziu paid the Xiu ruler twenty loads of maize each year, and every household in the province contributed one turkey hen, so the aggregate must have been considerable.

In one report from the Province of Mani the assessment is said to have been almost voluntary and only in acknowledgment of the Xiu lordship, the principal obligation being military service; but in another from the same area we are told that anyone who did not pay tribute was sacrificed.

It is not known whether there was a provincial council; the advisers of the halach uinic seem to have been the local officials of his capital. It is probable, however, that some of the batabs of other towns, especially those related to him, were consulted on provincial affairs.

No detailed description of what we might call the court of the halach uinic has come down to us. His household was no doubt similar to that of the batab but maintained on a larger scale, as he received sufficient tribute to live in considerable state. We know that when the Tutul Xiu ruler came to meet Montejo at Merida in 1542, he was carried in a litter and accompanied by an imposing retinue. The pomp and ceremony with which he was attended may be inferred from that which, as we shall see, was accorded to the ordinary batab.

The local town head was called the batab, who was appointed by the halach uinic in such provinces as we find the latter. A son usually succeeded his father to the position, if he was considered suitable, but in the Provinces of Ceh Pech and Mani many batabs were not the sons of their predecessors. Where there was no halach uinic, the rules of succession were probably the same as those which governed the territorial ruler.

The batab's functions were administrative, judicial, and military. Under him was a town council. He gave audience to petitioners; he saw to it that the houses of his town were kept in repair and that the fields were cleared, burned, and planted at the proper time, as designated by the priest, who kept track of the calendar. He acted as magistrate, trying criminals and deciding civil suits where both parties were of his own town. As we have already noted, cases where more than one town was involved were settled by the halach uinic. He had a small staff of deputies or assistants called *ah ḳulels,* who attended him at home and abroad and conveyed his wishes or orders to the people. When he held court, these men acted as advocates for the parties to the suit. Although they definitely ranked below the *ah cuch cabs,* they were important members of the town government.[6] In war the batab commanded the soldiers of his town, although there was also a special war chief called the *nacom.*

The batab's power varied apparently in the different states. Where he was the appointee of the halach uinic, he was naturally subject to the orders of that ruler. If the province was a confederacy of independent towns, as in Ah Canul and probably in Chakan, the chief check on his authority was the ah cuch cabs, who were members of the council and without whose assent nothing could be done. In the Province of Cupul were groups of towns, each dominated by the most powerful of the group. Although it is possible that this domination was confined to the exaction of tribute, I surmise that the authority of the subject batabs was limited by that of the ruling town.

Where there was a halach uinic over the batab, his town does not seem to have paid tribute to the latter but was obligated only to cultivate a field for him, garner the crop, build and repair his house, and perhaps supply him with domestic service. There are indications that he usually also had slaves who worked certain lands under his personal control. In his capacity of magistrate, however, he received certain gifts from petitioners and litigants according to their capacity to pay. At Sihunchen in northeastern Yucatan, where there was no territorial ruler, the batab received a certain amount of tribute consisting of food supplies and small cotton mantles, and this was probably typical of such towns.

---

[6] Motul dictionary, 1929, p. 527; San Francisco dictionary, Maya-Spanish, item, *ah ḳulel;* Crónica de Calkini, p. 11.

In the Cupul area, however, certain batabs who were overlords of other neighboring towns exacted tribute of considerable value. Besides the usual grain, other produce, and poultry, they received cacao, cotton mantles, and beads of red shell and green stone.

The batab was treated with great ceremony and attended by many people when he went abroad. When he visited the house of one of his townsmen to drink, the populace accompanied him, bowing before him, opening a lane for him to pass, and spreading their mantles in front of him. Even on less ceremonious occasions they protected his head from the sun with great fans of bright feathers. The cacique of Loche received Montejo in a reclining position and would speak to him only through a cotton cloth suspended between them like a curtain.

The members of the town council were the ah cuch cabs; they were also in charge of certain subdivisions of the town, collecting tribute and attending to other municipal affairs. As we have already noted, the ah cuch cab "had his vote like a regidor in the municipal government, and without his vote nothing could be done." We are also informed in a report from the Province of Ceh Pech that, "These (the batabs) divided the town into its wards like the districts of a parish (*colaciones*) and appointed a rich and capable man to take charge of each. It was their duty to attend to the tribute and services (communal labor?) at the proper time and to assemble the people of their wards for banquets and festivals as well as for war."[7]

In former times at Chichen Itza and also at Mayapan when the city was destroyed in the fifteenth century, these towns had been divided into four main quarters like the Acalan capital at Itzamkanac and as in the highlands of Mexico; but I am unable as yet to find evidence that the town wards in northern Yucatan at the time of the conquest corresponded to such a system. At Tenochtitlan the four main quarters were composed of a much larger number of smaller subdivisions called *calpullis*, which the Spaniards considered to be the wards of the town. In the few census lists that have come down to us from sixteenth-century Yucatan, families of many different patronymics lived in the same ward, so it would appear that these subdivisions were not based on the lineage groups.[8]

Another important official was the *holpop,* or *ah holpop,* whom the Spanish writers call an overseer (*mandón*) and sometimes even a cacique. In colonial times he had charge of the municipal building called the *popolna,* "where they assemble to discuss public business and learn to dance for the town festivals."

---

[7] Motul dictionary, 1929, p. 80; Vienna dictionary, f. 169r; Roys, 1940, p. 40; RY, 1: 137–38, 2: 211.
[8] AGM, Cuenta e visita del pueblo de Ppencuyut, 1584, Tierras 2809, no. 20.

Holpop means the "head of the mat," and the mat was a symbol of authority. The halach uinic and the batab are said to have governed the people through these officers, "who were like regidors or captains," and through them the people "negotiated with the lord for whatever they desired."[9] "These, and no others, consulted with the lord on matters and embassies from outside."[10] Two small towns in the Province of Mani are known to have been ruled by holpops instead of batabs. The political functions of the holpop seem to have ceased after the Spanish conquest, but we find him still acting as chief singer or chanter, in charge of the drums and other musical instruments, and presiding over weddings and assemblies in colonial times.

Lowest in the official scale was the *tupil* (Nahuatl *topile*), a term defined as *alguacil,* or minor peace officer. A number of tupils acted as carriers, when Nachi Cocom surveyed the borders of his province in 1545; and at Calkini they had the handling of the town stores. Evidently it was not a position filled by members of the nobility.

Besides the batab, there was a special war chief. He and the town priests should probably also be considered members of the town government, but here they will be discussed separately in the studies of war and religion.

[9] RY, 1: 90; Roys, 1940, pp. 39–40.
[10] RY, 1: 95–96.

Chapter 10. Warfare

IF WE TAKE into consideration the historical background of northern Yucatan, it is not surprising that the independent states, into which the Spaniards found the country divided, were constantly at war with one another. As we have seen, each so-called province was under the control of an aristocratic caste. Most, if not all, of its members believed themselves to be descended from the warlike Mexican adventurers, who had entered and dominated the country several centuries before; but this does not seem to have deterred them from making war on one another. This ruling class had, generally speaking, adopted most of the customs of the autochthonous population, and they all spoke its language, although they retained to some extent the religion and warlike traditions of the early invaders. Captives taken in war were desirable for sacrifice, but we may well infer from the reliefs on the older monuments that this was by no means a foreign innovation. Caciques and other leading men kept many slaves, and this supply of labor was recruited largely by means of warfare. It was the policy of each state to exploit its own commerce, as far as possible, at the expense of its neighbors. Finally, as we have already seen, the agricultural system involved letting the land revert to forest for a considerable number of years after two consecutive seasons in crop. This offered a temptation to an aggressive group of people living near a frontier to trespass across the boundary, cut the forest, and grow and harvest a crop, before the authorities of the neighboring province would be ready to interfere, particularly since it was not customary to make war during the growing season. With such agricultural conditions a considerable proportion of the population thus tended to live in scattered hamlets.

The most common weapons of warfare were the bow and arrow, dart, spear, and a kind of sword. The bow was of a hard wood called *chulul* (*Apoplanesia paniculata* Presl.). It was a little shorter than the height of a man, and strung with a henequen cord. Arrows were made of reeds. They were feathered, tipped with points of flint or sometimes fish "teeth," and the point was set in a piece of wood fitted into the end of the reed. Gomara tells us that two quivers of arrows were carried in war.

Their darts had fire-hardened or flint points and are said to have been about the height of a man. They were probably propelled by spear throwers, which are described by Landa and portrayed on monuments dating from the Mexican

65

period. Longer spears, 12 to 15 spans, seem to have been thrown by hand and also thrust.

The native sword was a stick of chulul wood 4 spans long and 3 fingers wide. In its grooved edges were set sharp blades of flint. The Spaniards called it a *macana,* said to be derived from the Mexican *macuahuitl,* but its Maya name was *hadzab,* literally "that with which one strikes a blow." There was also a short dagger of chulul, a span in length, and Landa tells of small axes of metal, probably copper, set into a wooden handle. We find occasional mention of the use of slings and stones. Although the Maya word *yumtun,* or *yuuntun,* is defined as a sling in three early Maya dictionaries, Landa denies its use but says that stones were thrown by hand with great force and accuracy.

Defensive covering consisted of shields, cotton body armor, and wooden helmets. The shield was called *chimal,* a Nahuatl word, and is said to have been round and constructed of rods of chulul closely bound side by side. It was made in two layers, the rods of the inner layer being set at right angles to those of the outer, and was covered or draped with deerskins.[1] The body was protected with twisted rolls of cotton cloth, a thick sleeveless jacket, or a very long broad strip of cloth tightly wound many times around the torso. Wooden helmets, probably ornamented with feathers, were worn by a few of the leaders.

The ordinary warrior, however, fought clothed with only a loincloth and adorned with war paint and feathers. The paint was most often black but sometimes red and white. The various arrangements of the hair possibly indicated the grade or rank of the individual. Skins of jaguars and pumas were worn by some, who may have been members of the military orders. Men of rank wore their jewelry. A Maya manuscript from Ah Canul says of a certain prominent warrior that, "When he went into battle, he put on his necklace of red shell beads, he put on his necklace of green stone beads, he fitted his shield to his arm, and with spear [in hand] he died in battle."[2]

Sharing the batab's command was a war chief called the nacom. He was installed in office with great ceremony and held the position for three years, during which he ate no meat but the flesh of fish and iguanas, was never intoxicated, remained continent, and had little intercourse with his fellow townsmen. He could not even be served his food by a woman. He probably had much influence in declaring war, for persons who had suffered injury away from home came to him to complain and seek revenge. Nacahun Noh, the war chief of Saci (Valladolid), received gifts of shell beads from people

[1] Oblong shields are also seen on the frescoes at Chichen Itza.
[2] Crónica de Calkini, p. 15.

living as far away as Tizimin who wished to conciliate him and avoid war with his town.[3]

Serving under the nacom were certain picked warriors called *holcans,* or braves. When these were not sufficient, however, other men could also be called out. The holcans were paid only in time of war, partly by the nacom personally and partly by the town; and only members of the active force shared in the spoils. Upon their return from a campaign, the holcans were permitted a certain license for a time, subjecting the town to more or less annoyance and demanding service and entertainment as their right.

Wars were short, and the usual time was between October and the end of January. This was the cool season, when there was little or no agricultural activity and when food would be found in the enemy's granaries.

Headed by the batab and the nacom the war party set out quietly, hoping for a surprise attack, although it was not customary to fight at night. They were preceded by scouts, known as "road weasels" or "army weasels," and, as soon as contact with the enemy was made, they blew whistles and conch shells, beat their wooden drums, and pounded large tortoise shells with deer-horn sticks. This uproar was accompanied by war cries and loud insults to the enemy, often of an obscene character *(palabras sucias).* If the nacom was killed or turned back, all the others slung their shields on their backs and re-treated. To bear one's shield on one's back *(cuch chimal)* became a figure of speech for being overcome or defeated in a dispute or for losing courage. Any-one who killed an enemy removed the jawbone, which was cleaned of flesh and worn as an armlet; and he who killed a batab or nacom was especially honored. It was most desired to take prisoners, who became the property of their captors. Those of rank were sacrificed, while plebeians—men, women and children—were enslaved. The hands of a prisoner were bound to a wooden collar or yoke, to which a longer rope was attached, and with this his captor led him home.

Surprise attacks were difficult, except for small war parties. Forest guards were stationed at various border sites and could give warning of an invasion. Battles often took place on the forest trails leading from one province to an-other. We find what are evidently references to such encounters in the Maya prophecies, where we read, "There shall be sadness over the flies and the large hairy flies [which swarm] at the crossroads."[4]

Barricades were set up on the main roads at strategic points in the thick forest, especially at the approaches to the towns. These were walls of dry stone

[3] Possibly such payments were compensatory damages for his fellow townsmen.
[4] Book of Chilam Balam of Tizimin, p. 25.

and palisades of heavy timbers bound together by lianas, and positions were constructed from which arrows could be shot and darts, spears, and stones could be hurled at the approaching enemy. Often the barriers were semicircular and camouflaged. Here the defenders waited quietly until the attackers had entered the trap and could be assailed from either side as well as from the front. During the conquest the palisades proved less effective, because the Spaniards with their metal swords and axes could cut the liana bindings and pull down the uprights. Nevertheless, these defenses gave the first invaders much trouble, until they later learned to detect the trap, divide their forces, and make flank attacks around the ends, while some of them made a show of assaulting the center.

City walls of dry stone have been found in the ruins of Tulum and Mayapan, and the Spaniards discovered a wall and ditch surrounding Champoton. Chamberlain and I have observed at Ake a ditch and the remains of a rampart which possibly enclosed the central part of the town only. Completely fortified sites may have been more common in southern Yucatan. Cortez found a Cehache town encircled by a wooden rampart and ditch; and Villagutierre tells of a town named Tulumqui farther south, which was defended by a hedge of agave.

It is of interest to note that the most frequent cause of war reported by encomenderos of towns in Ceh Pech, Hocaba, and Sotuta was to obtain slaves to sell. This suggests the possibility that, since they ordinarily fought with the neighboring provinces, they sold their captives and for their own service purchased slaves from more distant regions, who could less easily escape to their homes. In the Province of Cupul, the only area in which we hear of wars between two towns of the same state, war was sometimes due to quarrels over payments for goods sold on credit. Chancenote, the capital of Tazes, went to war to retaliate for injuries to its own citizens or those of its subject towns. In spite of these intestine dissensions, however, the Cupuls seem to have united when threatened by a common enemy, as in the case of the Spanish invasion.

Namo Cupul of Ekbalam frequently made war on the neighboring town of Yalcoba and sacrificed or enslaved his captives, although the batab of Yalcoba was probably also a member of the Cupul lineage.[5] The northern Cupul towns, especially those around Tizimin, were constantly at war with those of Ah Kin Chel and Chikincheel in their attempts to obtain access to the salt beds on the north coast. The latter province apparently even prevented the

---

[5] RY, 2: 161. A certain Pedro Cupul was governor of Yalcoba in 1565 (Residencia Quijada, AGI, Justicia 245).

Cupuls from coming to certain parts of the coast to trade.[6] Between Ah Kin Chel and Chikincheel was a considerable extent of coast distant from any town of importance, and it was probably a constant temptation to the Cupuls to raid the salt beds in this region. Even Popola in the center of the Cupul area warred with the city of Chauaca to the north and the Province of Sotuta to the west. On the whole, however, we hear little of hostilities between Sotuta and the Cupuls, although they had many disagreements over lands along their common border in colonial times.[7]

Ah Kin Chel fought with its neighbors on all sides. Besides its hostilities with the Cupul towns, it was attacked by Sotuta because it refused to sell the latter salt and fish. Its wars with Ceh Pech may have been caused by the slave raids of this neighbor, possibly by its own as well. Sotuta, too, seems to have been at war in nearly every quarter. The slave-raiding propensities of its Cocom rulers had been one of the causes of the revolution at Mayapan, and Nadzul Iuit of Hocaba, Sotuta's neighbor to the west, was equally noted for similar activities. There was also the old feud with the Xiu of Mani, who had betrayed and massacred the Cocom rulers, when Mayapan was destroyed. The experiences of the Spaniards with the Cochuahs indicate that they were also a warlike people, but as far as we can learn, they were for the most part on good terms with Sotuta and the Cupuls. The elaborate fortifications in the southernmost Cochuah towns suggest not resistance primarily to the Spaniards but rather hostile relations with Chetumal.

Little is recorded of wars between the provinces of the west, although we surmise that they, too, occasionally raided their neighbors for slaves and plunder. Chakan and Ah Canul possessed fisheries and salt beds, but it seems very possible that they maintained a more liberal commercial policy with their neighbors than did the coast peoples farther east.

We have no direct evidence of military alliances between the various independent states of Yucatan in pre-Spanish times; but there can be little doubt that such existed from the readiness with which the warriors of Cupul and Cochuah joined the Cocom of Sotuta in their attack on the Spaniards at Merida in 1542. In one case there appears to have been such an alliance with a nation living outside the Yucatan Peninsula. After the Spaniards were driven out of Chetumal on the southeast coast, an expedition of fifty war canoes from this region came to assist the natives living on the Ulua River in Honduras in their resistance to the Spanish invaders there. It seems probable that the towns

---

[6] RY, 2: 86, 90, 185, 208. Kikil and Hucbilchen warred with Chikincheel, Tecay and Zodzil with the people of the coast, Tizimin and Dzonot with Buctzotz and Dzilam, and Chochola (near Kikil) with Tepakan.

[7] *Ibid.*, 2: 46. "Noata" has been read as "Choaca," or Chauaca. Cf. Roys, 1939, pp. 11–16.

of southwestern Yucatan at times formed similar alliances with some of the towns of Tabasco. During the fifteenth century, when the Chontal-speaking Acalan descended the Usumacinta River and occupied Tixchel at the north end of Laguna de Terminos, they were driven back into the interior apparently by the united efforts of the Yucatecan Maya of Champoton, the Nahuatl-speaking inhabitants of Xicalango, and the Chontal of the town later known as Tabasquillo.

In the native literature the people of Emal on the north coast and of Uaymil, which was near Chetumal, are called "the guardians of the sands, the guardians of the sea." Since Mosquito Indians in canoes from Rio Tinto in northeastern Honduras were still making raids on the east coast of Yucatan down to the middle of the eighteenth century, it seems not unlikely that similar attacks took place in pre-Spanish times.[8]

[8] Roys, 1933, pp. 142, 156.

Chapter 11. Religion

THE RELIGIOUS beliefs and practices of the Maya were an important factor in the attitude of the Spaniards and natives toward one another from the very first and continued to affect their subsequent relations. The two races were impressed by the striking, if superficial, resemblances in their religious rites. Crosses, altars, and incense were sacred to both; confession of sin, baptism of children, fasting, continence, and the ceremonial consumption of fermented liquor were common practices.

One of the first things to arrest the attention of the Spaniards who navigated the coast of Yucatan was the religious architecture. They were enormously impressed by the large stone pyramid temples; and it is evident from the records of the early expeditions that they displayed considerable interest in what they found inside these buildings. Except on the Island of Cozumel, the first explorers tell little of conditions within the towns, but on Cape Catoche and at Campeche and Champoton they found temples by the seashore, evidently devoted to the worship of the gods of the fishermen and hunters of aquatic fowl. Similar shrines on Laguna de Terminos were also visited by traveling merchants, who doubtless frequented those on the Yucatan coast.

A monumental stairway ascended the pyramid temple. Sacrifices to the gods inside the temple were publicly performed either in the court below or on the terrace at the top. Descriptions of the interior are few and brief. On the walls were painted representations of deities, which the Spaniards considered hideous, and of sacred trees that resembled crosses. It seems not unlikely that these frescoes also portrayed ceremonial and historical scenes, which we find on the walls of earlier structures at Chichen Itza and Chacmultun. Altars were present, but we do not know that they were always found inside the temples; when Cortez cast the idols out of one at Cozumel and set up a shrine to the Virgin, he seems to have found it necessary to have the native masons construct an altar. Large stone tables supported by atlantean figures are still to be seen in the temples at Chichen Itza, and the Spaniards later found somewhat similar altars in use among the Itza at Tayasal. The principal feature of the Maya sanctuary was its many idols, but we know little of how they were arranged about the room. Some, as we have noted, were kept in wooden chests with gold votive objects. Bones of important rulers were preserved wrapped in mats. Here, too, were various religious accessories, such as

71

incense burners, often a clay bowl with an ornamental head on one side of the rim, and probably the covered clay plates or shallow bowls, in which the heart and blood of the sacrificial victim were offered to the idols.

Many important ceremonies were not performed at the temple, but in the private oratory of the batab or some other wealthy person of high rank. We have no description of such an oratory in northern Yucatan, but at Tayasal we read of one in the reception hall of the ruler, where idols, a large stone table with twelve seats for the priests, and some hieroglyphic books were arranged.

The Spaniards were struck with the vast number of idols on every hand: in the temples and smaller shrines, the oratories of the chiefs, and the homes of the common people, as well as on the roads, at the entrances to the towns, and on the stairways of the temples. They were mostly of clay, but some were of wood and perhaps a few of stone. The last probably included some jade images, and at Tayasal Villagutierre tells of a "coarse emerald" figure a span in height. The Spaniards thought most of them extraordinarily ugly and usually referred to them as *"demonios,"* partly no doubt because they were regarded as the work of the Author of Evil and partly because the faces of many of these figures bore a startling resemblance to those of the fiends portrayed in mediaeval Christian art.

In view of the prevalence of idolatry in Yucatan it is surprising to learn of a general tradition and belief that "they were not idolaters until Kukulcan, a Mexican captain, entered into these provinces; it was he that taught them idolatry."[1] Thompson has shown that the Chol Maya to the south, who had been less subject to Mexican influences, did not have idols but worshipped various features and forces of nature and that the Yucatecan Maya religion had evidently been of a somewhat similar character in pre-Mexican times. This is not to imply, however, that there was ever anything like a Mosaic taboo against portraying their deities, for on the buildings, stelae, and pottery of this earlier period we find many representations of the various Maya gods. In view of this, it is interesting that owing to Spanish influence idolatry has almost completely disappeared from Yucatan today, except for the worship of what was once the sacred tree, still painted green and now called "our lord Santa Cruz." Many of the personified powers of nature, however, still play an important part in the native religion.

Incomplete as our knowledge of Maya religion is, a full discussion of even those deities with which we have some acquaintance lies beyond the scope of this study. It is difficult to coordinate the descriptions by the sixteenth-century

[1] RY, 1: 270–71.

Spaniards with the representations on the older monuments and in the codices, or with the pottery idols that have been recovered; and it is sometimes equally perplexing to attempt to identify the supernatural beings still worshipped today with those described by the conquerors and missionaries. In a general way, perhaps, the Maya gods might be characterized by a certain moral duality of aspect. The same group of deities who furnished rain for the growing crops also sent the destructive hail and lightning.

The Maya cosmos, like that of the Mexicans, seems to have consisted of thirteen heavens and nine hells. In the native literature we frequently read of a group of thirteen gods called Oxlahun-ti-ku and another of nine gods known as Bolon-ti-ku. They are evidently the deities of the thirteen heavens and nine hells, especially since the Bolon-ti-ku appear to be of a malevolent character. We can not identify the members of these groups, but it seems probable that the sky god, Itzamna, was chief of the former, and that such deities as Cumhau, "the prince of devils," and the death god, Uac-mitun-ahau, were prominent among the latter. Another general classification might be made distinguishing the personified forces of nature from deified human beings; but the line can not be sharply drawn here, for even Itzamna is said to have once been a man. Among the deified persons, however, were some who seem to have had a definite historical existence.

The natives told the Spaniards that they had once worshipped a supreme deity called Hunabku ("only God"), "the only living and true God, the greatest of the gods of the people of Yucatan, of whom there was no image, because, they said, there was no conception of his form, since he was incorporeal." His name is also given as Colop-u-uich-kin,[2] which suggests a sun god. In any case, the story made a profound impression on the Spaniards.

At the time of the conquest the head of the Yucatecan Maya pantheon was the sky god, Itzamna. *Itzam* means a large land or water lizard, and the name might perhaps be translated as "house of the lizard." The association is confirmed by the Maya symbol for the sky, which is a lizard monster with astronomical signs on its long snakelike body, and a face, apparently that of the god himself, seems to look forth from between the jaws of another lizard monster, which, however, lacks the astronomical symbols. The god has the face of an old man with a Roman nose and an almost toothless mouth. One source makes Itzamna the son of Kinich Ahau ("sun-eyed or sun-faced lord"), the sun god, whereas two others state that he was formerly a man. All agree that he was the inventor of writing.[3] Itzamna and Kinich Ahau are given as names

[2] Motul dictionary, 1929, p. 404; Vienna dictionary, f. 129r.
[3] Vienna dictionary, f. 129r; Lopez de Cogolludo, 1867-68, bk. 4, ch. 8; Beltran de Santa Rosa, 1859, pp. 16-17.

of the same personage, and the faces of these two gods resemble one another, although the latter can usually be distinguished by a curved symbol over the nose. It seems likely that both represented different aspects of the same deity. Itzamna was the great food-giver, and in this aspect he was often called Itzamna Kauil, since *kauil* is a word for food. In times of drought and famine they prayed to him, along with the rain gods, to send rain for the crops. As the first priest and inventor of writing, he was also one of the gods of medicine and invoked as Kinich Ahau Itzamna at a special festival of priests, medicine men, and magicians, when they ritually cleansed their books and read the prophecy for the coming year.

As already explained, Maya culture was founded on agriculture. When the crops failed and any surplus food had been consumed, the people scattered to the forests to eke out a miserable existence on such wild fruits, roots, and game as could be found, and chaos prevailed until the rains came again and the orderly course of civilized life could be resumed.[4] Consequently the daily religion of the rank and file of the population centered around the rain and wind gods, on whose favor the crops depended. These were the deities who were, and still are, invoked when the bush is cut and burned, the fields are planted, and the grain is growing. Today, in addition to their other names, they are called the guardians of the forest, of the fertile wild lands, and of the fields; and it seems probable that these or other very similar appellations have always expressed the popular conception of the agricultural gods. Forest and field are closely related, since the forest of one year is the cultivated field of the next.

There were three classes or sets of agricultural deities, each set composed of four individuals, who were thought of as being at the four cardinal points. They were the Chacs, or rain gods, the Pauahtuns, or wind gods, and the Bacabs, or sky bearers. Each was distinguished by the color ascribed to his cardinal point. The Red Chac, the Red Pauahtun, and the Red Bacab were at the east, the white at the north, the black at the west, and the yellow at the south. These colored gods ruled each year by turn in the order named.

According to the Book of Chilam Balam of Chumayel, the world had once been destroyed by a flood and the sky had fallen. Only the four Bacabs survived, and they were set at the four world quarters to hold up the sky under the present dispensation. It seems very possible that each Bacab, Pauahtun, and Chac represented various aspects of the same deity. Their identities and functions merge. Landa tells us that they were all different names for the Bacabs, and Cogolludo refers to the Bacabs as wind gods as well as sky

[4] Roys, 1939, pp. 54, 191.

bearets. What the wind gods and sky bearers looked like is difficult to determine. We find sculptured reliefs of what are evidently sky bearers at Chichen Itza, but they are so Mexican in character that it seems doubtful that they portrayed the conception of the ordinary Maya farmer. As for the Chacs, although there has been some dissent, it is at present generally agreed that they are the gods with a long pendulous nose and projecting tusks so frequently depicted in the codices and on the monuments and pottery. The face is believed to be that of a stylized serpent, and we sometimes find this head on a serpent body. The importance of the Chacs may be inferred from the fact that the façade of one of the large temples at Kabah is a solid mass of Chac masks.

Closely related to the gods of field and forest, and perhaps simply another aspect of the same religious concept, are the red, white, black, and yellow Muzencabs, or bee gods. They are not mentioned under this name by the Spanish writers; Landa makes the Bacabs, especially Hobnil, the Yellow Bacab, the patrons of the beekeepers. Nevertheless the Muzencabs play an important part in the mythology and ritual of the native literature. The modern Maya still invoke them in their prayers and believe them to be certain supernatural bees, who dwell at the ruins of Coba in eastern Yucatan. I have identified the insect-like diving god of this site and others in eastern Yucatan with these deities.

Also set up at the cardinal points of the world were four trees, known as the red, white, black and yellow *imix che,* which might be translated as "tree of abundance." On each of these trees was perched a bird. There was also a fifth sacred tree called the green or first tree of the world *(yaxcheilcab),* which is probably to be identified with the mythical ceiba of the modern Maya. It rises to heaven from the center of the world. The stylized representations of these trees were probably the crosses which the Spaniards found everywhere in Yucatan and to which the natives prayed as a god of rain. It is plain that they were closely associated with the Chacs, and they may well have been personified, as the cross is in Yucatan today. The significance of the symbolic birds is difficult to determine.

Although some of them had their inimical aspects, the deities we have described were on the whole beneficent; but there was a god who brought nothing but evil. This was the ruler of the underworld, who was named Cumhau or Hunhau and described in the Motul dictionary as "Lucifer, prince of the devils." He appears to be the same as the regent of certain unlucky years, who was called Uac-mitun-ahau (lord of the sixth hell?). The image accompanying him bore a skull, a corpse, and a buzzard as his symbols, and a dance called the "dance of the devil" was performed in his honor. He seems to have been

called also Ah Puch, Xibalba, and Cizin, but some of these names may have
indicated his various aspects. He is represented in the picture manuscripts as
a skeleton or as a man in the prime of life with a certain death mark on his
cheek and crossbones on his headdress and mantle. He usually wore a collar
of copper bells. He was greatly feared, for nearly everyone, good and bad alike,
went to his realm eventually, which was a gloomy, cold, and unhappy place.
The Indians told the Spaniards that the reason they sacrificed men and animals to the infernal furies was that their lives might be prolonged and they
should not go so soon to suffer the pains of hell. There was a paradise, but it
was accessible to comparatively few, such as suicides and the victims of human
sacrifice.

Class distinctions in Yucatan sometimes extended even to religion, for we
are told that every cacique or principal who had Indians subject to him had
certain gods, whom the common people were not allowed to worship directly.
If the latter wished to make offerings to these deities, they must do it through
their lord. There can be little doubt that we have here gods introduced by the
Mexican invaders. Chief among them was Kukulcan, the quetzal serpent,
whose Maya name is simply a translation of Quetzalcoatl, the well-known
Mexican culture hero. The Maya explained him as a Mexican captain, a great
lord who came with his followers from foreign parts to Yucatan and taught
the people to practice idolatry. It seems probable that the story is based on that
of a Mexican leader and his successors in Yucatan, who took the name of the
culture hero as a title. Landa speaks of him as a historic personage, who re-
established the government at Chichen Itza, founded the city of Mayapan, and
finally returned to Mexico, after which he was deified "on account of his being
a just statesman." In Mexico his temples were round, and we find the remains
of a few such structures in Yucatan, but here square pyramid temples with
stairways on all four sides are also ascribed to this deity. In Yucatan, as in
Mexico, he is frequently represented as a feathered serpent, but sometimes as a
mythical serpent bird. It is also possible that he is the old man with a conical
headdress, who appears in the Dresden Codex.

In the highlands of Mexico, besides being the wind god and the lord of the
planet Venus, he was the peaceful civilizer and the patron of such peaceful
arts as metal-, jade-, and featherwork. In the course of his travels, however, his
character seems to have changed, for in several of the frescoes at Chichen Itza
the plumed serpent with open jaws and a threatening attitude accompanies
a war chief, who advances with raised shield and poised dart.

At the time of the conquest there was each year a special five-day festival
by the lords and priests of the various provinces, who assembled at the temple

of Kukulcan at Mani to worship him with unusual pomp and ceremony, since he was the special patron of these warlike rulers.

This deity was connected in a way with the Spanish conquest. Just as the return of Quetzalcoatl from the east was foretold in Mexico, so in Yucatan there was a definite prophecy that he would one day come back to that country with the Itza. When the Spaniards appeared from that quarter bearing the cross, which so startlingly resembled one of the most sacred Maya symbols, there can be little doubt that many of the natives were enormously impressed. If the first Spaniards met with an unfriendly reception by some of the Yucatecan states, the same occurred to Cortez in Mexico, and yet we know that the Quetzalcoatl myth had an important influence on Montezuma's attitude toward the invaders. The Maya literature of the colonial period compares the Spanish invasion with that of the Itza, and to the native mind it must have seemed more than a coincidence that Montejo's first attempt to establish himself was at the old Itza capital associated with Kukulcan. If this effort was unsuccessful, the same was believed to have been true of the first Itza occupation of the site. It must be remembered also that the fulfillment of the prophecy was not generally desired by a great part of the native population; the Itza were remembered with anything but kindly feelings in much of northern Yucatan.

How much of the Xiu friendship for the Spaniards was due to the fact that their capital was the headquarters of the Kukulcan cult is hard to say. The Cocom, who regarded themselves as the descendants of the god, resisted the Spaniards bitterly; possibly the latter's friendship for the Xiu had something to do with this, for the Cocom and Xiu were old enemies. There can be little doubt that the Chel, Pech, and Ah Canul chiefs held Kukulcan in high esteem, but their friendly attitude toward the Europeans may have come partly from their position on the coast and a more direct knowledge of the Spanish successes in Mexico. We can only infer that although the Kukulcan prophecy was an important factor, the policy of the Yucatecan rulers toward the Spaniards was determined largely by practical considerations.

There were various goddesses. One named Ix Kanleox was said by Cogolludo to be the mother of the other gods and was evidently of some consequence, as she still appears in the prayers of the modern Maya. We hear most, however, of Ix Chel, the wife of the sun god and probably the moon goddess. She was the patroness of weaving, childbirth, medicine, and divination.[5] Possibly as the goddess of weaving, she was closely associated with the spider. When a child was born, the midwife placed her image beneath the bed of the mother, and at the annual festival of the doctors and diviners images of this goddess and

[5] Thompson, 1934, pp. 166–67. Ix Chel was also a goddess of illicit love.

certain divining stones called spiders (*am*) played an essential part. Her most important shrine was at Cozumel, where pilgrims came from far and near. In the sanctuary was a very large pottery idol set against the wall. From the adjoining room a priest is said to have crept into the image and, impersonating the goddess, answered the questions of her worshippers. Other gods were also healers, however. Kinich-kakmo ("sun-eyed fire macaw"), probably an aspect of the sun god, had formerly attracted to his shrine at Izamal hosts of pilgrims who sought relief from sickness and pestilence.

To the Spaniards the Maya gods seemed innumerable. Many, no doubt, represented various aspects of the same deity, but even so, there must have been a great number. We read of three war gods. Cit-chac-coh ("father red puma") was the patron of the annual warriors' festival; the image of Ah Chuy-kak ("suspended fire"?) was carried to war; the third, Kak-u-pacal ("fiery shield"),[6] was evidently a deified hero. He is named as one of a hundred valiant Itza captains from Mayapan who conquered the surrounding towns.

Ekchuuah was the patron of the merchants and cacao planters; and the hunters, fishers, tattooers, comedians, singers and poets, dancers, and lovers all had their own deities. There was a god and a goddess of intoxicating drink, and even suicides had a special patroness named Ix Tab ("the lady of the rope"), who took those who hanged themselves to a special paradise. If the upper class had gods of their own, "the common people also had their special idols, to which each sacrificed according to his occupation or calling."[7]

In addition to all these there were the lineage gods, or deified ancestors, whose existence has only recently come to light. Of the few whose names have come down to us only Zacalpuc is known as a historic personage. He was one of the early Mexican invaders and conquerors of eastern Yucatan. We are not specifically told that every lineage had a different god. Perhaps several of them worshipped the same deity, but I am inclined to believe that each had its own patron. If every Yucatecan patronymic represented a lineage, as seems to be the case, this would have vastly augmented their pantheon, for about 250 Yucatecan Maya patronymics have been recorded.

Formerly there had been at Mayapan a chief priest called the *ahaucan;* the word is a homonym for "chief teacher" and "rattlesnake," and the latter is frequently portrayed on the monuments of Chichen Itza. His office was hereditary in the May lineage. He examined candidates for the priesthood and appointed and invested in office the priests of the various towns. We have no record of any ecclesiastical organization at the time of the conquest, but it

---

[6] *Pacal* is an unusual word for shield (Vienna dictionary, f. 182r).
[7] RY, 1: 52.

Figure 5—CASA COLORADA, CHICHEN ITZA, FROM SOUTHEAST

Figure 6—BUILDING AT LABNA, SOUTHWEST OF THE PUUC

FIGURE 7—AIR VIEW OF THE TEMPLE OF THE WARRIORS AND THE CASTILLO, CHICHEN ITZA (AFTER RICKETSON AND KIDDER)

FIGURE 8—THE TEMPLE OF THE WARRIORS LOOKING FROM THE CASTILLO

seems most probable that something of the sort existed. It may have been purely a local matter, but the halach uinic's religious functions and the fact that he was compared with a bishop strongly suggest that there was some centralized control, at least in the provinces ruled by a halach uinic. Seventeen years after the conquest we find the town of Yaxcaba performing a certain sacrifice at the order of the cacique of Sotuta.

Among the priests were certain prophets called *chilans,* or interpreters; and indeed they were the interpreters of the gods. These were especially honored and on occasions carried in a litter like the temporal rulers. In two unpublished Maya manuscripts we read of the manner in which the chilan delivered his prophecy. He retired to the inner room of his house and lay motionless, apparently in a trance, while a supernatural being, perched on the roof, vouchsafed a solemn communication in "measured words." Other priests were assembled outside the room, and they appear to have heard the words but could not understand them. They waited with their faces bowed down to the floor, until the chilan came out and delivered the prophecy to them.[8]

The attitude of the local chilans was evidently an important factor in the reception accorded the Spaniards in the various parts of the country. In the Xiu Province of Mani a certain Chilam Balam had, years before, prophesied the coming of strangers from the east, who should be welcomed and not opposed, whereas in the Cupul and Cochuah areas, where the Spaniards were persistently and bitterly resisted, the chilans are said to have been the chief "agitators and rebels." If, as appears from the prophecies that have come down to us, the return of Kukulcan was associated with that of the Itza, in these regions especially there would be little desire to see the prediction fulfilled.

A priest who performed human sacrifices was called a nacom, the same title that was applied to the war chief. Evidently a chilan could fill this position, for the famous prophet Chilam Balam, was also called Nacom Balam.[9] Landa tells us that the office of nacom was not considered very honorable, but this is evidently an error, for in postconquest times, when the religious organization had more or less broken down, we find caciques and other important men performing this service. Finally there were four old men called chacs, who were appointed each year from the laity to assist in sacrifices and other ceremonies.

Although cotton vestments were sometimes worn, the usual costume of the priests was a long white sleeveless robe of bark cloth, the skirt often ornamented with snail shells. The headdress was a miterlike crown similar in form to that

[8] Book of Chilam Balam of Tizimin, pp. 13–14; Roys, 1933, p. 182.
[9] Codex Perez, p. 65.

worn by the Mexican rulers and seen on some of the warlike figures dating from the Mexican period in the reliefs at Chichen Itza. The hair was unkempt and smeared with sacrificial blood. The shells and pointed crown recall the representations of Quetzalcoatl and strongly suggest a Mexican origin for this costume. The unkempt hair smeared with blood was typical also of the Mexican priesthood. During baptismal ceremonies the priest wore a short red jacket of feather mosaic work with long feathers trailing from its edge, and on his head a crown of feathers.

The principal functions of the priests were to propitiate the gods and keep track of the calendar, telling the people when to celebrate religious festivals and when to burn and plant their fields, hunt, or go to war. They also officiated at various domestic ceremonies such as weddings, baptisms, and confession; and they preached sermons and enforced religious observances. In punishing religious delinquency they are said to have had more authority than the temporal rulers. Although Landa refers to the baptism of very young children, other sources seem to indicate that it may have been a puberty ceremony. As in the Christian religion, it was called "rebirth" (*caput zihil*).

We find no record of certain tribute being assigned to the temples as in Mexico. The compensation of the clergy is said to have been voluntary offerings of red and green beads, cotton cloth, cacao, game, poultry, maize, and other provisions. Many of these alleged gifts, however, may well have been regular fees for certain religious services, like the "presents" given to the judge in lieu of court fees.

As we have already noted, besides the temple ceremonies many were performed in private oratories. Tozzer believes that the temple ceremonial had declined at the time of the conquest and that the oratory and the lord's house seem to have taken the place of the temple. The festival of Ekchuuah was held in a cacao grove, and there can be little doubt that certain sacrifices to the rain and wind gods were held in the fields, like those which have survived to the present time.

Of the various rites perhaps the most important were those in honor of the new year; these began during the last five days of the old. The gods of the four cardinal points presided in turn over the year ascribed to their own world quarter. Elaborate formalities were observed in dismissing the old incumbents and installing the new in office. They took place at the temple, at the four entrances to the town, and in the private oratory of the patron of the festival. Human sacrifice was sometimes performed at the inauguration of the east year, and at that of the south year a spectacular fire-walking rite took place. There was a great dance, and a structure was built of bundles of faggots in the temple court. This was set on fire, and the burning coals were leveled off; then a priest dressed in his ceremonial bark-cloth robe and miter, singing and bearing an idol, passed over the fire barefoot and unscathed, sprinkling the coals with an aspergill of snakes' tails. He was accompanied by the dancers, some of whom suffered severely from burns, especially if they were unduly intoxicated.

Another important cult was that of the *katun,* a time period of approximately twenty years. There were thirteen katuns, each with its own number which recurred every 256 years, and the destiny of each was ruled by a certain god. Ten years before a katun began, its idol was placed in the temple opposite that of the reigning incumbent as the "guest" of the latter. Here it remained during these ten years and the succeeding twenty of its own period of office, but during the last ten years of this time it lost some of its power and its successor was its guest.

At some festivals human sacrifice was required, but more often animals and other offerings were sufficient, human victims being considered necessary only in times of public calamity, to avert drought and famine, to prevent the recurrence of a hurricane, or to prolong the life of a sick ruler. On ordinary occasions, when people prayed for rain, abundant crops, health, good hunting or fishing, and success in war, the clergy and laity alike offered their own blood, drawn from the ear, lip, tongue, and various parts of the body. There were also sacrifices of turkeys, dogs, and various wild animals, birds, and sometimes reptiles, as well as oblations of food, feathers, and precious stones. Copal resin was burned on all occasions and sometimes chicle, the gum of the rubber tree, or that of a species of Notoptera. Women prepared food offerings and sometimes burned incense, but they did not make sacrifices; and only on very rare occasions were certain old women admitted to the temple ceremonies.

With human sacrifice a certain sense of proportion was observed and it never became as common as in the highlands of Mexico. The victims were war prisoners of rank, slave men and women, including the humbler captives and persons enslaved for theft or some other crime, for whose purchase the community contributed funds, and finally many children. The last, as in Mexico, were especially acceptable to the agricultural deities. Of these many were purchased from neighboring towns or provinces, and during the two decades immediately following the Spanish conquest it was so customary to kidnap children from other districts for this purpose that it seems reasonable to ascribe the practice to pre-Spanish times as well. Gifts of children for sacrifice were also sent from one ruler to another. Men are said to have piously donated their own children at times, but from the instances cited in Landa's inquisition proceedings in 1562, it seems more likely that these were usually either their offspring by female slaves or orphaned relatives reared by wealthy men. In many cases persons designated for sacrifice were kept in wooden cages.

In front of the stairway in the temple court was a round stone dais with steps and on it a sacrificial stone four or five spans high. There was also a similar stone at the top of the pyramid in front of the temple cell. The victim's body was painted blue, a paper crown placed upon his head, and he was stretched on his back over the stone. His arms and legs were held by the four chacs, while the nacom excised his heart with a large flint knife, which was called the hand or arm of god. The heart was placed in a shallow covered bowl and given to the priest, who offered it to the idols inside the temple and smeared their mouths with the blood. Later the heart was often burned in the same receptacle. On a certain occasion, when the sacrifice was performed at the top of the pyramid, the body was thrown down the steep steps and flayed. A priest then put on the skin and danced in it, after which ceremonial cannibalism sometimes ensued; but more often the body was buried in the temple court. This was evidently an importation from Mexico, where a similar sacrifice was made to Xipe Totec, originally a maize god. The flaying of the victim is believed to have symbolized the husking of the corn.

There was another form of human sacrifice which was also apparently a foreign importation, since the bow and arrow were not known to the Yucatecan Maya until a comparatively late period. Here the victim was stripped, painted blue with a white bull's-eye marked over the heart, and made to dance with a troop of men armed with bows and arrows. Then the man or woman to be sacrificed was bound to a stake on the dais in the temple court. The priest struck the sexual organs of the victim with an arrow and smeared the face of the idol with the blood drawn, after which the archers rapidly danced past the dais, each shooting at the bull's-eye in turn.

Most readers will be familiar with the custom of casting live persons into the famous cenote at Chichen Itza at sunrise. One was expected to commune with the gods beneath the water and return at noon with a prophecy. We have no record of this being done elsewhere, but the records of Landa's inquisition state that the bodies of slain sacrificial victims were frequently thrown into wells or cenotes in other parts of the country.

From Mexican analogies it seems probable that the victim was supposed to impersonate the deity. The fantastic and especially brutal manner in which a little girl was sacrificed near Hocaba in early colonial times strongly suggests that in Yucatan, as in Mexico, some immolations were dramatic representations of mythological episodes in the lives of the gods. This is partly confirmed by another sacrifice, which also occurred during the second decade after the conquest, and in which the native ritual was modified by Christian doctrine in a manner hardly anticipated by the missionaries. Two little girls were bound to crosses in the church at Sotuta. The executioners are reported to have announced first, "Here you see the figure of Jesus Christ"; and later they said, "Let these girls die fixed to the cross as Jesus Christ died, who they·say was Our Lord, but we do not know he was." Then they were taken down from the crosses, and their hearts were excised and offered to the idols which had been brought for the occasion.[10] Landa's inquisition of 1562 was effective in putting an end to human sacrifice in regions governed by the Spaniards. Surreptitious idolatry was not abolished until some time later, but the fusion of Christian and pagan beliefs has continued down to the present time.

[10] Scholes and Adams, 1938, 1: 78, 80.

Chapter 12. Science and Learning

ANY ATTEMPT to make a detailed examination of Maya science would lie far beyond the scope of the present study. Volumes have been written about the intellectual achievements of the Maya, and indeed we have ample evidence that their knowledge of mathematics, chronology, and astronomy was truly amazing.

In many inscriptions and at least one of the hieroglyphic codices we find a day count, which goes back to a mythical era some 4000 years before the latest date recorded by this system. The current moon age is often given, together with the position of the last completed lunation in a lunar year of five or six months. Arithmetical calculations are frequently found involving many thousands of days, some of them running into millions; and evidence has been adduced to show the existence of corrective formulas, by which the 365-day Maya calendar year was kept in harmony with the 365.24-day tropical year. The Dresden Codex contains a set of tables covering the synodical revolutions of the planet Venus during more than three centuries; and in the same manuscript is another table recording successive lunations in groups of five or six moons each for a period of nearly thirty-three years. The latter is apparently a table of eclipse syzygies, and, whether or not the Maya were able to predict eclipses, they appear to have known when one was likely to occur. Perhaps the greatest mathematical achievement of the Maya was their independent discovery of numeral place-value notation and the use of a zero, which must have greatly facilitated their chronological and astronomical calculations.[1]

The inscriptions and codex which are the sources of a large part of this information, however, antedate the Spanish conquest by several centuries at least. There are some indications that the decadence of Maya architecture, which we have already noted, was accompanied by an intellectual decline; and it is impossible to say how much of this scientific knowledge still existed at the time of the conquest. Certainly, if it still survived, a great deal of it escaped the notice of the Spanish missionaries and settlers. The long day count, which for centuries was the framework for recording astronomical observations, had apparently fallen into disuse; and according to a colonial Maya manuscript certain foreigners, the Itza, had brought to an end a golden age, when everybody was happy, healthy, and good, when "in due measure did they recite the good

[1] Morley, 1915. *passim;* Thompson, 1936, pp. 45–57; Tozzer, 1941, p. 134; Teeple, 1930, pp. 70–80, 86.

prayers; in due measure they sought the lucky days, until they saw the good stars enter into their reign; then they kept watch while the reign of the good stars began."[2]

On the other hand, hieroglyphic writing was still in use, and the complicated calendar still functioned. The priests kept track of the calendar and informed the people when to prepare to burn and plant their fields, which would imply that they were able to compute the variation of the 365-day Maya year from the true solar year. Moreover the survival of the Dresden Codex suggests that a few erudite persons at least still understood the chronological calculations and astronomical tables which it contains.

Most of the Maya sciences were based on the calendar, which was a combination of three different day counts. The first was a ritual period of 260 days made up of twenty day names combined with the numbers 1 to 13 as coefficients. Names and numbers followed one another without interruption, and, since the least common multiple of 20 and 13 is 260, the same day and coefficient recurred every 260 days. Then there was a 365-day year composed of eighteen months of twenty days each, with a special period of five unlucky days added at the end. The number of the day of the month and the name of the month fixed the day within this year; but this position fell a day short of the agricultural season by nearly a day every four years, since there were no leap years. In the colonial Maya manuscripts the year itself is often designated by the name and coefficient of its first day, a device which may have been borrowed from Mexico, since it is rarely employed, if at all, in the older Maya inscriptions. A day was often designated by its name and coefficient followed by its position in the 365-day year; but this fixed it only within a cycle of fifty-two such years known as a Calendar Round. Additional information was needed to place it more definitely.

Longer periods of time, however, were not reckoned in terms of the 365-day year, but by a chronological year of 360 days called a *tun*. Each tun was divided into eighteen *uinals* of twenty days each, and twenty tuns constituted a *katun* of 7200 days, or nearly twenty solar years. In the old Long Count already mentioned we also find a period of twenty katuns, or 144,000 days, which modern scholars call a cycle, or *baktun;* but this period was unknown to the sixteenth-century Spanish writers, and only in a single instance have I found an apparent reference to it in a colonial Maya manuscript.[3]

At the time of the conquest the usual method of dating events appears to have been less precise, judged by the native books of the colonial period. Here the time of an event is often indicated by giving only the name and coefficient

[2] Book of Chilam Balam of Chumayel, Roys, 1933, p. 83.
[3] *Ibid.,* p. 83. In the same source we find a mention of three score and fifteen katuns. which would be the equivalent of three cycles, or baktuns, and fifteen katuns (*ibid.,* p. 79).

of the last day of the katun in which it occurred. The actual name of this closing day is always the same, Ahau, and only the coefficient varies; but for con-
venience I shall call the combination of day name and coefficient the name of
the katun.[4] Since a katun of the same name could recur only every thirteen
katuns, or approximately 256 years, an indication of this sort places the event
some time in a given katun but does not tell us in which katun round it occurred. The last must be determined in some other manner. An attempt to
accomplish this has been made in most of the Maya chronicles by setting down
a number of katun rounds, one after the other. These chronicles are of enormous
historical value; but they were evidently compiled after the end of the sixteenth
century, and there are indications that the native chroniclers sometimes confused the sequence of the katun rounds.

Since some religious ceremonies or festivals were determined by their position in the 260-day period, others were decided on their place in the 365-day
year, and still others were celebrated at the beginning, middle, or end of the
7200-day katun, it is obvious that the priest, whose duty it was to announce the
approach of these important occasions and prepare for them, must have had a
considerable knowledge of arithmetic.

For counting objects the Maya employed the vigesimal system so common among primitive peoples, the ascending units most commonly used being
1 (*hun*), 20 (*kal*), 400 (*bak*), and 8000 (*pic*). The Spaniards were impressed
with the facility and rapidity with which people counted cacao beans; cacao
was not sold by dry measure or weight, but by counting each kernel, possibly
in order to detect the substitution of an inferior species or of imitation kernels.
It was sold in 400-kernel lots and probably in quantities of 8000 also, as we
know was the case in Tabasco. The latter amount presumably constituted a
load. Father Beltran in his Maya grammar also mentions three higher ascending units. The first was one *calab*, or 160,000. The second was one *kinchil*, or
tzotzceh, which he defines as 1,000,000; but it probably meant 3,200,000, since
the next higher order was the *alau*, which he tells us equaled 64,000,000. Brinton
notes that among the Cakchiquel, a people of the Maya stock living in the highlands of Guatemala, the word *cala* had the specific meaning of twenty loads
of cacao beans. It seems difficult, however, to associate the two highest orders
with the enumeration of concrete objects.

This system of enumeration differed somewhat from that of the chronological count, as we find it recorded in the inscriptions and codices. The latter
count is not purely vigesimal, since the series is broken by the tun of 360 days,

---

[4] In the Books of Chilam Balam the name and coefficient of the closing day are really treated as the
name of the katun.

and its ascending units are found to be 1, 20, 360, 7200, and 144,000. Goodman, Teeple, and Thompson consider the tun to be the real basis of the Maya chronological system. From this point of view the time count would be strictly vigesimal, since the days and uinals would be simply fractions of the basic unit. This belief is supported not only by the word katun, which evidently has the literal meaning of twenty tuns, but also by the fact that a tun symbol enters into the composition of the glyph for every known higher unit in the Maya calendar.

For counting either objects or days, numbers under twenty were recorded by dots up to four, and by bars, each of which signified five. Nineteen, for example, would be three bars and four dots. Landa states that they made their counts "on the ground or on something smooth." Thompson suggests that counters may have been used, such as grains of maize, beans, or pebbles, and a short stick or bean pod could have taken the place of the bar. In the calendrical computations the day, uinal, tun, katun, and cycle are indicated either by glyphs or by their positions in ascending columns. Unfortunately, however, no counts for as many as twenty concrete objects have as yet been positively identified in hieroglyphic writing, so we do not know the symbols for the higher orders of anything except the time count.

The real character of Maya writing still remains somewhat debatable. As yet it has been possible to decipher with certainty only those glyphs which have a numerical, calendrical, or astronomical significance. Some other characters appear to designate certain deities and possibly a few of the objects depicted in the illustrations accompanying the hieroglyphic texts in the codices. The glyphs seem to be chiefly ideographic but contain a phonetic element, apparently including rebus forms.

The knowledge of this writing was confined to the priesthood and some members of the nobility, although the latter made no public use of the accomplishment. Since we are told that the priests were members of the aristocracy and not commoners, the principal key to Maya science was apparently in the hands of a ruling class of allegedly foreign origin.[5] Their books were made of bark paper from a species of Ficus, possibly *F. cotinifolia,* and covered with a smooth lime sizing, on which glyphs and pictorial illustrations were painted in various colors. A long sheet of this paper was folded like a screen between two boards, so that it resembled a bound volume.

Only three Maya hieroglyphic manuscripts have come down to us. Of these one was purchased in Austria for the Royal Public Library at Dresden; another,

---

[5] "And they did not teach these [their letters] to any except noble persons; and for this reason all the priests, who were those most concerned with them, were persons of rank" (RY, 1: 52).

the Tro-Cortesianus, is really one codex composed of two parts discovered separately in Spain; and the third, called the Peresianus, was found in the Imperial Library at Paris wrapped in a paper on which the name Perez was written. We have not the slightest information regarding their origin or how they came to be brought to Europe; and no Maya codex has as yet been found in America, although there is evidence that some still existed in Yucatan at the end of the seventeenth century. The Dresden Codex is apparently the oldest and has been thought to date from about A.D. 1100. Besides the dates and chronological computations already discussed, it deals sometimes with ceremonies of the 365-day year but more often with the 260-day period. These portions of the book are believed to be a religious and astrological almanac and concerned with ceremonies, rituals, and offerings, as well as showing the lucky or unlucky days for the various activities of life. The Codex Tro-Cortesianus is devoted almost entirely to the 260-day period. The third, the Codex Peresianus, although it treats of the Maya zodiac and much of it is astronomical and chronological, may possibly contain some prophetic material.

Strangely enough, the Maya did not employ their graphic system to write letters or contracts,[6] and lawsuits were settled entirely by word of mouth; nevertheless, their hieroglyphic literature seems to have covered nearly every branch of Maya science. Landa writes: "The sciences which they taught were computations of the years, months, and days, the festivals and ceremonies, the administration of the sacraments, the fateful days and seasons, their methods of divination and their prophecies, events and cures for diseases, and their antiquities and how to read and write with the letters and characters with which they wrote, and drawings which illustrate the meaning of the writings."[7] In another passage he tells us that genealogy was also one of their sciences.

Their "computations of the years, months, and days" are amply confirmed by the inscriptions and hieroglyphic codices that are extant. That these manuscripts also dealt with "the festivals and ceremonies" as well as "the administration of the sacraments" seems evident from the pictures accompanying the texts. What appears to be a survival of this type of literature is found in the so-called Books of Chilam Balam, written in Maya but with European script.[8] Here we see native almanacs, which continued to be used throughout the eighteenth century and probably even later. Although not entirely correct,

---

[6] Chi, 1941, p. 231.

[7] Landa, 1941, pp. 27–28.

[8] Tozzer, 1917; 1921, pp. 182–92; Roys, 1933, pp. 3–6. In explanation of this name Brinton (1890, p. 257) tells us that, "In whatever village it was written, or by whatever hand, it always was, and still is, called 'The Book of Chilam Balam.'" The reason for the name might be the frequency with which statements in the books are ascribed to this prophet. I have been unable to find this name given to such manuscripts by any of the Spanish or Indian colonial writers. In two of the Books of Chilam Balam we find the word *reportorio*, which, like *lunario*, means almanac (Roys, 1933, p. 147; Tizimin ms., p. 27).

these are mostly correlations of the Christian annual calendar with the Maya months and the 260-day period. Each day of the latter is designated as good or bad; some are also declared to be suitable for planting certain crops, hunting, hiving bees, or other undertakings. A number of them are specified as lucky or unlucky for certain professions or classes of persons; others are apt to bring disease. Accompanying these prognostics are occasional weather predictions and a few obscurely worded phrases which may refer to pagan ceremonies. Toward the end of the colonial period the names of the saints are added, and these native books tend more and more to resemble the contemporary Spanish almanacs; but in the Codex Perez is a fragment of an earlier form, in which all reference to the Christian calendar is omitted. Here the glyph of the day name is followed by its name, coefficient, and prediction written out in European script.

Of special interest are the prophecies of the katuns, which also appear in the Books of Chilam Balam. As we have already seen, these time periods were of nearly twenty years each, and in every thirteen katuns one of the same name came around again. The principal basis of these prophecies was the belief that whatever had happened in the past would be likely to recur in another katun of the same name. Consequently these prophecies are full of historical allusions, although unfortunately we are not told in which series of katuns the event occurred.

Some of the prognostics are auspicious, but a surprisingly large number of them are unfavorable. War, pestilence, drought, locusts, famine, riot, and political upheaval are freely predicted, during which the people will be obliged to leave their homes and find their food in the forests. Some misfortunes seem to be symbolized by the deities who brought them; and certain events are indicated by simply naming a prominent person or a place associated with the occurrence.

Two series of thirteen prophecies each have been found in these books. One was no doubt compiled in the seventeenth century, since it contains frequent references to colonial times, but the other is evidently older. One of its prophecies mentions the conquest, but in the remainder the allusions are almost entirely to events which occurred before the arrival of the Spaniards, and there is some indication that much of the material found in them was transcribed from hieroglyphic originals.

The people of one of the Yucatecan Maya states succeeded in maintaining their independence and preserving their culture intact until the end of the seventeenth century. These were the Itza, who lived on Lake Peten in what is now northern Guatemala. Until they were finally conquered, their only contacts with the Spaniards were when they were visited by Cortez in the early sixteenth century and by a very few missionaries during the seventeenth. Father Avendaño, who spent a short time with them in 1696, gives us a description of their hieroglyphic books of prophecy. These, he tells us, showed "not only the count of the said days and months and years, but also the ages [katuns] and prophecies which their idols and images announced to them, or, to speak more accurately, the devil by means of the worship which they pay to him in the form of some stones. These ages are thirteen in number; each age has its separate idol and its priest, with a separate prophecy of its events. These thirteen ages are divided into thirteen parts, which divide this kingdom of Yucatan and each age, with its idol, priest and prophecy, rules in one of these thirteen parts of this land, according as they have divided it."[9]

The katun prophecies of the Books of Chilam Balam correspond as closely with this description as could be expected in a manuscript written in European script. With each prophecy are associated a place name, a deity, and, in two of the manuscripts, a bearded face accompanied by a written personal name. The last may well represent the priests mentioned by Avendaño.

Two other kinds of prophecies are also recorded in these books. One is a series covering each of the twenty years of a certain katun, and the other consists of special predictions ascribed to certain noted prophets. The most famous of these men was Chilam Balam, who lived about the beginning of the sixteenth century. Most of these were believed in colonial times to foretell the coming of the Spaniards and the conversion of the natives to Christianity; but, as we have already noted, they seem rather to predict the return of the culture hero, Kukulcan.[10]

Many of the Spanish chroniclers tell us that the Maya wrote down their history in their hieroglyphic manuscripts, but the precise character of these records of past events is difficult to determine. As we have already seen, in four of the Maya chronicles a number of successive katun rounds are set down, and opposite the names of some katuns are historical entries, the times of which are implied by their positions in this long series. Unfortunately a few of the katun rounds seem to be duplicated, upsetting the chronological scheme.

---

[9] Means, 1917, p. 141.

[10] Roys, 1933, pp. 185–87. Brinton, following Carrillo Ancona, states that Chilam Balam was the designation of a class of priests (Brinton, 1882, p. 69; Carrillo Ancona, 1937, p. 13). As we have seen, this is true of the word chilan, or chilam, but Balam is now and always has been a common Maya family name. I believe that Balam was the patronymic of this prophet and not a generic term, because not only is he always mentioned as one certain person, but he is listed repeatedly with other prophets, whose actual names are given, such as Napuc Tun, Nahau Pech, Ah Kauil Chel, and Natzin Yabun Chan. Like Balam, the patronymics Tun, Pech, Chel, and Chan are all familiar Maya family names. Sometimes, it is true, this famous man is mentioned only by his title, but in such cases he is simply called the "chilam," the "profeta chilam," or "ah kin chilam," which means the "priest interpreter." (Cf. Roys, 1933, p. 164; Book of Chilam Balam of Tizimin, pp. 10, 13, 14, 18.)

It seems probable that these early seventeenth-century Maya writers compiled their chronicles from various fragmentary sources, some of which were no doubt hieroglyphic codices; but the character of these sources remains a problem. On the back of a letter in the Xiu family papers is a short historical record in Maya but in European script. At the end is a statement by a certain Don Juan Xiu that he copied it in 1685 from "an ancient book [of] characters, as they are called, annals." The entries cover the years from 1533 to 1545 and were evidently taken from a postconquest hieroglyphic manuscript.[11] A number of codices, which were either written or copied in early colonial times, have come down to us from Mexico but this is the only case even mentioned in Yucatan. One sixteenth-century writer tells us that some of the missionaries learned to read and write these characters. A considerable number of native books were seized and destroyed by the Franciscan friars, but we know that a few survived until the last part of the seventeenth century in northern Yucatan.

R. B. Weitzel suggests that the original form of a Maya chronicle was a folk song similar to the so-called second chronicle of the Book of Chilam Balam of Chumayel. Here are lists of events which took place in katuns of a given name, without specifying in which katun round they occurred. It appears to have been taken for granted that the reader would know where to place these episodes in Maya history.

It also seems very possible that many of the histories in hieroglyphic writing, to which the Spanish writers refer, were simply the katun prophecies with their historical allusions. History and prophecy were evidently closely associated in people's minds. Of the Itza on Lake Peten Villagutierre writes: "Because the king had read it in his *analtehes,* they knew of the provinces of Yucatan (analtehes and histories being one and the same thing)."[12] Avendaño had evidently seen some of these books in northern Yucatan. Upon his arrival at the Itza capital he immediately noticed a mask set in a stone column, which he identified as Ah Cocahmut, apparently one of the names of Itzamna. He explains that, "I came to recognize it, since I had already read about it in their old papers and had seen it in their *anahtes* which they use, which are books of the barks of trees, polished and covered with lime, in which by painted figures and characters, they have foretold their future events."[13]

Cogolludo, quoting Father Fuensalida who visited the Itza early in the

[11] Morley, 1920, pp. 471, 506–08.
[12] Villagutierre Soto-Mayor, 1701, bk. 6, ch. 4, translated *apud* Tozzer, 1941, p. 28. The Spanish writers spell the name for this type of book in various ways, but in the Maya text of the Tizimin manuscript it is written "anahte," which is no doubt correct.
[13] Avendaño, 1696, Bowditch translation, p. 67; cf. Roys, 1933, p. 153.

seventeenth century, tells us: "Those whom they call priests preserve to this day the prophecies (written in their ancient characters) in a book like a history which they call analte. In it they preserve the memory of whatever has happened to them since they settled in those lands."[14]

In the native Maya literature the anahte is also closely associated with prophecy. The prognostic for a certain year in the Book of Chilam Balam of Tizimin is accompanied by a statement, apparently ascribed to Chilam Balam, that "he copied it from the characters of the anahte, from the words of Ah Kin Chel, the first to understand it, when he saw it." Farther along in the same passage we also read: "As it is stated in the characters of the katun, in the anahte." Pio Perez defines anahte as follows: "The bark of trees [like] parchment, which the Indians used to write or paint their histories with hieroglyphics"; but I have been unable to find the word in any of the older Maya dictionaries.[15]

Several of the native books contain a mythological account of the creation of the world, in which some of the gods appear under their Mexican names. One such story was reported early in the seventeenth century, and we surmise that such narratives also formed a part of the hieroglyphic literature, but we have no direct evidence that this was so.[16]

The interest of the Yucatecan Maya in genealogy might well be expected of a people governed by a hereditary ruling class and among whom the lineage group was an important feature of their social organization. One of the proofs of a person's social rank was a knowledge of his ancestry, and the Chumayel questionnaire states: "So, also, these are the nobility, the lineage of the chiefs, who know whence come the men and the rulers of their government." "They are very particular," Landa also tells us, "about knowing the origin of their families, especially if they are the descendants of some family of Mayapan, and they find this out from the priests, since it is one of their sciences, and they are very proud of the men who have been distinguished in their families."[17]

Many personal names have been identified and deciphered in the Mexican picture writing, but none have as yet been recognized among the Maya glyphs; and we are still uncertain in regard to the manner in which Maya genealogies were recorded. Since people turned to the priests for information concerning their ancestry, it would seem probable that such matters were committed to writing. We know from the proceedings of Landa's inquisition in 1562 that they had books, in which the names of the deified ancestors of certain lineages

[14] Lopez de Cogolludo, 1867–68, bk. 9, ch. 14.
[15] Book of Chilam Balam of Tizimin, p. 11; Pio Perez, 1866–67, p. 11.
[16] Martinez H., 1913; Roys, 1933, pp. 98–107; Sanchez de Aguilar, 1937, p. 181; Thompson, 1932.
[17] Landa, 1941, p. 99.

were set down. The greatest of these gods was Zacalpuc, who was one of the early Mexican conquerors of eastern Yucatan and whose name is still invoked in the Maya prayers of the medicine men.

The healing art formed an important branch of Maya science, and the Spaniards were deeply impressed by the native remedies. "There is in this land," we read, "a great quantity of medicinal plants of various properties; and if there were a person in it who had knowledge of them, he would find them most useful and effective, for there is no disease to which the native Indians do not apply plants. However, if you ask them for an account of their properties, they can not give any other than that they are cold or hot and they are accustomed to employ them for the effect, for which they apply them. Nevertheless, there are many of great virtue for every sort of sickness and antidotes for poison; and on the other hand there are also some that are very poisonous and deadly."[18]

A large body of literature on the subject in both Maya and Spanish has survived from colonial times. Much is found in some of the Books of Chilam Balam, and a number of eighteenth- and early nineteenth-century Maya manuscripts are entirely devoted to the same material, of which a considerable part has been published and translated. European remedies are also found in these books, but most of the prescriptions are native. Some of the plants prescribed appear in the modern pharmacopoeias, but the curative value of the greater number is doubtful or imaginary. Insects, birds, and animals formed a part of the native materia medica. As among the modern Maya, plants were both taken internally and applied externally, either crushed and raw or in the form of boiled infusions. Chile, honey, and other ordinary food articles were ingredients of these restorative compounds. The Maya cured like with like. Crushed wasp nests were the remedy for certain skin eruptions, vines resembling snakes for snake bite, and a drink of burned feathers of a red parrot or a cardinal for "blood vomit," a term applied in colonial times to yellow fever. Bleeding of the affected part was also in common usage, both before and after the conquest.

Modern Maya medical practice confirms in some respects the account quoted above. Foods and medical preparations are believed to be "cold" or "hot," not because of their own temperatures but rather because of their alleged cooling or heating effects on the patient. A fever patient should take "cold" things, but a person with a chill or weakened by sickness or childbirth should take "hot" or "half cold" things. Peccary, wild turkey, Lima beans, and squash are among the very "cold" foods, whereas honey is very "hot."

Sickness was usually ascribed to some supernatural cause, sometimes to the

[18] RY, 1: 62.

gods as a punishment for sin, and often, apparently, to sorcerers. In the six-teenth-century Motul dictionary are special names for persons who are said to "throw" certain diseases. These are formed by adding the name of the disease to the term *ah pul*, "he who throws." Such persons made children scream or refuse the breast and caused diarrhea, strangury, bloody stools, tapeworms, lung diseases, or indeed almost any illness.

Prominent in Maya diagnosis were two features, which were regarded as accompanying the ordinary symptoms in a way difficult to understand. These are mentioned in the colonial Maya literature, and we learn more of them from Redfield's reports of the modern Indians and from the definitions found in the Motul dictionary. One was *kinam,* a mysterious force within the body which acts sometimes for good but more often for evil. A throbbing pain, a poison, the virtue of a plant or stone, fierceness in men or animals, and the quality of inspiring awe have all been called kinam. Then there was *tamcaz,* or *tancaz,* an equally mysterious power, which caused stiffening, spasm, epilepsy, frenzy, and apparently almost any nervous shock. In various incantations the tancaz is addressed with the honorific "thrice greeted," as though it were a person of superior rank or a spirit. Strangely enough, the same term also designated the Milky Way. Kinam and tancaz are frequently mentioned in the Ritual of the Bacabs, the only book of incantations left from the colonial period.

Maya medical manuscripts refer to snakes in the bowels, to a small venomous lizard believed to poison a person by simply touching his garment or to cause a dangerous headache by biting at the shadow of one's head, and to the "purple tancaz parrot." In the Book of Chilam Balam of Kaua is a pic-ture of this dreadful bird. According to popular belief today, it flies over the top of a house and vomits a substance which causes death if it falls into the mouth of a sleeping child. The modern Maya attribute many diseases to certain personified evil winds closely associated with the tancaz, but it is hard to tell whether or not this belief goes back to the time of the conquest. However, the Mexican-Maya culture hero, Quetzalcoatl-Kukulcan, who is known to have been a wind god in Mexico, was a god of fevers in Yucatan.

With such ideas concerning the nature and cause of disease, it is not strange that prayers, offerings, and incantations played an important part in Maya medicine. We have already seen that Itzamna and Ix Chel were the great patrons of the healing art, and their shrines at Izamal and Cozumel were famous centers of pilgrimage. We know also of human sacrifices performed at Sotuta to prolong the life of an ailing cacique. These matters were no doubt in the hands of the regular priesthood. Although in one passage Landa tells of "the priests, the physicians and sorcerers, who were all the same thing," he elsewhere draws a distinction and puts in a different class the "surgeons, or to be more accurate, sorcerers, who cured with herbs and many superstitious rites." These shaman healers had medicine bundles, which contained, among other things, small images of Ix Chel and certain divining stones called *am*. This is the name of a certain poisonous spider, which is associated with Ix Chel in one of the incantations, possibly because the latter was also the goddess of weaving. Divining was one of the features of medical science. Landa informs us that "the sorcerers and physicians" were accustomed to "cast lots so as to know the future in their own duties and in other things."

Among the modern Maya the shaman healer, known as a *yerbatero* (herb doctor) in Spanish, is called *ah men,* or *hmen.* The literal meaning of the phrase is "he who does or understands something." In the Motul dictionary, however, the term is defined as a skilled master of any craft or profession. Here a sorcerer is called *ah cunyah,* but the missionary author also tells us that the word *ah dzacyah,* literally "healer," although it can mean any professional physician, "ordinarily is taken in the bad sense for a sorcerer, who speaks with bad and idolatrous words." Even the specialist, who bound the abdomen of a woman who was ill or recovering from childbirth, was regarded as a sorcerer by the missionaries, so it would seem evident that surgery and medicine were usually, if not always, accompanied by incantations.

The only old collection of incantations was discovered by William Gates, who called it the Ritual of the Bacabs, probably because of its frequent mention of these deities. The actual manuscript dates only from the last half of the eighteenth century, but it may well be a copy of a much older book. From their archaic and symbolic language it would seem that these incantations are very ancient and might possibly have been transcribed from a hieroglyphic codex. Except for an occasional "Amen," they contain little that suggests European influence.

How much of the medicinal lore was formerly set down in glyphs is uncertain. Acosta writes that, "In the province of Yucatan, where is the so-called Bishopric of Honduras, there used to exist some books of leaves, bound or folded after a fashion, in which the learned Indians kept the distribution of their times and the knowledge of plants, animals and other things of nature and the ancient customs, in a way of great neatness and carefulness."[19]

Some incantations were evidently committed to hieroglyphic writing, for in dealing with the poisonous serpents of Yucatan, ". . . formerly in the time of their paganism they took measures to guard against this poison by exorcisms and incantations. There were great sorcerers, and they had their books to con-

---

[19] Acosta, 1590, bk. 6, ch. 6, *apud* Tozzer, 1941, p. 78.

jure and charm them; and these sorcerers, with the few words which they recited, charmed and tamed poisonous serpents. They caught them and took them in their hands, without their doing them any harm." [20]

Maya knowledge of the movements of the sun, moon, and planet Venus has already been briefly discussed. That of eclipse syzygies, if it still survived at the time of the conquest, was evidently confined to learned persons, for people generally thought that an eclipse was caused by the sun or moon being eaten by certain ants called *xulab*. In the colonial Maya literature we find long astrological treatises, but evidently they are mostly translations of contemporary Spanish almanacs. Probably to this enthusiasm for European astrology was due their increasing neglect of their own astronomical and astrological science at a time when they were still preserving many other old traditions. Some references to the native astronomy apparently occur in the katun prophecies, but they are few and obscure.

In one of the older Maya dictionaries we are told that Venus as a morning and an evening star was known as *noh ek* ("great star") and *xux ek* ("wasp star"). Elsewhere *chac ek* ("red star") is defined simply as the day star, which is of especial interest, since in the Venus tables of the Dresden Codex the character representing the planet is almost always the Venus symbol prefixed by the glyph believed to mean "red." Among the present Indians of British Honduras the morning star is called Santo Xulab or *noh ich* ("great eye" or "face"). [21]

I have not been able to find a Maya name for any of the other planets. *Xaman ek* ("north star") is defined in the dictionaries and said to be the "guide of the merchants"; and a constellation called *chimal ek* ("shield stars") is identified with Ursa Minor, or sometimes with two of its brighter stars, "the guards of the north" (*las guardas del norte*). This Maya stellar group was also known as *yah bakul pach xaman* ("that which girds the north") and *yah çutil* ("that which revolves"). [22]

A few other constellations are mentioned in the dictionaries. One of them is *tzab* ("the rattles of the snake") and is defined as the Pleiades. Another, *ac* or *ac ek* ("turtle stars"), comprised certain stars in Gemini along with others. A third, *zinaan ek* ("scorpion stars"), is said to be the sign Scorpio. These three are pictured in the Tro-Cortesianus and Peresianus Codices. In the latter we find them, along with ten other somewhat similar figures, each holding the sun in its mouth, which would seem to indicate the Maya had a zodiac composed of thirteen signs.

Maya astronomy was concerned with the apparent movements of the

[20] RY, 1: 66–67.
[21] Motul dictionary, 1929, p. 292; Vienna dictionary, f. 138*v*; Thompson, 1930, p. 63.
[22] Motul dictionary, 1929, pp. 311, 916; Vienna dictionary, f. 115*r*.

heavenly bodies. Some of the hieroglyphic texts have been interpreted as records of the siderial revolutions of the planets; but, as Thompson and Lawrence Roys have pointed out, this could hardly have been the case unless the Maya knew that the earth and planets revolved around the sun—a knowledge that they evidently never acquired.

As already noted, few glyphs except those concerning numbers, the calendar, or astronomical phenomena have been satisfactorily interpreted; and, although the undeciphered glyphs in the surviving codices remain more or less a matter of conjecture, they hardly seem to be sufficiently numerous to cover the large variety of subject matter, which reliable writers of the sixteenth and seventeenth centuries tell us was set down in hieroglyphics. There are two possible explanations which might account for this. One is the character of the Maya language. Not only do many homonyms appear in the older dictionaries, but, by various associations of ideas, a single root with its derivations is frequently expanded so that it may convey a very considerable number of different meanings. This suggests the possibility that the same glyph may have expressed a variety of ideas. The other is the limited range of subjects treated in the few Maya codices that we have. As we have seen, these appear to be confined to ceremonial, chronological, and astronomical treatises; and it seems not unlikely that, if we had any of the manuscripts dealing with other matters, such as past events, prophecy, or the healing art, they would be found to contain a wider variety of hieroglyphic symbols.

Chapter 13. Neighbors of the Yucatecan Maya

TABASCO

GEOGRAPHY

THE REGION WHICH the Spaniards called the Province of Tabasco is a hot moist alluvial plain extending roughly from what is now Laguna Tupilco to Tenosique on the Usumacinta River and lying between the Gulf of Mexico and the base of the Chiapas mountain range. The Aztec called the country Anahuac Xicalanco and included it among certain areas known as Nonoalco, "the place where the language changes," although the latter term is said to have covered a part of Yucatan as well. Tabasco was no doubt the land which the Yucatecan Maya Chronicle of Mani calls Nonoual. The name Tabasco was believed to have been derived from that of the ruler of Potonchan, one of the principal towns of the region. The province did not comprise the western part of what is now the State of Tabasco, but it did include the portion of the present state of Campeche lying south and west of Laguna de Terminos.

The landscape of Tabasco is very different from that of Yucatan. Besides the swamps and quagmires for which it is noted, the country is characterized by what Sapper calls tree savannas. Here the tropical rain forest is interspersed with savannas covered with high grass, especially where the rivers overflow the surrounding country during the rainy season. There are many lagoons, and the land is intersected by a network of rivers, creeks, and bayous, most of which were navigable for canoes, and there was little travel by land in pre-Spanish times.

Tabasco has changed in some respects since the sixteenth century, and it is difficult to follow on the modern maps the route over which Cortez passed in 1524 on his journey to Honduras. Fortunately we have a detailed map made by Melchior de Alfaro Santa Cruz in 1579, giving an excellent idea of the country as it appeared in his time. A list of towns compiled in 1582 gives the distances between many of them and the local missionary headquarters.[1] During the sixteenth century most of the water of the great Chiapas River appears to have flowed almost directly north into the Gulf of Mexico through what was known as the Rio de Dos Bocas. Even though it was in the dry season,

[1] Scholes et al., 1938, 2: 64–65.

Cortez' forces in 1524 were obliged to cross it in canoes fastened together in pairs, and in 1579 it is still described as a large river. Dampier, however, tells us that in 1676 the Dos Bocas was a small clear stream, which would not float a canoe above a league from its mouth; today it is known as the Rio Seco. At the present time the main outlet of the Chiapas River follows what was formerly merely a connecting link with the Grijalva. This has changed the character of a number of the lagoons, bayous, and smaller rivers, which are partly fed from the Grijalva; and the seasonal overflow of new areas is probably responsible for the change in location of towns like Huimango and Conduacan, which are no longer at their former sites. Certain towns, however, were moved for other reasons, some of them apparently because their nearness to the coast exposed them to the raids of filibusters.

Most of the inhabitants of Tabasco were a people of the Maya stock, whom the Mexicans, and later the Spaniards, called Chontal, a term which the Molina dictionary defines as foreigners. The same name was, however, also applied to peoples of southern Oaxaca and Nicaragua, whose languages are totally unlike the Chontal of Tabasco. The last is closely related to Yucatecan Maya and even more similar to Cholti and Chorti. Indeed, Chontal, Cholti, and Chorti have such a resemblance to one another that, as Thompson suggests, they might almost be considered little more than dialectic variants of a single language, which at the time of the conquest extended across the base of the Yucatan Peninsula to Copan in western Honduras. Two other languages were also found in Tabasco. One was Zoque, spoken in six towns near the base of the sierra, and the other, Nahuatl, spoken in eight towns south and southeast of the Chontalpa and at Xicalango near Laguna de Terminos. Most of the Tabasco towns are now known to us only by their Mexican names, and Nahuatl was spoken by a considerable number of the Chontal as a second language.

The political divisions of the country are not clear. Alfaro wrote in 1579, "It is not understood that they recognized any lord, unless it was Montezuma, who had, as has been stated, two armed forces of Mexicans, who were at Xicalango and Cimatan and who collected the tribute of Montezuma, which was cacao." It seems impossible to reconcile this statement with Sahagun's detailed account of the visits of Aztec merchants to these towns, in which the latter are shown to be on very friendly terms with the Mexican ruler but in no way subject to him. We can only surmise that the country was divided into groups of allied towns and that in some cases the most powerful community directed the political policy of the group to which it belonged, as we have already seen to be the case in Yucatan.

The western part of Tabasco was the most populous. Here was a district

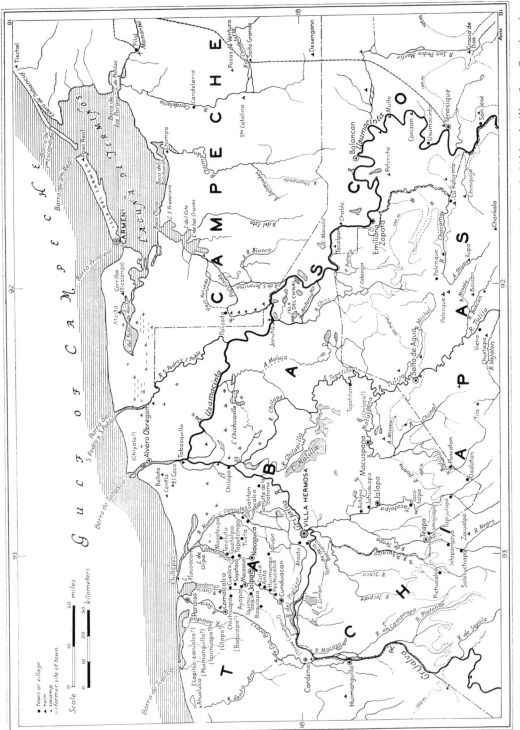

MAP 2—PROVINCE OF TABASCO. Based on Tulane-Carnegie map of "Archaeological Sites in the Maya Area" (1940) and map by Melchor de Alfaro Santa Cruz (1579).

which Cortez calls the Province of Copilco, named for the town of Copilco-zacualco, which, according to the Alfaro map and report, was six leagues west of the Rio de Dos Bocas and near the mouth of what was then called Rio Copilco. Also west of Dos Bocas were four other towns. Three of these, Huimangillo, Iquinuapa, and Boquiapa, are now to be found farther inland, and the fourth, Ulapa, has disappeared, as has Copilco-zacualco. These five towns probably spoke Chontal; in any case we are certain that east of Dos Bocas were twenty-three Chontal-speaking towns occupying a region known as the Chontalpa, most of which are still to be found on the modern maps. Among these was Copilco-teutitlan, the modern Copilco; Nacajuca may have been the most important, as it became the local missionary headquarters.

Cortez' province of Copilco ended at Nacajuca and seems to have comprised these twenty-eight towns. Immediately to the south was a group of five Nahuatl-speaking towns: Huimango, Culico, Anta, Jalupa, and Pechucalco. Of these Huimango was the largest and most important. All of them are still in the same region, but the location of Huimango has been changed.

A little farther south in the angle formed by the Grijalva and Dos Bocas rivers was a group which the Alfaro map shows as "three towns of the Cimatans." These were Mexican-speaking and were evidently Santiago Cimatan, Cuaquilteopa, and Conduaca. The first two have disappeared, but Conduaca still exists, although it has been moved a little farther north.[2] In spite of its swamps and quagmires the region was thickly populated at the time of the conquest. Cimatan was an important commercial center and, as we shall see, appears to have extended its political power over a considerable area. It continued to be hostile to the Spaniards for some time after the five Mexican towns adjoining the Chontalpa made peace.

Potonchan, at the mouth of the Grijalva, was another important commercial town. It was evidently Chontal-speaking, for the local name for canoe was "tahucup," and hucub is still the Chontal word for such a boat. Its jurisdiction no doubt extended over the neighboring towns of Cintla, Taxaual, and Chayala, and probably for some distance up the Grijalva River.[3]

When Cortez crossed the Grijalva on his journey to Honduras, he proceeded to a "province" called Zagoatan, or more properly Ciuatan. The Alfaro map shows "three towns called Çaguatanes" on a branch of the Grijalva, now the Rio Tacotalpa, which are evidently the modern Astapa, Jahuacapa, and Jalapa. Higher up this stream and also on another branch now called the Rio

[2] The existence of two suburbs of modern Conduacan named Cimatan and Cuculteupa indicates that all three towns were moved to this site. This was probably due to the increased flow of water in the Rio Grijalva.

[3] Lopez de Gomara, 1931, p. 306; Scholes et al., 1938, 2: 65.

FIGURE 9—FRESCO, THE TEMPLE OF THE WARRIORS (AFTER MORRIS, CHARLOT, AND MORRIS)

Teapa are the six Zoque-speaking towns already mentioned. There was still a population of several thousand in these six towns in 1579, and Dampier describes one of them, Tacotalpa, as "the best town on this river" in 1676. Around Teapa at the time of the conquest were many smaller settlements, and the region offered a determined resistance to the Spaniards. Godoy tells us that Teapa and a neighboring Zoque town in Chiapas called Ixtapangajoya were subject to Cimatan; and it seems very possible that the same was true of all the Zoque towns in Tabasco.[4]

Still farther to the east is a third large river flowing into the Grijalva, which retains its old name of Rio Chilapa. Strung out along this stream were four towns of moderate size. Whether they constituted a political group is uncertain, as they were some distance from one another. Of these Chilapa is now located on the main Grijalva River, Tepetzintila has disappeared, but Tepetitlan and Macuspana apparently still remain at their old sites. We do not know their size at the time of the conquest, but in 1579 they contained only 143 tributaries, or able-bodied married men, as compared with 325 in the Ciuatans and 658 in the Zoque towns.

The towns on the Usumacinta River seem to have been associated with Xicalango, a Nahuatl-speaking town, although some of them were certainly Chontal. Xicalango was the third important commercial town and situated at the ruined site now known as Cerrillos near Laguna de Pom, a short distance west of Laguna de Terminos. Here it commanded the trade route to Yucatan and through its subject town of Jonuta probably controlled much of the Usumacinta trade. There is, however, some evidence that Potonchan also had a share in this commerce.[5] Not far to the west was Atasta, but I do not know whether its inhabitants were Mexican or Chontal. Near the junction of the Usumacinta and Palizada was Jonuta, which may well have been Mexican, since the people of Xicalango were moved to this town in early colonial times.

Farther up the Usumacinta were seven towns, of which only Balancan and Tenosique are still to be found at their former sites. Two others, Ciuatecpan and Petenecte, also seem to have been not far from the junction of the Rio San Pedro Martyr, but Usumacinta is said to have been quite a distance down the river from Petenecte. Yucatecan Maya has been the language of Tenosique and the surrounding region in recent times, but we have a report of a petition presented by the authorities of Tenosique in 1605, which was written in Chontal.[6]

[4] The six Zoque towns in Tabasco were Tacotalpa, Tapijulapa, Puxcatan, Oxolotan, Tecomajiaca, and Teapa.
[5] Cortez obtained maps showing the route up the Usumacinta and to Honduras from merchants of both Xicalango and Potonchan (Lopez de Gomara, 1931, p. 409).
[6] Información de los malos tratamientos que los españoles hacen á los indios de la Provincia de Tabasco, 1605. AGI, Mexico 369.

Northeast of the Usumacinta towns was a large Chontal-speaking area known as Acalan. Its towns were located on the main stream and tributaries of a river variously known as Rio de Acalan and Rio de Sapotitan. The descriptions indicate that it can hardly be other than the modern Candelaria River. We have a list of seventy-six towns and villages. Many were no doubt small hamlets, but a number of them were places of some size, and the capital was a large town and a commercial center of considerable importance. Its Chontal name was Itzamkanac, but it is often mentioned by its Mexican name, Acalan. It is reported to have contained a number of temples and 900 houses, many of them with stone walls and thatched roofs. Cortez' Spanish soldiers and their horses are said to have been all quartered in a single building near the house of the ruler, which was probably either the unmarried men's quarters or the *tecpan*, or municipal building. By 1548 the place had shrunk to 200 houses, and in 1557 the inhabitants were moved to Tixchel on the coast, a short distance northeast of Laguna de Terminos. It is possible that the Chontal-speaking area extended to this region at the time of the conquest. The Acalan rulers had once occupied the site of Tixchel in pre-Spanish times, although they were unable to hold the area permanently.[7]

TOWNS AND BUILDINGS

The towns of Tabasco were not laid out regularly in streets, but it seems likely that, as in Yucatan, there were avenues leading from the center to the edge of the town. Bernal Diaz tells us that Potonchan and Cimatan were fortified with palisades of thick tree trunks, but it is only of the former that we have any general description. The early accounts agree that it was a populous town and occupied a large area, each dwelling being surrounded by a garden, and many of them set up on earth platforms on account of the fog and humidity from the river. The better houses were built of lime and brick. Since there was no native stone available within a distance of thirty leagues, it seems obvious that little, if indeed any, was used for building purposes. They made, however, an excellent concrete of burned shell and quartz sand, and figures of animals in imitation of sculptured stone have been found near the site.[8]

The mention of brick construction (*ladrillo*) is of special interest, for only in Tabasco do we find that burned bricks have been employed for structural purposes. Brick buildings dating from the period of the Old Empire have long been known at Comacalco on the Rio de Dos Bocas and on an island in Laguna

---

[7] Fray Lorenzo de Bienvenida to Prince Philip, Feb. 10, 1548. Cartas de Indias, 1877, p. 75; Paxbolon relación, AGI, Mexico 138.

[8] Seler, 1902–23, 5: 150–51; Brinton, 1896, p. 265.

de Mecoacan. At a ruined site believed to be that of Cintla near the mouth of the Grijalva River earth platforms have been found faced with mortar and ascended by stairs constructed of alternate layers of burned brick, mortar, and hard-pounded earth. These remains are more pertinent to the purpose of the present inquiry, for on one of the mounds Berendt discovered a broken vase, the handles of which represented figures of Spaniards. Consequently it would appear that the use of burned brick in this region continued down to the time of the conquest.

The roofs were mostly thatched, but some seem to have been covered with what Gomara calls *plancha* and Peter Martyr states were square flat stones. Possibly a flat, beamed roof topped with mortar or plaster was in use.

The more solidly built houses, however, do not seem to have long survived the conquest. All the later accounts tell us only of houses with pole or wattle walls and thatched roofs, which had always been the most common type. The descriptions are very similar to those of the houses in the interior of Yucatan. The walls were often daubed with clay on the outside, although in some cases this was not done on account of the humidity, and they were a sort of wattle or lattice like those described by Remesal at Campeche. Even as late as 1676 Dampier represented the native dwellings as "good large houses," the side walls of "mud or wattling, plastered on the inside and thatched with palm or palmetto leaves." Blom and La Farge give a sketch and brief description of the Indian houses near Comacalco. The walls are sometimes thatched with palm leaves, and, although the ground plan is not apsidal, the corners are rounded and the thatching poles and eaves are bent to carry out the curve.

We find some indication that there were many multiple-family houses. According to the tribute lists, twenty towns of the Chontalpa contained 390 houses in 1541. In 1579 the same towns contained 642 tributaries, which shows the number of able-bodied married men at that time. If we take into consideration the enormous decrease in population owing to European diseases and the dislocation of the native economic system during these thirty-eight years, it seems reasonable to believe that the houses of Tabasco contained from three to seven families each, such as we still find in Cozumel in 1570.[9]

Cortez established his headquarters at Potonchan in a square said to have been like a large courtyard with a great ceiba tree in its center. Here were three "houses of idols," probably pyramid temples since Bernal Diaz calls them *"cues,"* and some spacious halls large enough to house the Spanish forces. Gomara calls this building a "temple of the idols," and it has been considered a dependency of the chief temple. Its size suggests that it was a tecpan or the

---

[9] Autos fiscales, 1541. AGI, Justicia 195 (extracts by R. S. Chamberlain); RY, 1: 332–39.

unmarried men's quarters, either of which might probably have contained an oratory, which would explain the presence of the idols.[10]

We read of one feature of Potonchan, for which we have found no parallel in Yucatan. Gomara informs us that, "they had finer buildings outside the place than within it, for their recreation." Peter Martyr also states that, "astonishing things are told of the magnificence, the size and the beauty, of the country houses built by the natives round about, for their pleasure. They are constructed like ours, with courtyards shaded from the sun and with sumptuous apartments."[11] We are reminded of Pomar's description of the country places of the ruler of Texcoco. These buildings seem to have been at or near Cintla, where the famous battle was fought. Berendt and Seler report extensive remains in this locality, some of which, as we have seen, appear to have been occupied at the time of the conquest. There is a stretch of low marshy ground between these mounds and the site of Potonchan, and Cortez' forces found a causeway, with water on either side, by which they approached the scene of the battle. At Tixchel a paved road led through a mangrove swamp to a ruined site 4 km. inland.

AGRICULTURE AND FOOD

The most important product of Tabasco was cacao, for which the soil and climate are especially favorable. The trees require a hot damp atmosphere and are planted in groves shaded by other taller trees. The kernel was so highly esteemed as an article of food that it served as a medium of exchange in many parts of Middle America. It was grown everywhere in Tabasco except in the Zoque towns, where the weather is said to have been too cool. The cacao groves took much attention. In addition to the work of planting, caring for the trees, and gathering the crop, the grove needed continual watching, while the fruit was maturing, to protect it from the menace of monkeys, squirrels, parrots, and other animals and birds. The crop was an abundant one. In 1579, we are told, "he who gathers least gets ten or fifteen *cargas* or more, and others as much as fifty or more." The carga, or load, was probably about 42 kilos.[12]

Maize, beans, and squashes were also produced in large quantities, presumably by the milpa system of agriculture, which has already been noted in Yucatan and is still generally practiced in the lowlands and many other parts of Mexico, Guatemala, and Honduras. Tomatoes, chile, sweet potatoes, and other root crops were also extensively cultivated. Tobacco was grown and was taken medicinally, as well as carried in the mouth to ward off fatigue. It was

[10] For unmarried men's quarters in Tabasco, see Ximenez, 1929–31, bk. 2, ch. 37.
[11] Lopez de Gomara, 1931, p. 311; Anghiera (Eng. ed.), 1912, 2: 35.
[12] RY, 1: 367–70.

doubtless also smoked ceremonially, as in Yucatan. The tree calabash, mamey, aguacate, guava, a red zapote, and the sapodilla grew in the forests, and were probably also planted in the gardens around the houses.

Turkeys, and no doubt dogs as well, were raised for food. Turtles, manatees, and fish were taken in the rivers and lagoons; the last was an important article of diet. In the forests were deer, peccaries, rabbits, armadillos, coatis, iguanas, wild turkeys, and curassows, all of which seem to have been hunted for food.

The sixteenth-century reports do not mention the production of honey in Tabasco but state that the Spaniards imported all their wax from Yucatan. In 1676, however, Dampier observed both wild and domestic bees. The hives of the latter were hollow sections of tree trunks covered with a board at each end, but here they were set upright and not laid on their sides as in Yucatan. There was little salt in Tabasco. A few beds lay in some lagoons near Laguna de Terminos, but they could hardly have been of much importance. After the conquest they were completely neglected and all the salt consumed was imported from Yucatan.

INDUSTRY AND COMMERCE

The textile industry does not seem to have been very important. Bernal Diaz says that the local fabrics were coarse and of little value. Alfaro reports that much cloth was imported from Yucatan, and although cotton could be grown, it was not cultivated, spun, or woven, because the people devoted most of their time and attention to raising cacao and maize. In the latter part of the seventeenth century, however, Dampier tells us they were planting cotton for clothing.

Burned brick, as we have noted, has been found in various localities, and earthenware was probably made in most parts of the country. In the sixteenth century the descendants of the inhabitants of Potonchan, who had been moved a short distance up the river to Tabasquillo, still made a specialty of manufacturing pots and jars. Finely modeled clay heads and figurines, some of them apparently dating from a much earlier period, have turned up. As yet we know little of the quality of the pottery manufactured at the time of the conquest, but this appears to have been the area of an untempered ware, a rare thing in Middle America.

All the early Spanish accounts mention large numbers of canoes, and since transportation was mostly by water, it is evident that boat building was an important industry. Cedar was abundant, and it is probable that many of their boats were dugouts with a high bow and stern, not unlike the war canoes pictured in a fresco at Chichen Itza and the trading craft portrayed in the Dresden

Codex. The wooden ceremonial masks were probably carved of cedar, but the turquoise mosaic and gold leaf, with which some of them were covered, were imported. No metal was mined in Tabasco, but copper bells have been found at Bellota near the site of Potonchan, where Grijalva and Cortez obtained various gold objects, among which were gold crowns or headbands, necklaces, earplugs, and figures of dogs, ducks, and lizards. The last were probably votive objects like those found on the coast of Yucatan. Some of these are known to have been imported already manufactured, but it seems likely that many of them were made by local metal workers from imported sheets or plates of copper and gold. Bernal Diaz, however, tells us that not much gold was obtained here, only a few trinkets from their ancestors. Carved tortoise shell and finely tanned skins of the jaguar and cougar were also specialties of the country. A mineral gum, apparently produced from an oil seepage in certain springs, was used for glue, and in a culture where the principal tools were stone blades set in a wooden haft, such a waterproof cement must have been invaluable.

The internal trade of Tabasco centered mainly on maize, beans, chile, and squashes. Cacao-growing was so profitable that the producers were much inclined to buy their food staples, either from their neighbors or from the Zoque towns at the foot of the sierra. The people of the latter brought their produce down the rivers by canoe, and in return took back salt and other commodities from the coast country. Stone for the metates, or grinding stones, which every family possessed, could have been obtained from the region of Tixchel, the upper Usumacinta, or the sierra.

Foreign commerce with Yucatan and the trade route from Laguna de Terminos to this country have already been discussed. The Alfaro map shows inland waterways from Terminos to the Coatzacoalcos River. Ximenez describes in detail a direct route, by ponds and narrow swampy channels from Xicalango to the lower Rio San Pedro y San Pablo, which greatly shortened the journey to Potonchan, or Tabasco; but this fell into disuse after the removal of the people of Xicalango to Jonuta, and the Yucatan trade all followed the Rio Palizada to Laguna de Terminos.

Mention has also been made of Tabasco merchants, who traveled across the base of the Yucatan Peninsula to Honduras. There was evidently more than one route. In spite of the various rapids, the most convenient would appear to be up the Usumacinta and Rio de la Pasion by canoe, and thence overland to the Sarstoon River, which flows into the Gulf of Honduras. It was thought, says Cortez, that the entire trip could be made by water; and although this was not true, such a belief suggests that water transportation existed for most of the distance. Some merchants, however, made much of the journey by land. Rest houses were encountered along the route followed by Cortez, and at Tayasal on Lake Peten he was told of Tabasco merchants, who passed through that city on their way to the fairs. At Nito in Honduras an entire quarter of the town was occupied by Acalan traders and governed by a brother of the Acalan ruler.

Remesal describes the journey of Las Casas up the river to Tacotalpa and across the sierra to Chiapas by way of Teapa and Solosuchiapa. This was probably one of the old trade routes from the south, by which the so-called amber, or yellow topaz, nose beads from the region of Zinacatan, near the modern Ciudad Las Casas, were carried to Tabasco and Yucatan. The Zoque also had an important mine of the same stones near Tapalapa in northwestern Chiapas.

Sahagun gives an interesting account of the Aztec merchants who traveled through hostile territory to Tabasco. Their relations were with the Nahuatl-speaking towns of Cimatan and Xicalango. Before they arrived, they sent word ahead and were met in the enemy country, probably the Zoque area, by the friendly "lords" of Anahuac Xicalanco, who came out fully armed and conducted them to their towns. Since Cimatan lay among the bogs and swamps near the junction of the Rio de Dos Bocas and the upper Grijalva, I surmise that they were met by canoes some distance farther up the river and transported by water, first to Cimatan and then to Xicalango. From the highlands of Mexico they brought certain handsomely decorated garments, headbands and spindle cups of gold, earplugs of gold, crystal, obsidian, and copper, copper bells and needles, obsidian knives, razors, and lancets, cochineal, alum, rabbit hair, and slaves, including men, women, and children. In return they received carved jade, the so-called emeralds and other precious stones, red shells, tortoise-shell blades, apparently used for preparing chocolate, feathers, and jaguar and cougar skins. To this list of exports cacao, probably the most important of all, should be added.

GOVERNMENT

The sixteenth-century Spanish writers tell us little of government in Tabasco. We have already noted the probability that the country was divided into groups of towns, each group controlled by its most powerful member. Only in Acalan do we find a native account, which gives us some indication of the political organization of a large Chontal town. Here the capital, Itzamkanac, appears to have been divided into four quarters, each headed by its own chief, who held the title of *ahau*. Over them was a fifth ahau, whose office was hereditary and who was probably the supreme war chief. His authority, however, was definitely limited by the other four, and there was no doubt also a town council, but of the last we are given no information.[13] In Yucatan, as we have seen, there were many features of an intrusive Mexican culture ascribed to invaders from Tabasco, and many, if not all, of the ruling class considered themselves to be of Mexican descent. If such influences persisted in Yucatan, where only a sprinkling of Nahuatl words in the language and a few Mexican personal names survived to confirm the historical traditions, we may well believe that they were still stronger in Tabasco, where two of the most important cities, Cimatan and Xicalango, and a number of lesser towns were still Nahuatl-speaking at the time of the conquest.

Unlike Yucatan, at Xicalanco the chieftainship could descend in the female line in default of male heirs. "The inhabitants had a law that when a woman succeeded to the lordship, all honored and respected her, but she gave no commands or orders. A male relative, either the closest or the one most capable of command, governed in her stead; and even his hands were tied, for he could do nothing without the counsel and advice of the principal men (*mayores*), who came every day to his house or assembled on the square to discuss whatever came up."[14]

WARFARE

In Yucatan the practice of warfare had been strongly influenced by foreigners who came from Tabasco several centuries prior to the Spanish conquest, so it is not surprising that methods were very similar in both countries. In Tabasco also the various groups of towns fought with one another, and some captives were enslaved, while others were fattened, sacrificed, and ceremonially eaten.

Their weapons were long bows and arrows, darts with fire-hardened points, spears tipped with sharp bones and fish spines, wooden swords or clubs edged with flint blades, slings, and stones. We find little, if any, mention of stone arrow- or spearpoints, but it seems probable that they were imported, in view of the extensive commerce which the people of Tabasco carried on with their neighbors. Bernal Diaz states that the warriors of Cimatan were especially noted for their skill with the bow and arrow.

Defensive armor consisted of quilted and twisted cotton strips wound about the body and wooden shields and helmets. The last, which seem to have been more generally used than in Yucatan, were often handsomely decorated, as were the shields. Oviedo tells of a helmet plated with gold leaf and a shield covered with colored feathers and a gold plaque in the center. Many warriors also wore jaguar, cougar, and deer skins.

[13] Paxbolon relación, AGI, Mexico 138.
[14] Remesal, 1932, bk. 5, ch. 10, par. 3.

RELIGION

In the Spanish reports there are few particulars of the religion of Tabasco. Imposing temples are frequently mentioned, and there was a numerous priesthood, who, in addition to their religious authority, were consulted on important matters of state. They had gods for everything: the sun, maize, rain, winds, and war. These were represented by idols of clay, wood, and jade, and their worshippers sacrificed domestic animals, their own blood, and human victims to them. Cukulchan, who was the same as the Yucatecan Kukulcan and the Mexican Quetzalcoatl, was the god of the ruling caste here as in Yucatan. In addition to his other attributes I suspect that here, as in Cholula, he was a god of commerce and the patron of the merchants. Perhaps the most popular and widely worshipped deity was the goddess Ix Chel, whose famous shrine on Cozumel Island was visited by pilgrims from Tabasco. Not only was the site of Tixchel named for her, but as Seler has pointed out, the name of Ciuatecpan ("palace of the woman") on the Usumacinta and Ciuatan ("place of the woman"), which designated a group of important towns in central Tabasco, no doubt refer to the worship of the same goddess. It seems probable that she was the goddess to whom virgins were sacrificed at the Acalan town variously called Teutiercas and Teotilac.

At Itzamkanac, the Acalan capital, Cukulchan is stated to have been the god of the ruler, and four other principal deities are mentioned in connection with the four quarters of the town. One was Ikchaua, evidently the same as the Yucatecan Ekchuuah, who was the god of the cacao planters and merchants. Another was Tabay, a deity of the hunters in Yucatan. The third was Ix Chel and the fourth, an unidentified deity named Cabtanilcabtan. This religious pattern, consisting of a principal god of the town and others who were the patrons of the four quarters, may well have been typical of the larger cities of Tabasco.

ZOQUE, CHOL, AND OTHERS

On the gulf coast to the west of the Chontalpa was an area largely populated by Nahuatl-speaking peoples. Beyond the Coatzacoalcos River was the land where Grijalva obtained a large quantity of gold ornaments. Peter Martyr gives a glowing account of the region, and tells of courts of justice surrounded by walls, market places, and paved streets. Here lived a people known to the Aztec as the Olmeca Uixtotin, from among whom may have come the Nahuatl-speaking population of Tabasco, since the latter were known on the highlands of Mexico as the Olmeca Xicalanca. The name Olmeca has been translated as "rubber people." The Olmeca Uixtotin claimed to be descended from Quetzalcoatl. They were great merchants and very possibly the exporters of a fine orange pottery from the region of Veracruz. They wore rubber sandals and were armed with copper axes as well as bows and arrows. Among the Aztec they had the reputation of being great sorcerers.

In the mountains of northwestern Chiapas adjoining the group of Zoque towns in Tabasco was a large area inhabited by the same people. There is a wide range of temperature in this region, the climate varying according to the altitude. Here are many rivers, and fish was an important article of diet. The early missionaries report the production of maize, cotton, cochineal, honey, fruit, and some cacao. Near Tapalapa was a mine of the so-called amber, or yellow topaz, which was an important export.

We know little of their political or social organization, except that there was among them an upper class which prided itself on its noble status. Some of their towns were subject to the Chiapaneca, a small but powerful and ruthless nation, neither Mexican, Maya, nor Zoque, who occupied a stronghold on the Chiapas River. Others, who lived on the Tabasco border, were, as we have seen, subject to Cimatan. Most of them, however, appear to have lived in small independent groups of towns and villages.

Godoy describes the town of Ixtapangajoya as "very good and pleasant, with very good squares and houses and fine apartments." Thatched buildings with walls of daubed poles are still found in the area, and it seems probable that, like the Mixe, they also had walls of mass adobe packed between double rows of poles.

Their language is closely related to the Mixe of Oaxaca. Ciudad Real considers both to have been the same people; and it would appear that their basic cultures were very similar. The Mixe have always been considered to be a rude, stupid people of little culture, but Bancroft characterizes thé Zoque as "more rational in their behaviour, although they are ignorant and intemperate in their habits." They wore tufts of feathers and skins of green birds for ornament, as well as necklaces and nose- and earplugs of wood, gold, topaz, and other stones. Like Dampier's description of the Zoque towns in Tabasco, Gage gives a more flattering picture of the highland Zoque in the seventeenth century. The latter characterizes their "province" as the richest part of Chiapas and the people as "witty and ingenious." Larval silk had apparently been introduced among them, and he speaks highly of their colored silk fabrics, which were exported to Spain. Indeed, at this time both in Tabasco and Chiapas the Zoque were evidently more prosperous than many of the other peoples of Central America under Spanish colonial rule.

East of the Zoque towns of Tabasco and also bordering on the alluvial plain occupied by the Chontal were the Chol. Their descendants are still living at Tila, Tumbala, Palenque, and other towns of the present state of Chiapas. They retain their language, but no description of their culture at the time of the conquest is now available. Much of this area is rough and mountainous. Stephens describes the view from a hilltop at Tumbala, from which the Indian milpas could be seen "on almost inaccessible mountain heights, and in the deepest ravines." Only a century ago, although they had long been converted to Christianity, he found the Chol of this region wearing only the traditional loincloth, and he was impressed by their wild appearance.

Other Chol-speaking peoples, however, known in colonial times as the Lacandon, Acala, Manche Chol, and Toquegua, once occupied a belt of land extending to the southeast and east as far as the southern shore of the Gulf of Honduras. In connection with the Lacandon, it should be noted that, although the term is applied today to a people speaking Yucatecan Maya, Thompson has shown that in the sixteenth and seventeenth centuries the name designated a Chol-speaking people who then occupied the same area. Some accounts of the central and eastern Chol have been preserved, of which studies have been made by Tozzer and Thompson, and it seems probable that the culture of the western Chol was fundamentally the same. As Thompson has noted, the Chol are of considerable historical importance, not only as the occupants of the sites of many Old Empire cities and the possible descendants of their builders, but also because their culture was more purely Maya and less subject to Mexican influences than that of Tabasco and Yucatan.

The Chol Lacandon town of Dolores in eastern Chiapas consisted of 103 structures: 100 dwellings, two large communal buildings, and a still larger temple. The houses were thatched; the walls of poles and mud were sometimes calcimined. Many dwellings were enclosed on three sides and open in front. Among the Manche Chol a number of related families often occupied a single house, as in Yucatan.

The descriptions which we have of their personal ornaments, scarification, and body painting would probably apply almost equally well to what we have seen in Yucatan; and the same might be said of their clothing, except that besides their cotton garments, bark cloth was sometimes worn. The importance of agriculture is indicated by the name Chol, which means maize field. They cultivated maize, beans, squashes, cotton, and the other products already noted in northern Yucatan. To these should be added cacao, which was an important article of commerce. The central Chol, especially the Lacandon, were a warlike people and constantly raided their Christian neighbors in colonial times. The only weapons mentioned, however, were the bow and arrow.

Some of the Chol Lacandon and the Manche Chol did not have idols, but worshipped certain mountains, passes, crossroads, and river whirlpools. To these they sacrificed turkeys, offered their own blood, and burned copal incense and wax. The last is of special interest, as the Yucatecan Maya had a prejudice against burning beeswax. Among the Lacandon of Dolores, however, idols were venerated. They had gods of the river, maize fields, turkeys, cacao groves, and especially the lightning. We know that other Lacandon of this region sacrificed their war captives and that ceremonial cannibalism was practiced. There is little reference to a separate priesthood; and at Dolores the cacique exercised the functions of a chief priest.

In the heart of the Chol Lacandon country, east of Ocosingo and about 15 leagues southwest of Tenosique, Cogolludo describes a people who spoke Yucatecan Maya. Their material culture much resembled that of their Chol neighbors, but their religious organization was evidently Maya. Their idols were in the charge of a priest, who was assisted by an *ah kulel* (deputy) and an *ah kayom* (singer). They sacrificed dogs and captives taken in war, and these offerings were ceremonially eaten. Undoubtedly these people came from some region northeast of the Usumacinta River, but since we first hear of them during the seventeenth century, it is possible that they had been in this area only since the Spanish conquest of Yucatan. In any case, they would appear to have been the forerunners, if not the ancestors, of the Maya-speaking Lacandon, who now occupy the same country.

Of the eastern neighbors of the Chontal of Tenosique we have little, if indeed any, information. We can only surmise that they were Maya-speaking and were much like the people just described. Farther north, about three or four days' journey east of the Acalan, lived a people called Cehache by the Maya and Mazateca by the Mexicans. In either language the name means the "deer people." Bernal Diaz explains that among them the deer was a sacred animal and was not hunted. As far as we can tell, in language and culture they were a branch of the Yucatecan Maya; during the sixteenth and seventeenth centuries large numbers of fugitive Indians from northern Yucatan joined them. Cortez and Bernal Diaz passed through a number of their settlements and describe three of them as fortified towns with ditches and palisades. In the largest, called Tiac, there were three *barrios,* or subdivisions, each with its own palisade inside the main fortification. Like the Cupul towns of the north, some of these towns warred with one another, but their principal enemies were said to be the Lacandon.

HIBUERAS-HONDURAS

Attention has already been drawn to the importance of the commercial relations between Yucatan and Tabasco and the various peoples on the Caribbean slope of what are now the Republics of Guatemala and Honduras. The Spaniards called this region Hibueras and Honduras. The former was the West Indian word for the tree gourd, many of which were seen floating in the Bay of Amatique; and the latter owed its name to the great depth of the water off Cape Caxinas. Hibueras was the coast region from the Rio Dulce to the Ulua River and included the Ulua and Naco valleys; the name Ulua was sometimes loosely applied to the entire district. Honduras extended along the coast from a point about 10 leagues west of Trujillo to Cape Camaron. The hinterland was not very well defined, but it seems to have reached south to the mountains which separated this province from Salvador and Guatemala.[15]

On the Caribbean slope is a succession of river valleys running back from the sea and separated from one another by ranges of hills or mountains. On the mountains are pine and oak forests, but much of this coastal area is covered with tropical rain forest. In the valleys of the Ulua and Aguan and along much of the coast the rain forest is interspersed with savannas and stands of cohune palms. In many of these river basins, some distance back from the sea, are areas where the rainfall is light. Some of these, like the valley of the Motagua above Gualan, are semidesert, and the dry flats and slopes bear a scattered growth of thorny shrubs and cacti.

The larger rivers are an important feature of the country. Not only were they said to overflow and water the groves of cultivated trees along their banks, but they were navigable for canoe traffic a long distance inland and furnished easy transportation to the coast for the products of the inland tribes. One, the Rio Aguan, which runs almost parallel to the coast behind a range of mountains, was navigable for native craft for a distance of 40 leagues from its mouth.

Most of the people of Hibueras spoke a language of the Maya stock. Stone quotes a document of 1533, which states that from Copilco-zacualco in western Tabasco to the Ulua River the language was the same, and that they all traded with one another and considered themselves to be the same people.[16] As already noted, Chontal, Chol, and Chorti might well be considered little more than dialectic variants of the same language; and Ciudad Real, a famous linguist and the reputed author of the Motul dictionary, tells us that although he considers Chontal a different language from that of Yucatan, "in many words it agrees

[15] AGI, Indiferente General 1206, extract by R. S. Chamberlain.
[16] Stone, 1941, p. 14.

with Maya, and so knowing one, the other is easily understood."[17] We know that in the sixteenth century Chol was spoken along the Sarstoon River, on the north shore of Lake Izabal, and on the lower Rio Polochic; and at the beginning of the nineteenth century Chorti was still the language from Zacapa near the Motagua River to Copan in western Honduras. Just what language of the Maya stock was spoken east and southeast of the Rio Dulce is uncertain, but there can be little doubt that it was Chol, Chorti, or a closely related variant of the lowland Maya.

Somewhere near the lower Motagua River a heathen people known as the Toquegua were still living at the beginning of the seventeenth century. They may have been the descendants of the inhabitants of the Motagua valley; they still navigated the river with their canoes and traded with the Christianized Indians of the Bay of Amatique.[18] Toquegua sounds like a Mexican word and may have been a local descriptive term used by the Spanish settlers. To me it would seem to resemble the Aztec word *toquaeuayo*, which means scalp. If so, it might well refer to the hair arrangement of the Indians so designated, for many of the Maya peoples shaved the tops of their heads.

Near the mouth of the Rio Dulce was an important commercial center called Nito. Here an entire quarter of the town was occupied by merchants from Acalan and governed by a brother of Paxbolon, the Acalan ruler.[19] Although Nito was frequented by Chontal, Chol, and Yucatecan Maya traders, it seems possible that this was really a Nahua trading post. Chol cities of this character appear to have been practically nonexistent at the time of the conquest; and in this vicinity, as in Tabasco, we again begin to find Nahuatl names for Maya-speaking towns.[20] During most, if not all, of the long journey from Acalan to the Rio Dulce, Cortez' interpreter and Mexican allies had given him only Maya names for the settlements through which he passed; this is probably to be ascribed to the absence of Mexican trading colonies throughout this wide expanse of territory.

The importance of Nito was due to the extensive cacao-producing areas, which were accessible to it by water traffic. Close relations existed with the Chol on the Sarstoon River; among them Cortez found merchants from Nito, who had fled because of the Spanish occupation of the town. There was also evidently much commerce with the Chol, Kekchi, and Pokonchi in the valleys of the Polochic and Cahabon Rivers. The Polochic is navigable for canoes as

[17] Ciudad Real, translated by Noyes, 1932, p. 347.
[18] Fuentes y Guzman, 1932–33, bk. 6, ch. 4.
[19] Cortez, 5th letter, 1931, p. 127. The land on the east side of the river is thickly wooded, and I was unable to find this site.
[20] Diaz del Castillo (chs. 180–81) tells of Zinacan and Tenecintle on the Rio Polochic and of Cuyacan near the Motagua River.

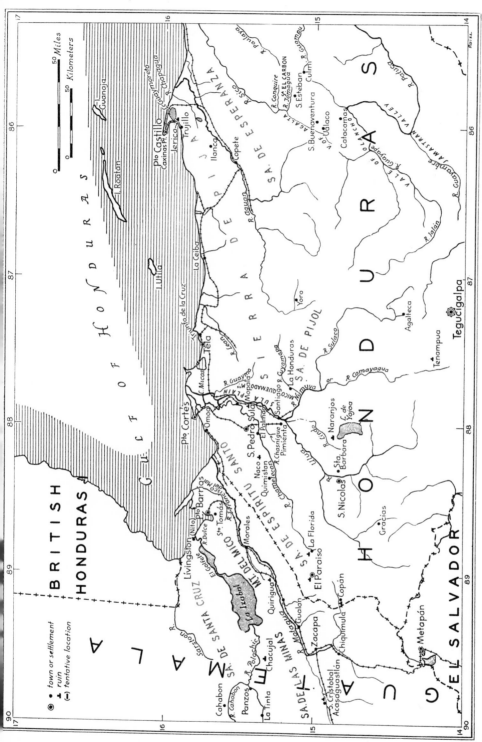

MAP 3—HIBUERAS-HONDURAS. Based on Stone, "Archaeology of the North Coast of Honduras" (1941) and Tulane-Carnegie map of "Archaeological Sites in the Maya Area" (1940)

FIGURE 10—EAGLE AND UNIDENTIFIED ANIMAL BELIEVED TO REPRESENT MEXI-
CAN MILITARY ORDERS IN YUCATAN, THE TEMPLE OF THE WARRIORS

FIGURE 11—SCULPTURED JAMB, KABAH

far as La Tinta, and the region was a prosperous one. The low hot valley has long been considered some of the best maize land in all Guatemala, and Cortez in his letter comments on the attractive cacao groves and fruit orchards that he observed on either side of this river. In this valley he found a large and old settlement called Chacujal. Here was a large plaza with temples and other buildings around it like those in Mexico, and Cortez says nothing like it had been seen since he left Acalan. This was perhaps an overstatement, since it is difficult to believe that it surpassed Tayasal, but in any case it was an imposing town. Although Marina, his interpreter, was with him, they had difficulty understanding the language, which was different from any hitherto heard, that is, Nahuatl, Chontal, Yucatecan Maya, and Chol. This is of especial interest, as it suggests that Chacujal was either a Poconchi or a Kekchi town. Maudslay locates the site near the main Polochic or south branch, but Ximenez believes Cortez followed the Rio Cahabon, which flows into it from the north. In either case Chacujal would be close to the edge of the Kekchi area as shown on Stoll's linguistic map. The Cahabon and Polochic Rivers formed one of the principal commercial outlets of Verapaz, where the highly prized quetzal plumage was obtained. Feathers as well as obsidian from the deposits near Coban were no doubt exported by this route.

A third important commercial tributary of Nito was the valley of the Motagua River. This was evidently the large stream which was said to be accessible to the Bay of Amatique by an inland waterway. The merchants of Nito told Cortez that they took this route during the stormy season, when they could not travel by sea, and one of them offered to escort some Spaniards to the river by this passage. The expedition was unsuccessful, and the party returned discouraged by the swamps into which they were led by the guide, although the latter seems to have acted in good faith. Some of the boats of the Spaniards probably drew more water than the native craft, and, as we have seen in Tabasco, the well-known inland waterway from Xicalango to the Rio San Pedro y San Pablo seemed to the Spaniards to be a difficult and inadequate route. Maudslay believes that the Nito trader attempted to take the Spaniards along a natural canal; probably he had in mind the course followed by the modern Canal de Los Angeles and the Rio San Francisco del Mar, which may well have been connected with the Motagua during the rainy season, when a considerable part of the region between the mouths of these rivers is still flooded.

The country near Nito was not thickly settled, but in the Motagua basin to the southeast the Spaniards found a number of prosperous settlements with maize fields and cacao groves, and it is quite probable that these plantations continued for a considerable distance up the river. The Motagua is navigable for canoes as far as Gualan, where swift rapids are encountered, but before that point is reached the climate changes and a dry belt begins. For merchants traveling by land Zacapa was only about a day's journey above Gualan. Here cacao was less plentiful than farther down the Motagua, but it was of a very fine quality. We may well believe that the obsidian, which was mined near Zacapa, was exported down the Motagua valley to the coast. It is of interest to note that at Acasaguastlan, not very much farther up the Motagua valley, was a colony of Nahuatl-speaking Pipil, presumably from the Pacific coast.[21] Canoes are still used at various points for crossing the Motagua between Gualan and Acasaguastlan, and it seems possible, in spite of the rapids and the shallow bars in the dry season, that the river was used for canoe traffic. We know that in pre-Spanish times merchants made use of water routes, which the Spaniards later considered impracticable. Lehmann indicates a line of Nahua influence and settlement, which passed close to Naco in Honduras and continued eastward to the Mexican-speaking colonies mentioned by Cortez a short distance south of Trujillo. Nito was visited by the Nahuatl-speaking traders from Xicalango, and we may well believe that the latter also had commercial relations with the Pipil living around Acasaguastlan.

East of the Motagua and across the Omoa Mountains lies the broad and fertile Sula valley in the basin of the lower Chamelcon and Ulua Rivers. This plain was a prosperous region and thickly populated at the time of the conquest. Here cacao, cassava, maize, and cultivated fruits were produced in large quantities. The Ulua River formed the eastern boundary of the Maya area. Trading canoes from Yucatan followed the coast to Ulua, and there had been close relations between the two countries. Long before the conquest the "lords" of Chichen Itza came by way of Ascension Bay to Honduras for cacao, feathers, and other commodities; and later, at the time of the fall of Mayapan, the son of the Cocom ruler of that city escaped the fate of the rest of the family, because he was absent in the land of Ulua on a trading expedition. Political relations between Yucatan and the Ulua region were greatly strengthened by the active part which the most prominent nobles and even the members of the ruling families took in this trade. After the first Spanish attempt to conquer the east coast of Yucatan was abandoned, Gonzalo Guèrrero, the famous renegade Spaniard who was shipwrecked there in 1511, first enslaved and later made chief captain of the ruler of Chetumal, came with a fleet of fifty war canoes to aid the Ulua people against the Spanish invaders. Here he was killed

21 Kidder, 1940, p. 124; Gann and Thompson, 1931, p. 201.

by a shot from an arquebus while defending a native fortress on the Ulua River.[22]

It is difficult to determine which of the lowland Maya peoples lived between the Omoa Mountains and the Ulua River, although it has been suggested that it was the Chorti. This surmise finds some confirmation in the report of Galindo, who states that the Chorti language extended to the Gulf of Honduras and infers from this and "other data" that Omoa was at one time subject to the rulers of Copan. Although the Old Empire city now known as Copan had long been in ruins, at the time of the conquest there was an important and well-fortified Chorti town of this name at or near the site, which offered a determined resistance to the Spaniards.

Reaching back into the Omoa Mountains west of the Rio Chamelcon was the prosperous, thickly settled valley of Naco, where the Spaniards were pleased by the wide roads bordered with fruit trees and impressed by the refinement and urbanity of the people. Here was the town of Naco, which was one of the most important commercial centers of Hibueras-Honduras. Although it lay in the Maya area, Naco was evidently a colony of Nahua traders at the time of the conquest, since a pottery definitely related to certain Mexican types has been found associated with Spanish artifacts at this site. It was said to be a town of Indians who had come from the Pacific coast.[23] At first sight this suggests the Pipil, some of whom, as we have seen, were living at Acasaguastlan. Strong, however, believes the Nahua influence at Naco to have been quite recent, and Thompson suggests the twelfth century A.D. for the Pipil occupation of the Pacific coast of Guatemala and Salvador. Another possibility is the Olmeca from southern Veracruz and whose name has also been associated with the Mexican-speaking towns of Tabasco. Torquemada tells us that some of them followed the Pipil and finally settled in Nicaragua. Montejo states that the town had a population of 10,000. We know little of its appearance; Bernal Diaz tells us that the Spanish soldiers were quartered in some large courts.

Naco would appear to be inhabited by one of a number of more or less isolated Mexican groups scattered over Honduras, who carried on an extensive trade with one another and with the Nahuatl-speaking Pipil on the Pacific coast. Bernal Diaz mentions the direct road which he followed from Nito to Naco, and reference has already been made to the long trade route, which extended from Tabasco through Nito and Naco to Nicaragua. Nahua colonies are known to have existed near Trujillo, in the Olancho valley, and near

[22] Tozzer, 1941, p. 8; communication from R. S. Chamberlain. In the report of his death his name is given as Gonzalo Aroça, but the reference to his past career makes it plain that he was Guerrero.

[23] RY, 1: 398–99, 411; Strong, 1940, p. 380; Stone, 1941, p. 97, quoting Documentos inéditos, 1864–84, 14: 244.

Comayagua, and there were doubtless others. Some of the Indians of Honduras even had a legend that the Mexican nation had originally come from that region. Nahuatl place names of non-Mexican towns are frequent in Honduras. Some of these may well have originated with the Mexican allies of the Spanish conquerors, but it seems evident that many were already in existence, when the Spaniards entered the country.[24]

The Ulua valley is of especial interest. It contained an admixture of cultural elements, so that it can hardly be considered to have belonged to any single ethnic group. As Strong has noted, the region was "a buffer area between two sets of linguistic stocks and cultural traditions, one derived from northern Central America and Mexico and the other, from southern Central America and eventually from South America."[25] The former culture is believed to have been based largely on the cultivation of maize, the latter on the production of cassava.

Beside the Maya and Nahua we also find a people known today as the Jicaque living in the Ulua valley. The name appears to be a corruption of a Mexican word and might be translated either as "the rude people" or "the former or older inhabitants." It may well have been originally a term applied by the newer Nahuatl-speaking people to the indigenous population generally. Spanish colonial writers apply the term to various heathen peoples in Honduras, so it is often difficult to tell just whom they mean when they refer to the Jicaque. A few of these people, speaking in the modern sense of the term, live near Palmar on the Rio Chamelcon, but since the Maya language penetrated as far as the Ulua, it seems likely that more of them occupied the eastern portion of the Sula plain beyond the latter river, also the valley of Yoro. Lehmann publishes a word list of the Jicaque of the Mountains of Lean y Mulia, the range separating the Yoro region from the Ulua valley and the Caribbean. They are said to have detested the English, so some of them must have lived not far from the coast. The same writer also quotes from a report of 1745, in which the country from the Ulua River to Trujillo is said to have been populated by the Jicaque. In the linguistic maps also this area is ascribed to the same people.

Most of the surviving Jicaque were converted to Christianity in the middle of the nineteenth century. They were visited by Habel shortly after this time and by Sapper a generation later. Both explorers describe the Jicaque as a tall people with a light skin, as compared with other Honduras Indians. Their garments were of beaten bark cloth, which was often dyed various colors. The men wore a sort of narrow poncho hanging to the thighs in front and to the knees

[24] Cf. Sapper (1897, pp. 349–53), who believes the contrary.
[25] Strong et al., 1938, p. 11.

behind. It was held together around the loins by a bark strip, into which they stuck their arrows, about 60 cm. long and tipped with three-edged points of hard wood. A narrow bark band worn around the head secured their long hair, which was parted in front and hung loosely over the shoulders. The women wore a narrow skirt and a long upper garment. Besides maize and beans, Sapper tells us, arrowroot was an important article of diet. The sixteenth-century writers furnish no description which can be definitely applied to the Jicaque, but from their general accounts of northern Honduras it seems likely that the nineteenth-century survivors were as little representative of their former culture as are the modern Lacandon, of Yucatecan civilization at the time of the conquest.

East of the Jicaque were the Paya, to whom ethnographers ascribe a large territory extending east from Trujillo almost to the Rio Patuca and south to the Valley of Olancho. Little more than 800 remained when Sapper visited them in 1898. Most of these lived north of the Valley of Olancho, and he reports a few on the Black River and its tributaries. At Culmi each family had a house in the village, but they lived mostly in scattered compounds outside the town. Their principal food is maize and especially sweet cassava. Like the Jicaque, they did not make tortillas until recently, but only tamales and various maize beverages. Their garments were formerly of bark cloth.

Paya culture at the time of the conquest was no doubt influenced by the Nahua colonies living in or on the edge of their territory. Only 7 leagues from Trujillo were the important towns of Chapagua and Papayeca, whose language, according to Cortez' own account, differed little from that of the highlands of Mexico. The names of some of their chiefs were unmistakably Mexican, such as Ce Coatl ("one serpent") and Mazatl ("deer"). Although only 2 leagues distant from one another, Chapagua had ten subject towns and Papayeca, eighteen.

There is reason to believe that the inhabitants of the Bay Islands were Paya. These islanders were employed as interpreters in 1622 by the Spanish missionaries among the mainland Paya, and although this evidence alone has not been considered conclusive, it finds confirmation in Stone's characterization of the archaeology of the Bay Islands as fundamentally Paya.

Here, it will be recalled, Columbus encountered a large trading canoe from Yucatan, and we may well believe that the plumage of the green yellow-headed species of parrot abundant on Guanaja Island was an important article of exchange. In colonial times a fine crystal was mined and exported from another of these islands; and it is very possible that this commerce goes back to pre-Spanish times. The deposit was well known as early as 1541. Beads of imported crystal have been found in graves at Chichen Itza, and translucent stone or glass is still used in Yucatan today for divining. In 1544 there were 60 houses on Guanaja and 150 on Utila, but by this time the population had greatly decreased.

There is excellent reason for Strong's belief that besides the Yucatecan Maya, the Chol or Chorti, the Jicaque from the Ulua, the Bay Islanders, and some of the coast tribes from Nicaragua were all engaged in trading along the coast. Down to the middle of the eighteenth century Mosquito Indians in canoes from the northeast coast of Honduras were still making raids on the east coast of Yucatan.

Trujillo was near the dividing line between the Jicaque and Paya, and an important Nahua group was reported a short distance to the south. Early descriptions of the region indicate that it was strongly influenced by the Nahua and Maya. The first bishop of Honduras refers to towns containing 1000 and 1500 houses and tells us that society was highly organized, "neither more nor less than the Mexican nation." The caciques and principals had much authority and were treated with great ceremony and respect. Indeed, they maintained such state that in order to impress them with his own importance Cortez felt obliged to wear his finest garments and jewelry and bring out his silver plate, when he was served in their presence.

South of the Sula valley, Yoro, and the northern part of the Valley of Olancho lived the Lenca, who occupied most of the remainder of Honduras and a portion of Salvador. As we have seen, however, there were Nahua settlements in this area, particularly in the Valley of Olancho and near Comayagua. Their culture was influenced by their Nahua and Maya neighbors, but it is, on the whole, to be associated with that of southern rather than northern Central America. Like the Jicaque and Paya, their linguistic affiliations are as yet uncertain, although a remote connection with Nahuatl, Maya, and Zoque has been suggested.

Herrera devotes a chapter to the manners and customs of Hibueras and Honduras, but unfortunately, except for his account of a few of the myths and religious beliefs and the practices of the Lenca in the valley of Cerquin, he gives us no idea which of the peoples of the country he is describing. A few of the traits and usages which he records may well be characteristic of a number of the tribes living east of the Maya area. Salt, he tells us, was difficult to obtain because the merchants who carried it were often killed on the road. The various tribes made war on one another with little provocation, especially at certain seasons of the year, and I infer that there was a truce during the growing and harvesting season. As in Yucatan, one of the principal reasons for making war was to capture slaves, who were employed in agricultural work. After peace was concluded, they resumed their usual commercial relations and "traded for birds, cloth, feather-work, salt, and achiote." He also tells us that those who differed in language were never at peace. This statement is no doubt altogether too sweeping, but it was probably true of certain peoples who were hereditary enemies. Such a condition, where it existed, would contribute to the commercial importance of the Nahua groups, who seem to have traded in every part of the country. The milpa system and the use of flint axes are mentioned; but, we are told, they also tilled the land with digging sticks and a sort of sharp spade. The former is described as having two projecting hooks or branches, one above the other, so that pressure could be applied by both arm and foot. This is of interest, since only a planting stick is reported from Yucatan. In the highlands of Guatemala and Mexico an implement which the Spaniards called a hoe (*azadon, coa*) was used; and Oviedo tells us that on the Pacific coast of Nicaragua a spade or hoe was made by setting a mother-of-pearl shell into a haft.

Some traits suggest influences from Mexico or northern Central America among people who seem to be neither Nahua nor Maya, although one can not always be certain of this. "The lord was chief justice in every town and had four deputies, who managed all affairs under him." Again, "they called their year *joalor,* that is, what passes away, dividing it into eighteen months of twenty days each, tho' they reckoned by nights, and in the day were ruled by the sun, observing his rising and going down."[26]

Of religious organization Herrera writes: "In the fields were little houses, long and narrow, and high from the ground, in which were their gods of stone, clay and wood, having faces of tigers and other creatures, and with them were old men naked, who liv'd an austere life, wearing their hair very long, wound in tresses about their heads. . . . None but the prime men might talk with those priests, because they held them in great veneration."[27] We know very little of temple architecture in Hibueras-Honduras at the time of the conquest, but this brief account may well be pertinent to various parts of the country. The priests probably wore a loincloth of some sort; Spanish writers often refer to men as going naked when they wore only this garment. Even so, the description would hardly apply to the Maya or Nahua, whose priests are usually said to have appeared in long robes.

[26] Herrera y Tordesillas (Eng. ed.), 1725–26, 4: 139, 141.
[27] *Ibid.,* 4: 139. This part of Herrera's account immediately follows a short geographical description of the Bay Islands, but it evidently refers to some part of the mainland, as it mentions a land journey of 20 leagues.

Chapter 14. Bibliographical Sketch

IN THE PRECEDING study not many specific citations from the better-known authorities have been made, especially when the information does not seem to be of a controversial character. For this reason I offer the following brief account of the more important of the literary sources which have been consulted in writing this sketch of Yucatecan Maya civilization as it existed at the time of the Spanish conquest. Bibliographical details of these and of the other sources on which this study is based will be found in the list of references at the end of the book.

The short and incomplete description of the geography and physiography of the Yucatan Peninsula is based largely on Lundell's monographs on the phytogeography of the peninsula and the vegetation of the Peten. These have been supplemented by Ricketson's and Kidder's aerial survey, Standley's and Bartlett's botanical studies, Thompson (1936a), Thompson, Pollock and Charlot (1932), Shattuck (1933), and Morley (1938). The last also contains an appendix on the physical-geological features of Peten by Hakon Wadell. Page has made a study of the climate of the peninsula.

Of especial interest are the reports of the three Spanish expeditions which sailed along the coast of Yucatan in 1517, 1518, and 1519 under Hernandez de Cordoba, Grijalva, and Cortez, and a fourth under Montejo, which invaded the peninsula from the east coast. Of these we have personal accounts by Cortez, by Juan Diaz, who was Grijalva's chaplain, and by Bernal Diaz, who accompanied the first three expeditions. Their narratives, which are only too brief so far as Yucatan is concerned, are supplemented by the histories of Peter Martyr d'Anghiera, Oviedo, and Gomara, who were well acquainted with a number of the men who took part in these discoveries and explorations. Here, at either first or second hand, we learn from contemporary sources the impression which the first Spaniards received of Yucatecan Maya culture at a time when it was as yet unaffected by contact with Europeans.

The earliest general account of the Maya and their civilization is that of the Franciscan missionary, Diego de Landa, who afterward became bishop of Yucatan. It was written about the year 1566 and is entitled Relación de las cosas de Yucatán. Tozzer observes in the introduction to his edition of this work: "The source material presented by Landa includes practically every phase of the social anthropology of the ancient Mayas, together with the history of the

Spanish discovery, the conquest and the ecclesiastical and native history together with the first accurate knowledge of the hieroglyphic writing. It is especially complete on Maya religion and rituals and, with the exception of Sahagun, there is no other manuscript of New Spain which covers adequately a similar range of subjects. The present copy of Landa is only a part of the original manuscript which is lost."

In spite of the stringent, and sometimes even cruel, measures he took to wipe out the pagan religion, Landa's attitude toward the natives is sympathetic; and indeed he was in an advantageous position to understand them. Not only was he an excellent Maya linguist, but he had come to Yucatan in 1549 and traveled extensively in the country at a time when a large part of the population was not as yet even nominally converted to Christianity, and prior to the political reorganization of the Indian pueblos by Lopez Medel in 1552. He himself acknowledges that Nachi Cocom, the last native ruler of Sotuta, had been one of his informants, and we know that Gaspar Antonio Chi was another.

The value of Landa's work is enormously enhanced by Professor Tozzer's annotated English edition. It is impeccably translated, and many of the notes are short ethnological and bibliographical essays on the subjects treated by the Franciscan. The latter's statements are compared not only with those of both the Spanish and the Maya writers of colonial times, but also with the ethnological studies of the modern natives. Wherever possible, Tozzer draws parallels with the pre-Columbian Maya picture manuscripts and sculptures. All this information is made available by a full index and a detailed syllabus covering every subject mentioned in the text and notes.

Second only to Landa's work is the collection entitled Relaciones de Yucatán. This contains a series of fifty reports written in 1579 and 1581 in reply to a long questionnaire, which had been sent out by the Council of the Indies in Spain. Two of them are by the corporations of Merida and Valladolid, and the remainder were written by individual encomenderos. Some of these men were old conquerors who had come with Montejo and who had some recollection of things as they were at the time of the conquest; and many of them had consulted the caciques of their tributary towns in making out the reports. Not only do these documents augment the ethnological material furnished by Landa, but they are of especial value for the ethnographical and historical information which they contain. Much of this was contributed by Gaspar Antonio Chi, who signs as joint author in a number of instances.

Chi was well educated by both native and European standards, consequently in his case there is not the psychological barrier which we encounter in studying the narratives of other native writers. The son of a pagan priest and the grandson of a former ruler of Mani, he was converted at the age of fifteen, educated by the missionaries, and later engaged in tutoring many of the children of the conquerors in Spanish and Latin grammar. Much of his life was spent as court interpreter at Merida. His own brief report is concerned chiefly with the native political organization and judiciary, but both this and his contributions to the writings of others are of enormous value.

Only a decade after the conquest Lopez Medel came from Guatemala to Yucatan, where he took over the government for a short time and instituted many important administrative reforms. The value of his short report is due to his competence as a trained observer, his extensive travels in the province, and his personal contact with the natives. Translations of the Chi and Lopez Medel reports are to be found in Tozzer's edition of Landa.

These accounts are supplemented by the valuable collection of contemporary documents published by Scholes and Adams and entitled *Don Diego Quijada, alcalde mayor de Yucatán, 1561–1565*. It contains the minutes of Landa's judicial investigation of idolatry in 1562 and adds greatly to our knowledge of the native religion.

Three important writers, who lived during the late sixteenth and early seventeenth centuries, have made important contributions to our knowledge of Maya culture, although, oddly enough, such information is only incidental to the avowed purpose of their works. Two of them were Franciscan missionaries, and the third was a creole priest. The first, Ciudad Real, was a famous Maya scholar who wrote an account of a journey of inspection by the commissary general of the Franciscan order, for whom he acted as traveling secretary. Lizana's book is largely a history of the statue of the Virgin at Izamal, to which many miracles were ascribed. The work of the third, Dr. Sanchez de Aguilar, is a bitter attack on the persistent idolatry of many natives and an impassioned plea for greater severity in the prosecution of such offenders.

Two Maya dictionaries dating from the same period also contain much ethnological material. One is the well-known Diccionario de Motul, which is probably the work of Ciudad Real. The other is a manuscript volume in the National Library at Vienna, but its authorship is still a matter of conjecture. Herrera's history, which first appeared about this time, contains an excellent chapter on the Yucatecan Maya, but it follows Landa very closely.

Lopez de Cogolludo, who wrote a history of Yucatan about the middle of the seventeenth century, devotes much space and attention to the Maya and their culture, especially their religion, apparently as a background for the accounts of missionary activities, which occupy a large part of his book. For this he has drawn heavily not only upon Chi, Lizana, and Sanchez de Aguilar, but also upon many important lost sources. Among these are the ordinances by Lopez Medel for the government of the natives, which he quotes in full, and a long report by Fuensalida, who visited the Itza capital on Lake Peten and other parts of southern Yucatan. Some of his descriptions of the pagan deities are remarkably similar to the definitions of the *"ydolos"* in the Vienna dictionary. Cogolludo's intolerance and his dislike for the Indians, which at times seems almost malicious, are so evident that one is at first inclined to distrust many of his statements, but a comparison with the available sources does much to inspire confidence in his reliability.

Two more important sources coincide with the conquest of the Itza at the end of the seventeenth century. One is the report of Father Avendaño, who visited them shortly before they were overcome; and his picture of this last surviving Maya city has a freshness to be compared only with that of the personal accounts of the early explorers. He was an accomplished linguist and was familiar with both the native colonial literature and the old picture manuscripts. Indeed, it is more than probable that he was able to read the hieroglyphic writing. The second source is Villagutierre's famous history of the conquest of the Itza, which is very full and is based upon the official records of the Spanish expedition.

The native Maya literature of colonial Yucatan has been discussed in Chapter 12. Brinton and Martinez Hernandez have published texts and translations of the Maya chronicles and the papers of the Pech family; and Perez Martinez has translated the chronicle of Ah Nakuk Pech. Various editions of the text and the translations of the Book of Chilam Balam of Chumayel are listed in the references. In addition to my Chumayel publication, I have published texts and translations of a large number of native medical prescriptions and a series of land documents covering almost the entire period. Photographic reproductions of many unpublished colonial Maya manuscripts are accessible in the Library of the Peabody Museum of Harvard University, the Newberry Library at Chicago, and the Library of Congress. In his Maya grammar Tozzer includes a complete bibliographical survey and appraisement of this literature and publishes interlinear translations of a number of Maya texts ranging from an ancient prophecy to a modern witch story.

For the brief inquiry into the state of Maya knowledge of mathematics and astronomy at the time of the conquest, I have chiefly consulted the epigraphic studies of Morley, Thompson, and Teeple.

Comparisons with the modern natives are based largely on Tozzer's *A comparative study of the Mayas and Lacandones,* Thompson's *Ethnology of the Mayas of southern and central British Honduras,* Redfield's and Villa's *Chan*

Kom, Redfield's *The folk culture of Yucatan*, Steggerda's *Maya Indians of Yucatan*, and Wauchope's *Modern Maya houses*.

Source material for the neighbors of the Yucatecan Maya is somewhat fragmentary. Besides the early chroniclers already mentioned, more or less information regarding Tabasco has been gleaned from Cortez' letters, Sahagun, Remesal, Ximenez, and Dampier. The most detailed description of the country in the sixteenth century, however, is to be found in official reports written by Alfaro Santa Cruz and other Spanish settlers in 1579 and published in Relaciones de Yucatán. Scholes has also discovered in the Spanish archives at Seville an important manuscript containing a narrative history of the Chontal of Acalan and Tixchel, which goes back six generations before Cortez. A study of these papers, which include both the Chontal text and a Spanish version, is now in course of preparation. Of the earlier writers who have described the Zoque, I am familiar only with Godoy, Herrera, Remesal, and Gage, but I surmise that a search would reveal others. There is a more extensive literature on the Chol, but the present sketch is derived chiefly from Tozzer (1913) and Thompson (1938), who have thoroughly covered the bibliography of these people.

For Hibueras-Honduras our sources of information are even less satisfactory than for Tabasco. Here the personal observations of Cortez and Bernal Diaz, brief as they are, assume important proportions. Bishop Pedraza's report, written in 1544 and published in Relaciones de Yucatán, is of no little value; but unfortunately for the purposes of this study, it is much more concerned with the Spanish colonists than with the Indians. Herrera writes at considerable length about native customs, but the area was occupied by a number of heterogeneous peoples differing widely in language and culture, and only rarely does this writer localize his descriptions. Lehmann's linguistic studies and the archaeological reports by Strong, Kidder, and Paul and by Stone contain valuable ethnographical information, which they have found in little-known documents; this is especially true of Stone (1941), who has given much attention to the colonial missionary annals. Our slight knowledge of the ethnology of the few surviving Indians in northern Honduras is largely due to the investigations of Habel and Sapper, who visited them when they still retained more of their native customs than at the present time.

PART II.

The Cacique System in Yucatan

Chapter 15. Preservation of Indian Nobility

WHEN THE SPANIARDS arrived in Yucatan, they found a hereditary aristocracy of long standing. This class was designated as *almehen,* or noble, and from its ranks were drawn the territorial rulers, the local town heads, or batabs, the higher officials who served under them, and probably the priesthood as well. Remarkable to state, instead of attempting to abolish this nobility, as might be expected from the diligent way in which they destroyed many other native institutions, the Spaniards saw in this Indian aristocracy a parallel of their own nobility, that seemed very much worth while to them. They not only allowed it to survive, but gave it definite and even liberal encouragement, a fact generally overlooked by historians.

The political structure of pre-Spanish Yucatan has already been discussed, but I will recapitulate with an oversimplified tabulation of this framework as a background for the interesting legal developments which occurred during the colonial period.[1]

1. The *halach uinic,* a term which might be literally translated as the "real man," was the political head of a Yucatecan independent state, such as the Xiu Province of Mani. He also had important religious functions. Some states, however, seem to have had no halach uinic but were governed by a federation of batabs.

2. A *batab,* or local chief, was responsible for each town of any importance. He had a staff of deputies, called *ah kulels,* who assisted him. The batab was at the head of the local military forces but had under him a *nacom,* or war chief, who was the active military leader.

3. Under the batab was a town council of considerable power. At least some of its members, called *ah cuchcabs,* were heads of subdivisions of the town.

4. A priesthood interlocked with the general scheme, acting in an advisory capacity in certain civil matters, in addition to its religious functions.

Although the preservation of native nobility in Yucatan in colonial times has received little, if any, attention from historians, we nevertheless find references to caciques and natural lords in the Relaciones de Yucatán, to Indian hidalgos in the Pech papers, census lists and baptismal records, and to almehens, or nobles, in the Book of Chilam Balam of Chumayel, the Titles of Ebtun, and the Mani land treaty. The *probanzas,* or proofs of nobility, in the Xiu

---

[1] Ch. 9, *supra;* Roys, 1933, app. E; 1939, pp. 43–44.

family papers, however, constitute the principal source of information for the manner in which the institution was maintained in Yucatan.[2]

The Xiu had from the first avoided any clash with the Spanish invaders and had finally come to the aid of the latter, when they first established themselves at Merida and were being sorely pressed by hosts of enemies. The Xiu ruler, who rendered this assistance, died a few years later and was succeeded apparently by his younger brother, Don Francisco de Montejo Xiu, who played so important a part in the Mani land treaty of 1557. The latter seems to have been well liked by the Spanish civil officials, with whom he always cooperated, but he never got on well with the Franciscan missionaries, who were his bitter enemies and several times made serious trouble for him. Whether or not he left any male heirs is unknown, but in any case the caciqueship reverted to the descendants of the elder brother, who had moved to Yaxakumche adjoining the larger town of Oxkutzcab.[3]

The Xiu probanzas begin with a family tree and a copy of the Mani land treaty. The latter was no doubt inserted to show the extent of the former state once ruled over by this family. These papers consist largely of a number of series of documents, which follow a certain set form. At irregular intervals the head of the family presented a Maya petition to the Spanish official, who was called the defender, or protector, of the natives. This petition was a request for confirmation of the rights, privileges, and exemptions hereditary in the family, which had been granted by previous Governors of Yucatan. The original grant has not been preserved. The defender addressed a similar petition, written in Spanish, to the Governor, who then issued a third document, a decree in Spanish, granting the petitions. This was later presented to the Indian authorities at Yaxakumche, who, in turn, executed an acceptance in Maya, in which they promised to obey the Governor's decree. This procedure was generally followed during a long period, although we find minor variations. Sometimes a visiting judge issued the decree; in later years the latter was accompanied by a legal opinion by the attorney for the natives, and we no longer find the acceptance by the town authorities. Other papers in the collection include the record of a judicial inquiry regarding the noble status of the family, commissions to the head as captain of the native militia and as local governor of his own or some other town, a permit to bear firearms and a number of birth certificates.[4]

[2] RY, *passim;* Brinton, 1882, pp. 216, 222, 225; Martinez Hernandez, 1926, *passim;* AGI, Contaduría 920, 1688; Roys, 1933, 1939, 1941; Books of baptism, churches of Oxkutzcab and Mama, Yucatan; Crónica de Oxkutzcab.
[3] Morley, 1941; Scholes and Adams, 1938, 1: xlvii.
[4] Morley, 1941; Roys, 1941. Throughout this study the title of the Governor of Yucatan is capitalized to distinguish his office from the governorship of an Indian town.

Figure 12—NEMECIO XIU AND HIS FAMILY

Figure 13—MAYA INDIAN, QUINTANA ROO
(photograph by Frances Rhoads Morley)

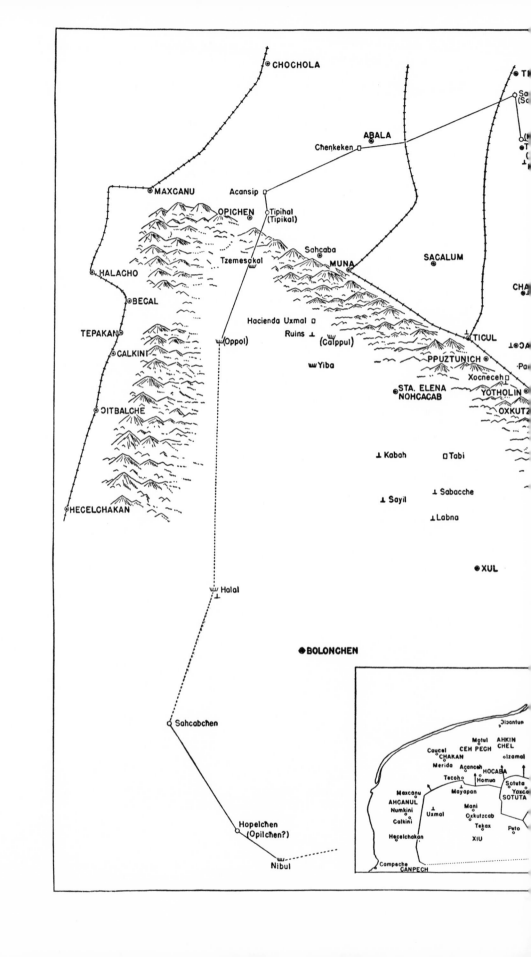

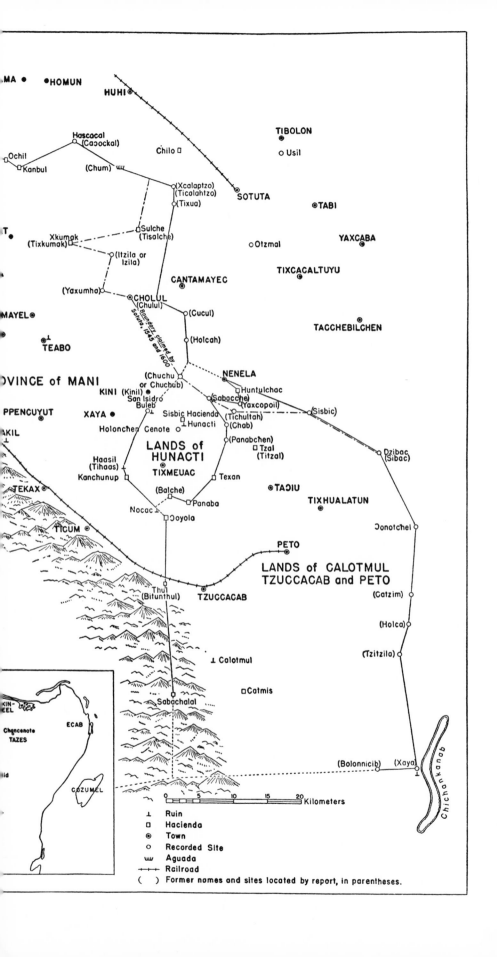

MA ●   ●HOMUN

HUHI ◉

Hascacal
(Caɔockal)   Chilo □

Ochil ○   TIBOLON ◉
Kanbul ○   (Chum) ⌇⌇   ○ Usil

                              ○(Xcalaptzo)
                              (Ticalahtzo)
                              ○(Tixua)   SOTUTA ◉

T ●   ◉ TABI

Xkumak □   □Sulche   YAXCABA ◉
(Tixkumak)   (Tisalche)   ○Otzmal

                    ○(Itzila or
                      Izila)   TIXCACALTUYU ◉

(Yaxumha)○   ◉CHOLUL   CANTAMAYEC ◉
MAYEL ◉   (Chulul)
                              ○(Cucul)   TACCHEBILCHEN ◉

TEABO ⊥
                              ○(Holcah)

OVINCE of MANI   (Chuchu   ◉NENELA
                      or Chuchub)○   □Huntulchac
      KINI (Kinil) ●   San Isidro □(Sabacche)
PPENCUYUT ●   Buleb ○   ○(Yaxcopoil)   ○ Sisbic
      XAYA ●   Sisbic Hacienda (Tichultah)○
AKIL   Holonchen Cenote ○ □Hunacti ○(Chab)
⊥   ○(Panabchen)   ○Dzibac
         LANDS of   □ Tzal   (Sibac)
         HUNACTI   (Titzal)
      Haasil ⊥   TIXMEUAC ◉
      (Tihaas)   □ Texan
TEKAX ◉ Kanchunup
              (Balche)   ● TAƆIU
                ○—□Panaba   TIXHUALATUN ◉
      Nocac ⊥ □Ɔoyola
TICUM ◉   ○Ɔonotchel

                    PETO ◉
                                   LANDS of CALOTMUL
         Thul   TZUCCACAB and PETO
      (Bitunthul) TZUCCACAB ◉   ○(Gatzim)

                                          ○(Holca)
              ⊥ Calotmul
                                          ○(Tzitzila)
                    □Catmis

              Sabachalal

                                   (Bolonnicib)○ ○(Xaya)
                                                      ⊥

         0   5   10   15   20
         |————————————————| Kilometers

         ⊥   Ruin
         □   Hacienda
         ◉   Town
         ○   Recorded Site
         ⌇⌇   Aguada
         ┼┼┼   Railroad
         ( ) Former names and sites located by report, in parentheses.

(inset map)
KIN...
EEL
Chancenote
TAZES   ECAB

id

COZUMEL

Chichankanab

FIGURE 14

FIGURE 15

FIGURE 16

FIGURE 17

MAYA INDIANS OF QUINTANA ROO
(photograph by Frances Rhoads Morley)

The Xiu probanzas are more complete than any Indian family records available in Mexico, but they leave many things unexplained. The Xiu were caciques and natural lords, and their papers barely mention the lesser nobility, the hidalgos. Also it is to be surmised that they obtained from time to time various permits, which have not been preserved. These would be for special privileges, like Don Juan Xiu's license to own a gun. No Indian documents of this sort have been found in the archives of Yucatan corresponding to the vast collection in the National Archives of Mexico. Although allowance must be made for the differences which existed in the character of the country and its population, many of the Mexican documents help to fill the gaps in our knowledge of the preservation of native nobility in Yucatan.[5]

Solorzano, the famous jurist and commentator on Spanish colonial law, gives the following account of the manner in which Spanish recognition of Indian nobility originated:

Although the dominion, government and general protection of all the extensive provinces of the New World belong to our Catholic Kings of Spain, by the just titles and principles which I have stated in the first book of this *Política,* nevertheless it was always their royal will that in the towns of Indians there, which were found to have some form of organized government, or in which such was later set up in the manner stated in the preceding chapters, there should be maintained to rule and govern them particularly those petty kings or captains who did this in the time of their paganism, or those who may prove themselves to be their descendants.[6]

In the Island of Hispaniola, which was the first to be discovered and settled by Don Cristobal Colon, they called them caciques in their language, and hence our own people generally continued to apply this name to the others whom they found in the same office in other regions, although (as it can be understood) each would be designated differently in his own language.[7]

In the laws of Burgos, the most important of the early statutes dealing with Indian affairs and enacted in 1512 for the Islands of Hispaniola and Puerto Rico, we read that "since it is just that caciques and their wives should be better treated and dressed than [other] Indians," a portion of the revenue is to be applied for this purpose. It is also provided that each cacique shall have a certain number of personal servants, according to the number of Indians he has under him.[8] In a law dated 1516 specifying the amount of tribute the Indians were to pay, we find exception made for caciques, "for whom and for whose

---

[5] Roys, 1941, docs. 35–39; AGM, Indios, Mercedes. Copies of documents furnished by France V. Scholes of the Division of Historical Research, Carnegie Institution of Washington.

[6] Solorzano, 1776, bk. 2, ch. 27, art. 1.

[7] *Ibid.,* art. 2.

[8] Hussey, 1932, p. 316.

wives there shall be maintained the preeminences and honors which their Indians owe them."[9]

This attitude on the part of the Spanish government was maintained, in spite of some temporary legislation to the contrary,[10] and in 1557 Philip II formulated a definite policy in the matter: "In the time of their infidelity certain natives of the Indies were caciques and lords of towns; and since it is just that they should preserve their rights after their conversion to our holy Catholic faith, and that their having submitted to us should not lessen their rank: we command our royal *audiencias*[11] that if these caciques or *principales*,[12] descendants of the first ones, claim to succeed to that sort of lordship or *cacicazgo*[13] and attempt to bring an action in the matter, they shall be allowed to do so, and the parties concerned shall be summoned and heard with all dispatch."[14]

Solorzano tells us that at one time, ". . . in New Spain the viceroys, considering these cacicazgos to be offices for the administration of justice and government, judged it to be better that they should be bestowed and conferred by choice rather than by succession; and so they actually proceeded to put this into practice and execution, and entirely at their own volition."[15] I can not find, however, that this was ever attempted in Yucatan, and in 1614 the hereditary character of this dignity was further confirmed by Philip III: "Since the discovery of the Indies it has been a matter of possession and custom that sons should succeed their fathers in the cacicazgos: we command that there shall be no change made in this respect, and that the viceroys, audiencias and governors shall not have discretionary power to take these away from some persons and give them to others; leaving the matter of succession to the former law and custom."[16]

In Yucatan, as far as the descendants of a halach uinic were concerned, this manner of succession was more or less in accordance with pre-Spanish usage;[17] but it was not always the rule in the case of the batab, who was appointed by

[9] Altolaguirre y Duvale, 1928, 2: 281.

[10] Recopilación de leyes de los reynos de las Indias (hereafter cited as Recopilación), 1774, bk. 6, tit. 7, law 5; Altolaguirre y Duvale, 1928, 2: 328.

[11] A certain superior court and administrative commission. Yucatan was for a time under the Audiencia of Guatemala, but during most of the colonial period subject to that of Mexico.

[12] The term *principal* apparently designated any Indian of recognized noble status in Mexico, but it also can mean the head of a *barrio,* or subdivision of a town. In Yucatan alcaldes and regidors are referred to in general as principals; but, as in Mexico, the term is also specifically applied to the official in charge of a barrio. "Principales of a town in general, *nucbe uinicob, u chun thanob.* Principal of the town, like the regidor, who has charge of some subdivision, *ah cuchcab.*" Vienna dictionary, f. 169r. Cf. Lopez de Cogolludo, 1867–68, bk. 4, ch. 17.

[13] The dignity or office of a cacique and his territory.

[14] Recopilación, 1774, bk. 6, tit. 7, law 1.

[15] Solorzano, 1776, bk. 2, ch. 27, art. 15.

[16] Recopilación, 1774, bk. 6, tit. 7, law 3.

[17] Ch. 9, *supra.*

the halach uinic.[18] Landa tells us that the "lords" confirmed the sons in their fathers' offices if they were acceptable.[19] This was often done, but not always. In the chronicles of the Pech family we read of a certain Ah Tunal Pech of Maxtunil, who had come from Motul, the capital of the so-called Province of Ceh Pech and the residence of Naum Pech, the halach uinic. Ah Tunal Pech had three sons: Ah Macan Pech, batab of Yaxkukul, Ixkil Itzam Pech, batab of Conkal, and Ah Kom Pech of Xulcumchel, whose son, Nakuk Pech was appointed batab of Chicxulub by Naum Pech.[20] It would seem likely that natural heirs were supplanted in some of these cases.

The Xiu of Oxkutzcab, however, were not only caciques but also had the status of *señores naturales,* or natural lords,[21] being descended from a family of territorial rulers. The last halach uinic of the Province of Mani was Kukum Xiu, baptized Francisco de Montejo Xiu. I can not learn that he left any descendants, but the line of his elder brother, Melchor Xiu, enjoyed the title of cacique and natural lord together with the rights and privileges already noted.

[18] Roys, 1933, app. E.
[19] Landa, 1941, p. 27.
[20] Brinton, 1882, pp. 216–41.
[21] "The concept of the *señor natural* was applied in the Indies with reference to the dominion and position held by native rulers and lords and to the relation of these lords to the king of Castile." Chamberlain, 1939, p. 131.

Chapter 16. The Cacique System

TO ME IT WOULD APPEAR that the cacique system and local government of the Indians in Yucatan were largely the result of the administrative policy developed in New Spain. By 1542, the year of the conquest in Yucatan, the reorganization of the Indian towns seems to have been effected over a very considerable portion of the Mexican area. In Yucatan a similar reorganization was carried out in 1552 by Tomas Lopez, *oidor* of the Audiencia of Guatemala.[1] At this time he inaugurated the policy of concentrating a large part of the rural inhabitants in towns near the convents,[2] thus anticipating the civil congregation in New Spain by about forty years.[3]

Reduced to its simplest features, Indian municipal government was organized in the following manner. We find a governor, who was chosen by the town, but his actual appointment was made by the Spanish authorities, to whom he must be *persona grata*. There were usually two alcaldes, petty justices with very limited judicial and somewhat more extensive police powers, and three or more *regidores,* or councillors, according to the size of the town. Some towns had *parcialidades,* or wards, each of which was in the charge of an official called a principal. We also find a sort of steward called *mayor domo* and a town clerk. Certain minor police were called *alguaciles,* also known as *tupiles* in Yucatan and *topiles* in Mexico.[4]

Apparently at the head of this organization in a great many Indian towns was the cacique. In Mexico, where salaries were sometimes paid, his was greater than that of the governor.[5] During the sixteenth and the first part of the seventeenth centuries we are told that he governed his town, was obeyed by the governor, alcaldes, and principals, and "had charge and care of the good treatment of the natives and of the things concerning the good government" of the town.[6] It is difficult to determine the precise duties and powers of the cacique as distinguished from those of the local governor, and in many respects this must be left an open question. The executive functions enumerated in Don Juan Xiu's commissions as governor of Oxkutzcab and Maxcanu[7] are so many

---

[1] One of the judges of this superior court.
[2] Roys, 1939, p. 10.
[3] Simpson, 1934, p. 32.
[4] Cf. Roys, 1939, pp. 44–46.
[5] AGM, Indios, vol. 1, nos. 287, 298 (1583, 1581).
[6] Roys, 1941, docs. 4, 17b; AGM, Mercedes, vol. 1, f. 288r (1551).
[7] Roys, 1941, docs. 41, 42.

that we can not but wonder what was left for the cacique.[8] In some cases at least, it was considered advantageous in Mexico to have both a cacique and a governor. In 1542 Viceroy de Mendoza was informed by the town of "Cocopetlaynca" that "it was fitting and necessary that there be provided in the said town a cacique and a governor, who should have charge of its government and be employed with the things conducive to the good of the commonwealth." He accordingly appointed Don Cristobal cacique and a certain Mateo governor, both of whom had been chosen by the town.[9] I believe that the functions of the cacique, as such, must have diminished greatly between this time and 1665, the date of Don Juan Xiu's commission as governor of Oxkutzcab.

In both Yucatan and Mexico the first caciques, in the colonial sense of the term, appear to have been the native chiefs whom the Spaniards found, or believed they found, ruling the various towns. This was in accordance with the policy outlined by Solorzano and confirmed by Philip II and Philip III.[10] In the Mexican archives we find a number of caciques claiming descent from pre-Spanish rulers, such as the *"cazonci"* of Michoacan, the *"casa de Ocotepec"* in Huexotcinco, and the *"casa del rey Guaguela"* in Oaxaca.[11]

In Yucatan the general policy was evidently to recognize the former territorial rulers, or halach uinics, and the town batabs as caciques. In the case of the former it is well known that Nachi Cocom (Juan Cocom) of Sotuta and Kukum Xiu (Francisco de Montejo Xiu) of Mani became caciques; and there are excellent reasons for believing that the descendants of Naum Pech, halach uinic of Ceh Pech, became caciques of Motul,[12] and that Francisco Namon Iuit, cacique of Hocaba, was the son of Naum Iuit, the former territorial ruler.[13] After the halach uinics, the local batabs were the persons most eligible for recognition as caciques. Ah Kin Euan, priest and also "temporal ruler" of Caucel, became Cacique Don Francisco Euan.[14] Batab Camal of Sisal, later Don Juan Camal, was cacique and governor of that town.[15] Antonio Pech, cacique of Chuburna, was the son of Ah Tzam Pech, the pre-Spanish "cacique" of the town.[16] Nakuk Pech, batab of Chicxulub, and Ah Macan Pech, batab of Yaxkukul, make it clear in their narratives from their mention of their heredi-

---

[8] The matter is further complicated by the occasional tendency of Yucatecan Spanish writers to refer to the town executive as a cacique, when he is nothing more than governor. Lopez de Cogolludo, 1867–68, bk. 4, ch. 17: Vienna dictionary, f. 32r.

[9] AGM, Mercedes, vol. 1, f. 29r.

[10] Cf. ch. 15, *supra*.

[11] AGM, Mercedes, vol. 1, f. 18r; Indios, vol. 2, no. 786; vol. 4, no. 399; vol. 20, no. 216a; and vol. 25, no. 117.

[12] Martinez H., 1926, p. 25; Los caciques yndios to the Crown, AGI, Mexico 367; RY, 1: 76.

[13] *Ibid.*, 1: 89; Scholes and Adams, 1939, 1: 150.

[14] Lopez de Cogolludo, 1867–68, bk. 5, ch. 6. Cf. Roys, 1933, p. 146.

[15] RY, 2: 202; AGI, Sebastian Vasquez pesquisa, 1565, Justicia 245. Nakuk Pech refers to him as Ah Kul Camal (Brinton, 1882, p. 205).

[16] RY, 1: 278.

tary nobility, probanzas, and exemption from taxes that they had been made caciques, although the actual term is not employed.[17]

It would appear, however, that a considerable number of the colonial caciques were descended from officials subordinate to the batab in rank. It was a period of disorganization, and the Spaniards probably found the latter temporarily in command at their towns. At Tekanto the cacique, Juan Po, was the son of a Nacom (war chief) Po, whom the Spaniards regarded as "the principal cacique."[18] At Citilcum and Cauich the alleged "principal cacique" was an ah kulel called Ah Kul Can, who was succeeded by his son, Francisco Can.[19] In a similar case at Sudzal and Chalante the encomendero explains, "They have been governed by some Indians who said they were principals and lords, because many caciques who were natural lords have died of diseases."[20]

During the decade intervening between the conquest and the arrival of Lopez Medel in 1552, the Spaniards, in spite of the oppression and excessive exploitation which occurred, appear to have made little, if indeed any, attempt to alter the native form of local government. Generally speaking, I believe, the old batab continued to govern his town with the aid of his ah kulels and ah cuchcabs. The fact that several halach uinics were created governors of their provinces indicates that the towns remained more or less subject to them for a time at least, even after Lopez Medel's reorganization.[21]

Barring the concentration of rural dwellers in the towns, which in many cases caused great distress, Lopez Medel's reforms seem to have been effected without much trouble.[22] Leaving aside the change in religion, which of course was a serious matter, I am led to believe from the continued use of much of the old Maya terminology, the narratives of the Pech family,[23] and the little evidence we have of serious friction, such as occurred in Mexico,[24] that this local political reorganization did not represent so violent a change as might be expected.[25] The same group of local aristocrats, or *almehenob*, continued to control the humble commoners; and the former batab with his chief men, or *nucteil uinicob*, became the cacique and principals of the new dispensation.[26]

Many Yucatecan caciques at the time of the reorganization were made governors of their towns, and during the remainder of the century we fre-

---

[17] Brinton, 1882, pp. 216, 222; Martinez H., 1926, pp. 5, 22.
[18] RY, 1: 116.
[19] Written "alcucan." This caciqueship did not remain in the family. *Ibid.*, 1: 221–22.
[20] *Ibid.*, 1: 247.
[21] Ch. 14, *supra;* Scholes and Adams, 1938, 1: x.
[22] *Ibid.*, 1: xviii–xix; Roys, 1939, pp. 10–11.
[23] Brinton, 1882, pp. 193–241; Martinez H., 1926.
[24] Zurita, 1891, pp. 100–108.
[25] Roys, 1939, pp. 43–46.
[26] Brinton, 1882, pp. 222, 239–40.

quently find either a cacique or one of his relatives in this position.[27] Not only would the cacique's prestige and influence as leader of the local native nobility tend to place him in the governorship, but the Spanish administration encouraged the procedure in both Mexico and Yucatan. Zurita mentions this practice,[28] and in 1551 Viceroy de Velasco appointed a relative of the minor son of a deceased cacique to serve as governor until such time as the boy should become of age to fill the office.[29] The same may be inferred in Yucatan from cases apparently cited as exceptions to the usual procedure. In 1581, we are told, the governor of Mococha was an Indian principal of the town, because the person to whom the caciqueship belonged was not adequate for the position.[30] Similarly at Tixkokob the governor was a man from San Cristobal, a suburb of Merida, "because, although the said town has a natural cacique, he has not been entrusted with the government of the said town, since he is not capable of it."[31]

As has already been noted, prior to the political reorganization of the Indian towns by Lopez Medel the local executive was called the cacique by the Spaniards and the batab by the natives.[32] With the creation of a formal and hereditary caciqueship by the Spanish administration, the Maya title of the incumbent continued to be that of batab, irrespective of whether or not he became the town governor. For the historian, however, the situation is complicated by the fact that when the cacique acted as governor, in both Spanish and Maya documents we find him referred to and signing as *gobernador,* and not as cacique or batab. This condition lasted until the end of the sixteenth century and possibly longer, but a time finally came when any governor, even though he was not a hereditary cacique, might be officially designated as cacique or batab, as well as governor. Consequently the meaning of the terms cacique and batab depends on when they are employed, and I shall attempt to trace their history.

The Motul dictionary, believed to have been written during the latter part of the sixteenth century, defines the term batab simply as cacique, but it elsewhere implies that it was still a hereditary title at that time.[33] In the Mani land treaty of 1557 the batab of Maxcanu is mentioned. All the other principal par-

[27] In the Mani land treaty eight governors of towns in this province and seven others from outside are cited by name. Of the former all except Alonso Xiu of Tekit are elsewhere stated to be caciques (Scholes and Adams, 1938, 1: 33, 166, 180, 196, 217; RY, 1: 158). Of the latter five are known to be caciques, and there is reason for surmising that the same is true of at least one other, Gonzalo Tuyu of Tixcacaltuyu. Carta de diez caciques, 1877; Scholes and Adams, 1938, 1: 46, 108, 150.

[28] Zurita, 1891, p. 105.

[29] AGM, Mercedes, vol. 3, f. 263v (1551).

[30] "Porque a quien viene el cacicazgo del dicho pueblo no tiene suffiçiencia para ello" (RY, 1: 282).

[31] Ibid., 1: 281.

[32] Ch. 15, *supra.*

[33] Martinez H., 1929, p. 142. "You come of the lineage of caciques" (*ibid.,* p. 331).

ticipants appear only as governors, although, as we have seen, most of them were also caciques. Since the Spanish translation of the document translates his title as cacique,[34] he was evidently called batab because he was only cacique and not governor of Maxcanu. In Landa's inquisition proceedings of 1562 we read of a Batab Che, one of the caciques of Xocchel, who was probably not governor of the town.[35]

We find two Maya letters to the King dated February 11 and 12, 1567, and signed by a number of batabs of towns in the Province of Ceh Pech. One letter is stated to be from the caciques and Indians and the other, from the Indian caciques of Yucatan. In these requests for more Franciscan missionaries the caciques are evidently writing ex officio, for although we know that a considerable number of them were also governors of their towns, all but one sign as batabs.[36] In a very similar Maya letter from the Province of Ah Canul dated February 11, 1557, the ten signers are designated as "caciques," but five of them and the son of a sixth are elsewhere stated to be batabs.[37] Among the receipts for compensation made to various Indian towns by the widow of Dr. Quijada in 1572, quite a number of batabs are mentioned. Most of these, but by no means all of them, were also governors, as some towns have more than one batab.[38]

Very much like the case of the batab of Maxcanu in the Mani land treaty of 1557, we find in the Ebtun version of a land agreement made in 1600 among six towns in eastern Yucatan that all but one of the principal participants were governors and appear as such in the documents, although there is reason to believe that at least two of them were also caciques. The single exception, Don Juan Chi of Kaua, is called batab in the Maya text and cacique in the contemporary Spanish translation.[39] In the Sotuta version of this agreement, however, a significant change, or at least an amplification, of the meaning of the term batab is foreshadowed. Here, in an order by Governor Velasco, the word *gobernadores* is translated into Maya as *batabob* by the famous Indian interpreter, Gaspar Antonio Chi. This is the first case I know of in which town governors, as such, are called batabs.[40]

Coronel, in his Maya grammar first published in 1620, translates the word

---

[34] Appendix, *infra*; Crónica de Mani, f. 3.
[35] Scholes and Adams, 1938, 1: 141.
[36] Melchor Pech, apparently the successor of Naum Pech who was halach uinic of Ceh Pech, signs as governor of the Province of Motul. Two others sign as batab and governor, and seven of the remaining twenty-one signers are elsewhere stated to be governors. They were probably not all governors, however, since two are batabs of Telchac. A town might have several caciques, but only one governor. AGI, Mexico 367, ff. 62–63, 70–71; Residencia de Quijada, Justicia 245, 247.
[37] Carta de diez caciques, 1877, 1929; AGI, Residencia de Quijada, Justicia 247; Crónica de Calkini, p. 35.
[38] AGI, Residencia de Quijada, Justicia 247. Cf. Scholes and Adams, 1938, 1: xcix.
[39] Roys, 1939, pp. 78, 82, 84, 86.
[40] Documentos de tierras de Sotuta, p. 422.

batab as "gobernador."[41] In 1631 we find the governor of Cuncunul designated as batab in the text of a Maya document, but he signs as Don Cristobal Cupul, "gobernador." It is very probable that he was also a cacique and the son of Don Fabian Cupul,[42] but here he is only validating an ordinary land transfer, which was part of the routine business of a town governor.[43] In 1638, however, in another Maya land transfer where Don Gaspar Un of Ebtun similarly appears as batab in the text and signs as gobernador, there is no reason whatever to believe that he was a hereditary cacique.[44] There are three wills executed before Don Miguel Canche of Cacalchen in 1653 and 1654. In one of these he is called the governor, but he appears as batab in the other two.[45] In 1660 Antonio Camal, governor of Ebtun, both appears in the text and signs a land transfer as batab. Here, acting with the alcaldes and regidors he appears to be following the usual routine of a town governor. From 1669 on, we find the terms batab and gobernador employed indifferently to designate the town governor in documents from every part of Yucatan.[46] Even after the close of the colonial period, Estanislao Couoh, constitutional alcalde of Ebtun, signed a legal document in 1829 as batab.[47]

In addition to the Relaciones de Yucatan and the Motul dictionary, we might cite another late sixteenth-century source which mention caciques. It is a Maya letter addressed to the King and somewhat similar to the one sent by the ten caciques of the Province of Ah Canul in 1567.[48] It is dated January 8, 1580, and the accompanying Spanish translation is signed by the interpreter and twelve Indians who bear the title of don and appear each as the cacique of his respective town.[49] Here again are a number of persons acting ex officio as caciques.

In the Vienna dictionary, however, we find a new conception of the word cacique similar to the change we have already noted in the meaning of the term batab. This manuscript, which is written in more than one hand, is undated, but its calligraphy has been tentatively ascribed to the end of the sixteenth century or the beginning of the seventeenth.[50] Here we read: "Cacique,

---

[41] *"Macx bátab uayé? Who is governor here?"* He also translates batab as cacique, however. *"Pay batab:* call the cacique." *"Hal ti batab ca u tzecte:* tell the cacique to chastise him." Coronel, 1929, pp. 5, 27, 53.

[42] In a land treaty of 1600 Don Fabian Cupul appears as both governor and batab of Cuncunul (Roys, 1939, pp. 428–30).

[43] Roys, 1939, p. 242.

[44] *Ibid.,* p. 224.

[45] Libro de Cacalchen. Cf. Tozzer, 1921, p. 204.

[46] Cf. Roys, 1939, *passim;* 1941, docs. 34, 48, 60, 74; AGI, Residencia de Aldana, pza. 17, Escribanía de Cámara 315A.

[47] Roys, 1939, p. 388.

[48] Carta de diez caciques, 1929.

[49] AGI, Mexico 104 (58-6-18).

[50] Priego de Arjona, 1939, p. 6.

who governs the town: *batab*. [Example:] I was cacique, at present I am not. *Batab en cuchi.*"[51] It seems clear that the temporary character of the governorship is indicated here. The hereditary cacique was rarely deprived of his office, and then only for serious offenses and after due process of law.

In 1641, however, we have a dated document showing that the title cacique was applied to the town governor as such, even though he was not a hereditary cacique. Attesting the noble status of the father and grandfather of Don Juan Xiu, a certain Martin Ɔiu testified before the judge receptor that when he was "cacique" of Yaxakumche, he never collected tribute from them.[52] Not only do we know that it was the business of the town governor and his alcaldes to collect such tribute in Yaxakumche,[53] but it also seems evident from this entire series of documents that the Xiu were the only family of hereditary caciques in the municipality. As the witness testified in Maya, the language is that of the judge receptor; and the fact that it is so employed by a court officer in a formal legal document would seem to indicate that the term had already for some time been popularly used to designate the governor.

Writing about 1656, Cogolludo, after briefly explaining the origin of the hereditary caciqueship, informs us, "Now for some years past there is not so much attention to this, and they appoint as caciques those whom they consider, perhaps, to be most suitable for the government of the towns, although they are not descended from those who were lords." He goes on to tell of the alcaldes, regidors, and other local officials who aid the "cacique" to govern the town.[54] Cogolludo had no doubt observed that among the town governors of Yucatan the number of those who were also hereditary caciques had been steadily diminishing for some time past. It is plain, however, that he now designates the governor as a cacique, regardless of whether or not it is a hereditary cacique who fills the office. In the series of 1669 documents already cited,[55] just as in the Maya texts batab and gobernador both designate the town governor, so in the Spanish documents we find the terms cacique and gobernador expressing the same meaning. From this time on, the town governor was called the cacique frequently, regardless of his hereditary status.[56]

In the meantime the Xiu of Yaxakumche continue to appear in their probanzas as "caciques and natural lords" until 1645.[57] Subsequently we find

---

[51] Vienna dictionary, f. 32r. The number of pagan deities described in this dictionary suggests that it was written at a fairly early period.
[52] Roys, 1941, doc. 17.
[53] *Ibid.*, doc. 11.
[54] Lopez de Cogolludo, 1867–68, bk. 4, ch. 17.
[55] AGI, Residencia de Aldana, pza. 17, Escribanía de Cámara 315A.
[56] Cf. note 46, *supra*.
[57] Roys, 1941, doc. 23.

them designated as "natural lords" or "hidalgos and natural lords" until 1717.[58] From that time until 1752 they are called "hidalgos and descendants of natural lords,"[59] after which they appear only as hidalgos.

Between the Xiu documents and the Titles of Ebtun, we are able to trace the hereditary caciqueship down to Don Lucas Tun of Cuncunul, who died in 1699. His son, Diego, inherited the title of don and is called an almehen in Maya; but he is usually designated as choirmaster and never as cacique.[60] In an extensive report made in 1766 we find a reference to the numerous hidalgos of Yucatan who are exempted from paying tribute, but here the word cacique is evidently applied only to the town governor.[61] In the absence of other evidence available, I infer from the preceding that some time during the first part of the eighteenth century the term cacique, like natural lord, fell into disuse as a hereditary title in Yucatan, and that the descendants of the hereditary caciques were now called hidalgos.[62]

In Mexico the meaning of cacique does not appear to have changed as it did in Yucatan. In a large number of documents in the Archivo General de la Nación dealing with caciques and Indian governors from 1542 to 1744, a governor is called a cacique only when he is also a hereditary cacique. In the latter case he is almost always cited as "cacique and governor," so there is no ambiguity in the designation.[63]

The term *señor natural,* or natural lord, expresses an old Spanish concept, which was fully formed and generally comprehended by the middle of the thirteenth century. It implied a rightful lord, who was obeyed by his subjects and acknowledged by other lords and their peoples. Chamberlain, to whom we are indebted for the history of this title, cites its use in 1554 as applied to native rulers in Mexico.[64]

[58] *Ibid.,* doc. 71. Sometimes they are called the descendants of caciques and natural lords (docs. 25, 37)..
[59] *Ibid.,* doc. 92.
[60] Roys, 1939, pp. 24, 127, 135, 147.
[61] Scholes et al., 1938a, pp. 10, 16.
[62] Cf. note 59, *supra.*
[63] AGM, Mercedes, vols. 1–3; Indios, vols. 1–4, 11, 15–17, 20, 25, 30, 35, 40, 45, 55.
[64] Chamberlain, 1939, pp. 130–32.

Chapter 17. Functions and Powers of the Cacique

T HE MOST SERIOUS problem connected with this study is that of the powers and duties of the cacique. We read much of his honors, privileges, and exemptions but little of his actual functions. As I have already noted, originally the Yucatecan cacique was expected to be the governor, unless he was an unsuitable person to hold the position. Later, although he continued to be especially eligible for the office, the cacique was only occasionally governor; and it is difficult to determine what is meant when we read that he governed his town and was obeyed by the governor and other local officials, or when, as in Mexico, he is said to have "charge and care of the good treatment of the natives and of the things concerning the good government" of the town.[1] Lacking other evidence, we can attempt to trace only such activities as we find the cacique carrying on, when he did not also occupy some other office.

Accounts of the functions of caciques, as such, are unfortunately rare in the records of Yucatan. The ordinances of Lopez Medel in 1552 charge caciques with certain duties, but practically all of these, such as assessing and collecting tribute, keeping up religious schools and infirmaries, protecting legacies, and making people attend church, seem to be the duty of the governor in subsequent times.[2] His reorganization was very recent at this time, however, and it is probable that practically all the governors were also caciques.

Although many caciques were convicted of idolatry in Landa's inquisition, the Franciscan missionaries seem to have looked to this class for support, possibly owing to the fact that the members of this order were more apt to know Maya than were the secular clergy and more familiar with native customs than were other Spaniards. This may well account for the joint letters from caciques to the Crown in 1567 and 1580, asking that more Franciscan friars be sent to Yucatan.[3] In Don Juan Xiu's petition in 1662 for a permit to have a gun, his principal reason is that it will aid him to capture fugitive pagan Indians in the forests and bring them to the towns to be baptized. He states that he is accustomed to do this when occasion offers, and as there is no record of his having

---

[1] Ch. 16, note 6, *supra*.
[2] Lopez de Cogolludo, 1867–68, bk. 5, chs. 16–19.
[3] Diego Pech, cacique of Euan, and Luis Pech, cacique of Muxupip, who signed one of the 1567 letters, had been accused in 1562 of being present at a human sacrifice about four years before (Scholes and Adams, 1938, 1: 162).

142

as yet been either town governor or captain of the native militia at this time, we can only infer that this was one of his activities as cacique.[4]

Although he no longer inherited his father's title of cacique, Don Diego Jacinto Tun of Cuncunul successfully defended in the court at Merida his town's title to an outlying tract of land, which had been seized by an aggressive Spaniard. It must be admitted that the town afterward refused to reimburse him for the money he had expended.[5]

After the middle of the eighteenth century a further duty was imposed on the Xiu hidalgos. They were evidently obligated to belong to the native militia, and in all the grants from 1752 on they are charged to be provided with firearms and have them in readiness when needed for the service of the King.[6]

In Mexico a somewhat wider range of activities of caciques is recorded. They evidently had a regular position in the *cabildo,* or town corporation, for in 1591 a cacique and natural lord complained that the alcaldes, regidors, and principals not only prevented him from being governor but also excluded him from elections. In a similar complaint, dated 1724, it is stated that the petitioners should "be heeded as such caciques and admitted to the elections."[7]

The other acts of caciques, which have been recorded, are concerned more with emergencies than with the usual procedure of municipal government. In 1583 the cacique, instead of the governor, of Xilotepec collected tribute in a persistently hostile area *(tierra de guerra).*[8] In 1590 a cacique in the Oaxaca district made an accusation to the Spanish authorities that the alcaldes, regidors, and other principals of his town were guilty of habitual drunkenness and neglect of duty. This resulted in an order for an investigation and the punishment of those who should be found guilty.[9] In the same year a favorable reply was made to the request by the caciques of four small poverty-stricken villages near Tonala that official visits of inspection may be less frequent.[10] In 1591 Don Francisco Montezuma, cacique of Tepexi de la Seda, was ordered by the viceroy to protect the people of his town from abuse by certain Spanish and mestizo shepherds.[11] In 1638 a favorable response was given to the complaint

[4] Roys, 1941, docs. 36–39.
[5] Roys, 1939, pp. 147, 159.
[6] Roys, 1941, doc. 93 and *passim.* Such instructions continued after the Cisteil insurrection of 1761 in spite of the strict prohibition of Indians' owning firearms (Molina Solis, 1904–13, 3: 244). Caciques in Mexico were still obliged in 1743 to obtain a license to own such arms (AGM, Indios, vol. 55, no. 118).
[7] AGM, Indios, vol. 3, no. 345; vol. 50, no. 121.
[8] *Ibid.,* vol. 2, no. 108.
[9] *Ibid.,* vol. 3, no. 183.
[10] *Ibid.,* vol. 4, no. 199.
[11] *Ibid.,* vol. 4, no. 36.

by the cacique of a town near Puebla regarding the interference in municipal elections by the Spanish clergy.[12]

In the eighteenth century the caciques of Mexico evidently still maintained their prestige and authority unimpaired. In 1721 the cacique of Penjamo, in the name of the governor, alcaldes, and other natives of the town, successfully appealed to the viceroy in behalf of the local Indian tanners for relief from the interference of Spaniards and other outsiders who were controlling the leather business, and from illegal excise taxes on their sales in neighboring districts, since Indians were exempted from such impositions. The same year the cacique of "Tepespa" near Teotihuacan was in charge of rebuilding certain masonry bridges on the road to Otumba, collecting and disbursing the funds for this project. In this year we also find Don Diego Montezuma, "cacique principal" of Octupa, insisting on his right to select the alcalde from his *barrio*, or ward. In 1722 two caciques of "Theolouica" near Quauhtitlan, in the name of the principals and other inhabitants, petitioned the viceroy and prevented the illegal re-election of the governor of their town. In 1743, during a disputed election at Xilotepec, the Spanish authorities ordered that the governor's wand be turned over to a suitable person, preferably the cacique, who was to supervise the community until the difficulty was settled.[13]

All these things are recorded from Mexico, but I believe that most of them could equally well have occurred, at least prior to the eighteenth century, in Yucatan, where we know that Don Juan Xiu was sent to Maxcanu to replace a local governor who was neglectful of his duties.[14] Zurita has much to say of the confusion which occurred in the Indian towns of Mexico, after the "lords," as he calls them, had lost their earlier powers and apparently before the Spanish administration had put their new status and compensation on a firm legal basis.[15] The evidence seems to indicate that in both Yucatan and Mexico the cacique was a person whose noble status and personal and inherited prestige enabled him to intervene in behalf of either the Spanish administration, the clergy, or his own town, when things were not running smoothly or an emergency occurred.

There can be little doubt that the hereditary caciques of Mexico enjoyed more power and prestige than those of Yucatan. The very fact that the Yucatecan town governor came to be called a cacique strongly suggests a certain loss of prestige for the real cacique, which he did not suffer in Mexico.[16] Also

[12] *Ibid.*, vol. 11, no. 8.
[13] *Ibid.*, vol. 45, nos. 54, 58, 68, 102; vol. 55, no. 166.
[14] Roys, 1941, doc. 42.
[15] Zurita, 1891, pp. 102–05.
[16] Although various reasons could be cited to account for this difference, I find it difficult to explain.

the compensation of the Xiu cacique and the governor of Yaxakumche was approximately the same.[17] In Mexico, in two of the three cases where a comparison is possible, we find the remuneration of the cacique very much greater than that of the town governor.[18]

Although it is true that in Yucatan some caciques inherited, bought, and sold land, as did other Indians,[19] there is no evidence in the probanzas that the Yaxakumche Xiu were large landowners. Indeed, a letter from one member of the family to another refers to their poverty.[20] Probably this is not to be taken too literally, but it suggests at least that they were not wealthy.

In Mexico, on the other hand, many caciques owned lands which were often extensive.[21] We also find caciques possessing a sugar factory,[22] salt beds and fisheries,[23] a smelter,[24] and large herds of cattle.[25] In documents relating to the succession of caciques we read of properties belonging to the caciqueship itself.[26] These were probably mostly lands or houses, but they may have included other possessions. One *cacica,* or woman cacique, of "San Juan Suchitepeque de la Mistteceriaja" near Guajuapa was very wealthy. Although married to a cacique, she possessed several cacicazgos in her own right. One consisted of thirty-one towns or villages and had a value of 130,000 pesos. Another contained six towns and included a hacienda of irrigated lands with sixty laborers and tenant farmers. A third was composed of towns and grazing lands of sufficient value to warrant a mortgage of 10,000 pesos.[27]

[17] Roys, 1941, docs. 8, 41, 42.
[18] In Tutepec the cacique's salary in 1580 was 120 pesos and that of the governor, 40 pesos (AGM, Indios, vol. 1, no. 224). In 1581 the cacique and natural lord of Coyoacan received 300 pesos and the governor, also called *gobernador coadjutor,* 100 pesos (*ibid.,* vol. 1, no. 298). In 1583 the small town of Cococolco, however, paid its cacique and natural lord only 12 pesos, whereas the governor received 10 pesos (*ibid.,* vol. 1, no. 287).
[19] Roys, 1939, pp. 24–25.
[20] Roys, 1941, doc. 53.
[21] AGM, Indios, vol. 2, nos. 464, 786; vol. 3, nos. 32, 80, 396; vol. 4, nos. 96, 217, 454; vol. 15, no. 36; vol. 17, nos. 14, 293; vol. 35, no. 159; vol. 40, nos. 90, 173; vol. 55, nos. 70, 308.
[22] *Ibid.,* vol. 30, no. 270.
[23] *Ibid.,* vol. 17, no. 14; vol. 30, no. 378.
[24] *Ibid.,* vol. 25, no. 130.
[25] *Ibid.,* vol. 17, nos. 14, 240; vol. 40, nos. 141, 176, 181, 185, 194.
[26] *Ibid.,* vol. 2, nos. 261, 322; vol. 3, nos. 272, 345, 693; vol. 4, no. 500.
[27] *Ibid.,* vol. 45, no. 75, Jan. 15, 1722. Evidently the modern Suchixtepec and Huajuapan in Oaxaca are meant.

Chapter 18. Compensation of Caciques

THE XIU PROBANZAS are chiefly concerned with compensation, exemptions and privileges, and the same is true of many of the cacique documents in the Mexican archives. It is difficult to find any additional material advantage possessed by the cacique who also had the status of natural lord. The amount of compensation appears to have depended rather on the number of inhabitants in the cacicazgo than on the cacique's status as a natural lord.[1]

In the first set of Xiu probanzas that has come down to us, dated 1608, the protector of the Indians petitions the Governor of Yucatan to order the town of Yaxakumche to perform certain services for Don Pedro Xiu, who is stated to be cacique and natural lord. A cornfield is to be cultivated for his support and that of his family; each week he is to be furnished with a man and a woman servant; and the various buildings comprising his home are to be repaired or rebuilt whenever necessary. The Governor of Yucatan issued an order in fulfillment of this petition and the town authorities acknowledged receipt of the order.[2] There are other documents mentioning the same services, issued in 1624 and 1652,[3] after which we find similar papers citing the cornfield and domestic service, but not the repair and renewal of the houses, until 1688.[4] At this time the acknowledgment by the town authorities states that they can furnish only the woman servant who has done this work for the past seven years and are unable to supply a man.[5] After 1688 there is no further mention of either cornfield or servants, and it is difficult to determine how much longer such services were continued.

Since our knowledge of compensation and services to caciques in Yucatan is derived almost entirely from the Xiu probanzas, it is of interest to examine the situation in Mexico. Here, in some towns, caciques were compensated with a salary in terms of money, and there is no mention of a cornfield or servants.[6] In other cases the cacique received money as well as the products of a field and the services of a man and a woman servant.[7] More often, apparently, the compensation of the cacique consisted of the products of a field and of domestic

---

[1] Ch. 17, note 18, *supra.*
[2] Roys, 1941, docs. 4, 5, 6.
[3] *Ibid.,* docs. 8, 25.
[4] *Ibid.,* doc. 56.
[5] *Ibid.,* doc. 60.
[6] Cf. ch. 17, note 18, *supra;* AGM, Indios, vol. 1, nos. 143, 232.
[7] AGM, Indios, vol. 1, nos. 161, 254, 284, 287.

service only. The latter was usually that of one man and one woman, as at Yaxakumche, but in a few cases two or three of each were furnished. Sometimes the town paid their wages and sometimes the cacique did; in other cases they were ordered to be paid according to custom.[8] Caciques were also granted the services of Indians to cultivate their own agricultural lands, but they themselves were obliged to pay the wages of these men.[9] I have found only two orders to repair caciques' houses in Mexico. Payment for the labor is mentioned, but it appears to be left to established custom whether the cacique or the town paid the wages.[10]

[8] For caciques: *ibid.,* vol. 2, nos. 261, 458, 627, 881. For natural lords: *ibid.,* vol. 1, nos. 126, 162, 179; vol. 2, no. 627; vol. 3, no. 968; vol. 4, nos. 196, 399, 418. In a few cases caciques are stated to have received wood, poultry, and cacao also.

[9] *Ibid.,* vol. 2, no. 464; vol. 4, no. 454.

[10] *Ibid.,* vol. 3, nos. 511, 950. The preceding references to compensation and services to caciques and natural lords in Mexico have been found only in sixteenth-century documents.

Chapter 19. Privileges of Caciques

EXEMPTION FROM PAYING TRIBUTE

AMONG THE VARIOUS privileges enjoyed by the Xiu of Yaxakumche was freedom from paying tribute. This favor was permitted to the wife or widow and the daughters-in-law of the head of the family as well as to his own children.[1] In the eighteenth century the exemption was extended even to distant cousins of the same name who lived in other towns. All of these, however, were descendants in the male line of Don Juan Xiu, who was head of the family from 1640 to 1688.[2] In only a single recorded case was the courtesy given to the son of a Xiu woman This was Bonifacio Uc, the son of Don Juan's sister Petrona, who together with his wife was exempted from tribute.[3]

Solorzano refers to a similar exemption of caciques in Peru and states that he understands it to be the same in other provinces. In explanation he tells us: "The above exemption is not conceded to them so much by virtue of such government or jurisdiction (for neither this nor being a lord of vassals is ordinarily sufficient for exemption from taxes or tribute according to the decisions of many authors) as it is by virtue of being nobles and held and reputed as such among their own people, both themselves and their ancestors from the time of their paganism."[4] Solorzano's statement, however, is not quite so broad an assertion as would appear from the above translation. He employs the term *pechos,* which I have translated as taxes but which really means taxes not applicable to nobles and contributions other than those paid to the king. Consequently he is probably not referring to exemption from all taxes whatsoever. In Mexico instances occurred in 1679, 1687, and 1690 where payment of royal taxes *(tributos reales)* by caciques appears to have been a regular procedure.[5] In Yucatan, however, a report of 1766 states, "Besides the tributary Indians, there is a great number of them in the province in the class of hidalgos, who do not pay tribute and are enrolled as militia."[6]

---

[1] Roys, 1941, docs. 10–12, 43, 56, 64, 72.
[2] *Ibid.,* docs. 103–112.
[3] *Ibid.,* doc. 56.
[4] Solorzano, 1776, bk. 2, ch. 21, art. 41.
[5] AGM, Indios, vol. 25, f. 342*v*; vol. 30, nos. 55, 342.
[6] Scholes et al., 1938a, p. 10.

EXEMPTION FROM PERSONAL SERVICES

An important exemption enjoyed by caciques and other recognized native nobility was freedom from personal services and compulsory labor for Spaniards. Such labor was a serious burden to the natives everywhere, although it was less so in Yucatan than in Mexico, where the mines were worked largely by forced labor and many Indians died from insufficient food and overwork. Nevertheless even in Yucatan the natives were often compelled to neglect their farms and were badly treated. Compensation was supposed to be obligatory by law, but even where it was paid, the Indians usually considered it inadequate. Abuses were especially flagrant in the larger towns, such as Campeche and Merida. Dampier tells us that, "For there even the poorer and rascally sort of people, that are not able to hire one of these poor creatures, will by violence drag them to do their drudgery for nothing, after they have work'd all day for their masters: nay, they often take them out of the market from their business; or at least enjoyn them to come to their houses when their market is ended: and they dare not refuse to do it."[7]

This is evidently one of the exemptions and immunities so frequently cited in the Xiu probanzas. Direct references to it occur in 1752 and thereafter, when we are told that the Xiu hidalgos were not liable for personal services other than those performed within the town and for its benefit. I venture to doubt that the head of the family was ever at any time called upon to perform manual labor; nor were the Xiu hidalgos compelled to fill any town offices beneath those of alcalde and regidor.[8] I infer from this that the duties of the alguacil were regarded as menial.

A similar exemption existed in Mexico, where in 1591 a cacique in Michoacan complained that certain principals were attempting to make him pay tribute and perform personal services. The viceroy, however, declared him exempt from such obligations.[9] In Mexican documents of 1582 and 1583 we find protests by principals at being compelled to take part in "personal services and manual labor, which are and have been the obligation of *macehuales* (common Indians) and not of principals."[10] It was also stated that "this is neither lawful nor permitted, and that it is not only a notable injury, but would destroy the pre-eminence and credit *(nombre)* belonging to themselves and their children."[11] In 1648 a cacique in Michoacan was confirmed in his succession to a cacicazgo and his claim to freedom from tribute and personal services.[12]

[7] Dampier, 1906, 2: 209.
[8] Roys, 1941, docs. 93, 94, 101, 102.
[9] AGM, Indios, vol. 3, no. 446.
[10] *Ibid.*, vol. 2, no. 242.
[11] *Ibid.*, vol. 2, no. 420.
[12] *Ibid.*, vol. 15, cuad. 1, no. 65.

PREFERMENT FOR HONORABLE EMPLOYMENTS

Another noteworthy privilege of caciques was that they were considered especially eligible to such public offices as were open to natives, particularly those of governor, alcalde, and regidor of an Indian town. We have already seen how during the sixteenth century in both Yucatan and Mexico it was considered more or less a matter of course for the cacique to be governor of his town.[13] After 1600 it is difficult to determine how frequently hereditary caciques were governors in Yucatan, because of the tendency there to refer to a governor as a cacique, regardless of his inherited status.[14]

Of the Xiu heads of the Yaxakumche family the probanzas record that Don Pedro was governor of his town at one time, and there is little doubt that he was governor of Tekax at the time of the famous riots there in 1609.[15] I can not find that Don Juan Xiu was ever governor of his own town, but we know he served in this capacity at Oxkutzcab and Maxcanu.[16] The governor of Yaxakumche in 1608 was a Don Francisco Xiu;[17] I surmise that he was a brother of the cacique, Don Pedro, but there is some doubt as to his identity. Don Pedro also had a father named Francisco, but the latter must have been dead in 1608. Don Pedro was now cacique and head of the family, and neither in the Yucatecan records nor in the cacique documents from the Mexican archives have I found anyone succeeding to this position prior to the death of his father. No Xiu hidalgo appears as a governor during the eighteenth century; nor is any recorded as alcalde or regidor in the documents of this collection or in four other sources in which the names of such persons are given.[18] Although it seems probable that members of the family held the latter offices during some of the many years for which we have no record, I can not help surmising that the Xiu were not popular at Yaxakumche.

Indians of rank enjoyed the same preference in Mexico. In a document of 1701 it is stated: "And just as a difference is made between noblemen and plebeians in regard to offices and dignities, so it is the same with caciques in respect to macehual Indians, who paid tribute to them as nobles in the time of their paganism."[19] The following year a royal cedula of 1697 to this effect was quoted in full.[20]

13 Ch. 16, *supra.*
14 Cf. ch. 16, note 54, *supra.*
15 Lopez de Cogolludo, 1867–68, bk. 9, ch. 1; AGI, the Tekax trial, 1609–10, no. 2, Escribanía de Cámara 305A.
16 Roys, 1941, docs. 41, 42.
17 *Ibid.,* doc. 6.
18 Roys, 1941, docs. 6, 9, 17a, 22, 30, 34, 48, 60, 74, 79, 85, 90; AGI, Residencia C. de Sosa, 1674. pza. 1, Escribanía de Cámara 319C; Res. Arechaga, 1684, pza. 1, *ibid.,* 321A; Res. Tello de Guzman, 1688. pza. 1, *ibid.,* 321B; Res. Barcena, pza. 1, *ibid.,* 321A.
19 AGM, Indios, vol. 35, no. 75; cf. *ibid.,* vol. 30, no. 322 (1690).
20 Royal cedula, Madrid, Mar. 26, 1697, *apud* AGM, Indios, vol. 35, no. 103.

The question naturally arises whether common Indians, or macehuals as they were called in both Yucatan and Mexico, were eligible to the governorship. There can be little doubt that only nobles were governors in Yucatan during the sixteenth century; but the evidence is less positive for the remainder of the colonial period. During this time at Ebtun I have found only seven different surnames in the governorship, and of the twenty governors whose names have come down to us fourteen were confined to three surnames, the Camals, Nauats, and Nohs. Of four other names, one was probably that of a noble lineage from a nearby town, and the remaining three correspond to old landholding families of Ebtun.[21] I infer from this that the governorship at Ebtun was restricted to a few prominent families who were noble. It must be admitted, however, that a different condition existed at Yaxakumche where eight surnames were distributed among the twelve governors whose names have come down to us. This was surely too many noble lineages for a small community, which probably numbered less than 500 inhabitants in 1688. Among these governors we find a Don Francisco Pacab, and the Pacabs were a well-known noble family of Oxkutzcab. It seems possible that just as Don Juan Xiu was elected governor of Oxkutzcab, so some of these Yaxakumche governors were caciques or hidalgos from the large adjoining town, which had a population of 860 married Indian men, or perhaps a total of 3400 persons, in 1688.[22]

The Book of Chilam Balam of Chumayel contains a questionnaire or ritual which seems pertinent to this question.[23] It is a series of questions demanded by the halach uinic of certain town officials, including the batab; and in its present form it probably dates from the early seventeenth century. The object of this inquiry is to ascertain "whether they are of the lineage of rulers, whether they are of the lineage of batabs, that they may prove it." The questions all have a hidden meaning. The "green jaguar seated over the sun to drink its blood" means a green chile placed on a fried egg; the "brains of the sky" are copal gum; and the "flower of the night" is a star. Those of the proper lineage know these things, but the ignorant are shown to be impostors and meet with an unpleasant death, which is described in detail. The answers are called the "language of Zuyua," and Zuyua, a legendary Nahuatl place name, was the symbol of the Mexican origin of the ruling class in Yucatan. The implication seems to be that only the descendants of the Zuyua people should hold important offices and not the autochthonous plebeians.

Most of this, no doubt, goes back to pre-Spanish times, but some of the ques-

[21] Roys, 1939, p. 47.
[22] AGI, Contaduría 920, 1688.
[23] Roys, 1933, pp. 88–98.

tions pertain to things introduced by the Spaniards, such as a horse and a candle, indicating that this interrogation had not fallen entirely into disuse in colonial times. The ritual is addressed to the Governor of Yucatan, suggesting that to the native mind it resembled the *residencia,* or accounting, required of Spanish officials. To what extent this ritual was employed in colonial times remains a question; we find it in an eighteenth-century Maya manuscript. In any case it appears to constitute a threat to the commoner who aspired to an office above his station.

In the Mexican documents most of the references to Indian governors state that they are caciques or principals. In a few cases the hereditary status of the governor is not mentioned; and in one of these, where the governor of Cuernavaca in 1618, described only as a *natural* (native) of the town, is conceded the right to wear Spanish dress, sword and poniard apparently only during his governorship, the possibility is suggested that he did not have the rank of cacique or principal. Such persons usually enjoyed this privilege for life.[24]

Whether or not this was true, however, we know that in course of time a wealthy or intriguing macehual was sometimes able to insinuate himself into the governorship, although the practice evidently did not meet with general approval. In 1690 there was a complaint from "Osolotepeque" in Oaxaca that a certain macehual had represented himself as Don Feliciano Garcia, constituting himself a cacique and principal without being one, and that his father, likewise a macehual, had been made governor apparently through the machinations of the local beneficiary.[25] In 1745, however, the viceroy ordered the town of Coyotepec in Oaxaca to accept as governor a certain Sebastian de Dios Zurita, native of the town, in spite of the fact that he had lost the election by one vote, and "notwithstanding his not being a cacique." This was because of his devotion and generosity to the local church.[26]

The Laws of the Indies state that mestizos could not be caciques. They must be removed and the caciqueship given to Indians in the established manner.[27] I believe that this also applied to governors of Indian towns, as the term cacique is sometimes loosely employed in these laws. I have not found the question raised in Yucatan; and it seems probable that there were not many mestizo caciques or governors in Mexico. In 1620, however, the guardian of the convent at Tula complained of a mestizo governor of the town that he had maneuvered the election of certain unsuitable town officials.[28] In 1721 at a

---

[24] AGM, Indios, vol. 7, no. 307.
[25] *Ibid.,* vol. 30, no. 372. This is the modern Santa Maria Ozolotepec.
[26] *Ibid.,* vol. 55, no. 363.
[27] Recopilación, 1774, bk. 6, tit. 7, law 6.
[28] AGM, Indios, vol. 9, no. 274.

town near Teotitlan del Camino a wealthy cacique and exgovernor complained of an attempt by the natives to depose him from his rank and prevent him from holding office under the pretext that he was a mestizo. He cited his services to the church and town and proved himself to be a legitimate cacique, but it seems not unlikely that he was of mixed blood.[29] In 1743 three Robredo brothers, mestizo caciques of Ixquimilpan, successfully appealed to the viceroy, complaining that their right to the governorship of the town was being infringed by a certain Quesada family, who wrongly claimed to be caciques and had won over the electorate.[30]

PERMISSION TO RIDE A HORSE, WEAR SPANISH DRESS, AND BEAR ARMS

Three privileges of caciques and other recognized Indian nobles are frequently associated in the Mexican documents. These are the right to ride a horse with saddle and bridle, to wear Spanish dress, and to bear certain arms, usually sword and dagger. None of these are specifically mentioned in the Xiu probanzas, but there can be little doubt that this illustrious family enjoyed all of them. I infer either that the Xiu were so well known as important caciques and natural lords that special permits were not necessary in their cases, or that their rights in these respects had been well established before the date of our first probanza. In the cacique documents of Mexico licenses to do these things are more numerous perhaps than any other class of papers. Indian governors were also allowed these privileges, but whether this was as governors or as principals is uncertain.

Indians generally were not allowed to ride horses, but we find Diego Quijada, alcalde mayor of Yucatan from 1561 to 1565, granting this privilege to Indian governors, who were no doubt all native nobles at this time, and similar licenses were issued still earlier in Mexico.[31] In 1542 one governor was granted this privilege because he was old and fat; another governor and a cacique were allowed to ride because of their military record in New Galicia; and a cacique was permitted to ride a mare instead of a horse, because he was old and heavy and had rheumatism.[32] Later we sometimes find the privilege restricted to riding a pony, "notwithstanding the decree that Indians may not ride horses."[33] Even after 1600, principals were occasionally required to give a

---

29 *Ibid.,* vol. 45, no. 11.
30 *Ibid.,* vol. 55, no. 178.
31 AGI, Residencia de Quijada, Justicia 245 (communication from F. V. Scholes).
32 AGM, Mercedes, vol. 1, ff. 95, 118, 122, 137.
33 AGM, Indios, vol. 2, no. 465; vol. 3, nos. 252, 273, 565.

reason for riding, such as having to accompany trains of pack animals.[34] In the documents accessible to me I have not found permits to ride horses later than 1690.

After the conquest the Christianized Indians were obliged to discard their former native costume. Commoners had always dressed plainly. Their clothing consisted of little besides a cotton loincloth, which was wound several times about the hips, the ends hanging down in front and behind, sandals of deerskin or agave, and, when needed, a square cotton mantle knotted over one shoulder. The body was painted with red ochre; earplugs were worn; and the hair was cut like a crest in front, shaved on top, and the remainder, left long, was braided and often wound about the head. The nobles wore the same garments but added a sleeveless jacket, and the loincloth and mantle were woven or embroidered more elaborately. Some of their mantles were adorned with feather-work. They also wore a yellow bead in the nose,[35] necklaces and wristlets of shell or greenish stone beads, and sometimes carved pendants, presumably of shell or jade. In colonial times the Indians generally were made to wear cotton shirts and drawers but retained the sandals and mantle, which was now known as a *tilma* (Nahuatl *tilmatli*). An effort was made to get them to wear straw hats, but it was some time before they all adopted this change. They were no longer permitted to paint or tattoo themselves, and were obliged to cut their hair short.[36]

If the distinction between nobles and plebeians was to be preserved, it was obvious that there should be some difference in dress; and already in 1581 we find the native upper class in Yucatan dressing like Spaniards and wearing felt hats and stockings or boots.[37] In 1691 a Mexican cacique complained that the priests and some people of his town would not allow him to go about in cloak and wide breeches but compelled him to wear a tilma like "low class people" *(gente vil)*.[38] Indeed, in Yucatan certain class distinctions in dress have continued to be enforced almost down to the present time, although the institution of native nobility appears to be completely forgotten.[39]

As early as 1510 legislation was enacted forbidding Indians to have metal arms,[40] but an exception was later made in favor of caciques, principals, and governors. In 1542 the cacique of Coyoacan was allowed to wear a sword,[41] and subsequently many licenses were issued to these members of the native

[34] *Ibid.*, vol. 30, no. 322.
[35] Vienna dictionary, f. 53*v*.
[36] RY, 1: 82, 83, 96, 97, 123, 149, 188, 298.
[37] *Ibid.*, 1: 82, 298.
[38] AGM, Indios, vol. 30, no. 477.
[39] Redfield, 1938, p. 521.
[40] Altolaguirre y Duvále, 1928, p. 345.
[41] AGM, Mercedes, vol. 1, f. 95*r*.

ruling caste to wear sword and dagger. Some of the permits state that the applicant may wear Spanish dress and these weapons; others seem to take the Spanish dress for granted and allow him to bear such arms only when wearing this costume.[42] This is sometimes declared to be for his adornment and defense or for the luster of his person.[43] Occasionally the reason is given that the applicant travels through the country with cattle or with pack trains,[44] but more often it appears to be simply to enhance his social prestige, especially when the right to wear a sword belt is included in the permit.[45] Although I have found such permission granted as late as 1743,[46] after 1690 such applications seem to be less frequent than requests to have a gun.

A license to own and carry a gun was a very different matter from the permission to wear sword and dagger and not so readily granted, even to important caciques. Some reason besides the rank of the applicant was usually required, and more formalities were observed in complying with such a request. The permit to Don Juan Xiu is as yet the only one that has survived from Yucatan. When he applied for this privilege in 1660, he showed that he was a reliable and law-abiding person of noble lineage, citing at length the services of his ancestors in punishing rebellious natives and his own need for this weapon in the service of God and the King, when he went into the forests to recover fugitive apostates and return them to their homes where they would be made to lead Christian lives. He first petitioned Nicolas de Cardenas, an official interpreter, to translate his petition. Then the protector of the natives brought the petition before the Governor of Yucatan together with one of his own to the same effect, presenting at the same time the Xiu book of probanzas. Whereupon the Governor granted a license to Don Juan to own the gun, which the latter apparently had already possessed for some time past.[47]

I do not know whether permits of this sort were granted in Yucatan or Mexico during the sixteenth century. The first instance I have encountered occurred in 1619, when the cacique and governor of "Acanbaro" in Mexico petitioned to have a gun because he collected tribute at a considerable distance from his town, and the country was infested by many negro, mulatto, and mestizo herdsmen, who often robbed people on the road. He was allowed to carry a gun when collecting tribute, but only outside of town and during the time he was governor.[48] I infer, however, that once an Indian noble obtained

---

[42] AGM, Indios, vol. 2, nos. 214, 684; vol. 3, nos. 191, 679; vol. 16, no. 14.
[43] *Ibid.*, vol. 3, no. 191; vol. 7, no. 6; vol. 30, no. 339.
[44] *Ibid.*, vol. 7, nos. 67, 68; vol. 11, no. 318.
[45] *Ibid.*, vol. 11, nos. 5, 318.
[46] *Ibid.*, vol. 55, no. 191.
[47] Roys, 1941, docs. 35, 36, 37, 38.
[48] AGM, Indios, vol. 7, no. 362.

lawful possession of a firearm, he was apt to keep it indefinitely, for in 1639 a principal and exgovernor, who had been allowed to have a gun for the same purpose during his governorship, was now permitted to retain this weapon.[49]

During the seventeenth century practically all such permits that I have found among the Mexican documents were to caciques and to principals who were, or had been, in charge of tribute as governor or alcalde. In one case two exgovernors at Agua del Venado in the vicinity of hostile Chichimeca were permitted to have firearms which they obviously needed for defense.[50] After 1700 we find licenses issued to caciques who are cattle men and traveling merchants and who need such protection on the road. In one case musket, pistols, and knife are included in the permit, while in another it is restricted to a long musket and a *cuchillo del monte* (hunting knife).[51]

In the Xiu probanzas for 1759 and the years following we encounter what seems at first to be a radical modification of this policy. Here in the Governor's order confirming the rank and privileges of the family they are required to have their guns ready for the King's service. The original Spanish order merely mentions arms, but the Maya version plainly states that guns *(ɔonob)* are meant. The explanation for this is that the Xiu were now members of the militia. What little we know of this phase of hidalgo activities in Yucatan will be discussed farther on.[52]

SPECIAL STATUS IN THE COURTS

There were still other privileges and exemptions of Indian nobles in Yucatan and Mexico, which would tend to protect them in the courts, especially if they incurred the enmity of a local Spanish official. Laws favoring Indians were only too frequently disregarded in actual practice, but a study of the cacique documents of Yucatan and Mexico gives us the impression that, although caciques sometimes suffered in this respect, the legal regulations were more often observed in their case. In one such law we read: "No *juez ordinario* [a judge of the lower court] shall imprison a cacique or principal except for a serious crime committed during the time that the judge, *corregidor* [a certain magistrate], or alcalde exercises jurisdiction, and in such case he shall forthwith send the brief to the royal audiencia of the district."[53] This would prevent intimidation of the cacique by imprisonment on a trivial charge or by reviving

[49] *Ibid.*, vol. 11, no. 335.
[50] *Ibid.*, vol. 7, no. 362; vol. 11, no. 335; vol. 15, cuad. 2, no. 31; vol. 16, nos. 15, 103; vol. 25, no. 386; vol. 30, no. 279.
[51] *Ibid.*, vol. 40, no. 141; vol. 55, nos. 301, 369.
[52] Roys, 1941, docs. 93, 95.
[53] Recopilación, 1774, bk. 6, tit. 7, law 12.

or trumping up some old accusation difficult to disprove. Pressure could still be exerted upon him by exiling him from his town for insufficient cause, but even in this situation it was easier for him to obtain redress than if he were in prison.

In 1702 the Archbishop of Mexico cited a recent royal cedula and ordered that the cacique of Teutila should be allowed to enjoy "all the privileges or exemptions, preferences and honors *(fueros, preeminencias y honras)* which it is customary to bestow upon the noble hidalgos of Castile."[54] If this order was to be taken literally, we should expect it to imply immunity from being made to retract or put to torture, as this was a prerogative of Spanish nobility.[55] I have been unable, however, to find such exemptions specifically granted to caciques or other Indian nobles, although no complaints have been noted on this score subsequent to Landa's inquisition in 1562.

COATS OF ARMS

It is of interest to note that royal grants of coats of arms were sometimes made to Indians of rank. This occurred in Mexico and Guatemala, although no record of the practice has come down to us from Yucatan. As early as April 14, 1523, Charles V granted a coat of arms to Don Diego de Mendoza de Austria y Moctezuma, son of the ill-fated Cuauhtemoc. Besides such familiar heraldic devices as sword, shield, lance, and helmet, it bore a crowned eagle, a cactus, and a fortress over water, probably referring to Tenochtitlan and its rulers, from whom Don Diego was descended. On the escutcheon was also a pair of native shoes or sandals embroidered in green, yellow and white, possibly a symbol of his rank. Charles V also granted escutcheons to a cacique of Xochimilco in 1534 and to a cacique of Coyoacan in 1551. In 1543 coats of arms were bestowed by the same monarch on caciques of Sacatepec, Tecucitlan, Tecpanatitlan (now Solola), Chichicastenango, and Atitlan in Guatemala. Most of the escutcheons I have cited bore pious legends, such as "Credo in Deum patrem" and "Ave Maria."[56] Fuentes y Guzman reproduces a coat of arms granted by Charles V to the Tlaxcalan auxiliaries of Alvarado in Guatemala.[57] Also in the Book of Chilam Balam of Chumayel there is one of conventional design evidently intended for Yucatan, as its Maya legends include the names of a number of the more important towns of the peninsula.[58] I doubt, however, that it was ever an authorized escutcheon.

[54] Royal cedula, Madrid, Mar. 6, 1697, *apud* AGM, Indios, vol. 35, no. 103.
[55] AGM, Indios, vol. 35, no. 129.
[56] AGM, Vinculos, vol. 80 (1721), vol. 240, exp. 10 (1707), vol. 272, exp. 11 (1588); AGI, Guatemala 393, lib. R2, ff. 203–05.
[57] Fuentes y Guzman, 1932–33, 3: 48.
[58] Roys, 1933, p. 86.

In pre-Spanish Mexico shields and mantles were decorated with designs and symbols. Some of these were of a mythological character, others probably represented certain military orders; but it is likely that certain of them stood for the social or military rank of the bearers and were in effect a sort of title of nobility. We also find devices on Yucatecan shields, especially in the sculptures dating from what is called the Mexican period, but little information has come down to us about them. The Mexican military orders seem to have been carried to Yucatan, and the Xiu, like most of the other ruling families, were of Mexican origin, so we might well surmise that they possessed some characteristic insignia in pagan times.[59] It is difficult to say why so illustrious a family of rulers, and one which had furnished such signal assistance to the Spanish cause, was not honored with a coat of arms, but none is recorded in their papers.

THE TITLE OF DON

In Yucatan and Mexico, as elsewhere in Spanish America, caciques and Indian governors of towns had the title of don. This honor was also extended to certain other native nobles, but practice varied somewhat according to the time and place.

In Yucatan, apparently, a cacique head of a family and also a governor, even after his office expired, held this title for life. It was usually, though not always, extended to the wives of governors and sometimes to the brothers and sisters of a cacique. For wives of caciques usage differed considerably: the widow of Don Alonso Xiu was called doña, but neither of the two wives of his son Don Juan enjoyed the distinction. One of these, an Indian woman, is cited only before he became a governor, and the other was a mestiza. At an early period the two sons of Don Pedro Pech (Ah Macan Pech), cacique of Yax-kukul, were called dons; but Don Pedro's sister, Ix Cakuk Pech, who was baptized Ursula Pech, did not bear the title.[60] In 1640 Don Juan Xiu's two sisters had this title,[61] but it is difficult to determine whether brothers and sisters of a cacique always enjoyed it. Don Fabian Cupul, governor and probably also cacique of Cuncunul in 1600, had a son, Diego, but after the father's death the latter is not called don, although it is stated that he was an almehen. I infer that he was a younger brother of the son who succeeded to the caciqueship.[62]

During the seventeenth century even the oldest son and heir of a cacique in

[59] Seler, 1902–23, 2: 509–619; Roys, 1933, app. F.
[60] Martinez H., 1926, p. 22.
[61] Roys, 1941, doc. 13.
[62] Roys, 1939, pp. 121–25.

Yucatan does not appear to have been called don until he succeeded his father. In Cuncunul the only son and heir of Cacique Don Lucas Tun did not sign himself as don until his father's death. Also a son of Cacique Don Juan Cocom of Sotuta in 1600 was not entitled don, but we can not be certain that he was the oldest son.[63] In the baptismal certificates of his sons, dated 1680 and 1682, Roque, the oldest son and heir of Don Juan Xiu, is not given the title.[64] In 1710, however, not only Roque, who was now the head of the family, but also his brother, Juan Antonio, and his sons, Juan and Diego, all appear as dons.[65]

From 1722 on, several of the more important members of the Xiu family are designated as dons in the probanzas. Others are listed without the title until 1764. Thereafter long lists appear, all the males being entitled don, although a considerable number of them were only distantly related to the head of the family and were living in other towns. All of them, however, were descendants in the direct male line from the first Don Juan Xiu, who succeeded to the caciqueship in 1640.[66] We also find lists of Xiu women, but not until 1779 were they given the title of doña.[67] By this time the heads of the family had long ceased to be caciques but were all designated as hidalgos.

Some of the lesser Indian nobility of Yucatan, who were not caciques, bore the title of don long before the time when the privilege was extended to so many Xiu hidalgos. Doña Catalina Cime, the widow of Don Alonso Xiu, had remarried, and in 1640 she was the wife of Don Francisco Ku, a hidalgo of Ppencuyut, who had his own proofs of nobility.[68] It is evident, however, that many recognized Indian nobles did not merit this distinction. In the tax rolls of 1688 are lists of hidalgos, at Tzucila and Chancenote, who are not called dons, and the same is true of a number of persons, mentioned in the Titles of Ebtun, who are designated as almehen.[69]

In the Mexican documents already cited and many others, caciques are almost always entitled don. A few exceptions occur, particularly in 1741, 1743, and 1745, for which I am unable to account.[70] For Mexican principals we find the same situation which we have already encountered in regard to the hidalgos of Yucatan. Some were dons, and others were not.[71] How and where this line

[63] *Ibid.*, pp. 83, 129.
[64] Roys, 1941, docs. 61, 62.
[65] *Ibid.*, doc. 64; cf. doc. 80.
[66] *Ibid.*, docs. 75, 86, 91, 95, 99, 103 and *passim*.
[67] *Ibid.*, doc. 111.
[68] *Ibid.*, doc. 13.
[69] AGI, Contaduría 920; Roys, 1939, pp. 121, 243, 245, 291, 333, 357. Before making the present study, I believed that all the native nobles in Yucatan who were recognized by the Spanish authorities had the title of don (*ibid.*, pp. 23, 291).
[70] AGM, Indios, vol. 55, nos. 14, 118, 301.
[71] *Ibid.*, *passim*.

was drawn between these two classes of the lesser nobility remains an open question. I can only surmise that some Indian families of the upper class, although they enjoyed the rank and prerogatives of the native nobility, were not considered to be of sufficiently illustrious lineage and descent to merit the title of don.

Chapter 20. Succession of Caciques

AMONG THE XIU PAPERS is the record of a judicial inquiry into the right of the first Don Juan Xiu and his two sisters to succeed, he to the rank and they to the status of caciques and native lords. This took place in 1641, some years after the death of their father, Don Alonso, which had occurred prior to the petition of his widow in 1632.[1] It is the only record of an investigation of this sort that has come down to us from Yucatan. One reason for the inquiry may have been that a number of years had elapsed since the death of their father, and it is possible that they had been living with their mother, who was remarried to a hidalgo of Ppencuyut. As a matter of fact, Don Juan's oldest son, Roque, and Petrona's son, Bonifacio Uc, were baptized at the latter town and not at Oxkutzcab. However, orders for such investigations are not infrequent in the cacique documents of Mexico; and Solorzano discusses the matter as one in which he had had some personal experience.

In regard to deciding on claims to native nobility, Solorzano tells us: "The thing which offers the greatest difficulties is in the examination of matters of descent and relationship in connection with these caciqueships; for, since the witnesses for the most part are from among the Indians themselves who are of so pliant a disposition, every claimant always proves the things which form the subject of the inquiry."[2] He states that he has acted as judge in a number of such cases, and that he deferred rather to such proofs as, "apart from the witnesses, were based on the documentary evidence of the old census lists and polls of the towns, upon repartimientos which were made in former times of the actual Indians and upon attestations derived from the books of baptisms and marriages of previous caciques, which are found in those of the offices of secretaries of governments and in other public archives; and considering it all, I gave decision [according to] what appeared to me to bear and contain in itself the greatest clarity and appearance of truth."[3] Solorzano's account gives us some idea of the scrutiny which the probanzas of caciques must have received from time to time before they were confirmed. This writer evidently had a poor opinion of such oral testimony as we find in the hearing of 1641, but would have regarded the decrees in favor of the father and grandfather of the petitioners as more valid evidence.

[1] Roys, 1941, docs. 10, 11.
[2] Solorzano, 1776, bk. 2, ch. 27, art. 33.
[3] *Ibid.*, art. 25.

Some time in 1640, probably early in October, Don Juan Xiu, who was evidently now of age to succeed to the caciqueship, petitioned the advocate general and the protector of the natives to present his case to the lieutenant general. He wished his probanza to be signed and authorities of Yaxakumche ordered to furnish him and his sisters with domestic service and to cultivate a field for their support. The advocate then petitioned the lieutenant general that evidence be taken to establish the Xiu claims and, in the event of a favorable decision, the record of the proceedings should be delivered to these petitioners.[4] The lieutenant general granted the petition October 16, 1640, and the following month a judge receptor cited the authorities of Yaxakumche to appear before him. This officer, whom we might perhaps call a delegate judge, was at the town at the time, but what happened further on this occasion does not appear in the records.[5] It seems very probable to me that at this hearing the town authorities maintained an unfriendly attitude toward the Xiu petitioners and the evidence was unsatisfactory. We know that there was no justification for their attempt to levy tribute on Don Alonso's widow in 1632. Solorzano plainly states: "The wives of the caciques themselves shall enjoy the same privilege [exemption from tribute], even though they be widows (where it is customary for women to pay tribute), because it is evident that they enjoy and preserve it [this privilege], so long as they do not remarry, through the persons and dignities of their husbands."[6]

There can be little doubt that the Yaxakumche authorities were well aware of this legislation, which was promptly enforced as soon as Catalina Cime complained to the protector of the natives. The town had apparently for some years been free from the burden of supporting the Xiu family and was not eager to reassume the obligation now. We may well infer that Don Juan and his sisters were not popular in their town, both from the baptism of Petrona's and his own sons at Ppencuyut in 1645 and 1646 and from the absence of any convincing evidence that he was ever elected governor of Yaxakumche,[7] in spite of the prominence he achieved as governor and captain of the militia at Oxkutzcab and Maxcanu. In any case, whatever the reason, the hearing was postponed until May 13 of the following year and held at the town of Tekax 4 leagues distant from Yaxakumche.

Here three friendly witnesses, one of whom was an exgovernor of Yaxakumche, testified in behalf of Don Juan and his sisters. The sum and substance

---

[4] Roys, 1941, docs. 13, 14.
[5] *Ibid.*, docs. 15, 16.
[6] Solorzano, 1776, bk. 2, ch. 21, art. 43.
[7] In one of the Xiu papers Don Juan Xiu is referred to as governor of Yaxakumche, but it is evidently a clerical error, as he is known to have been governor of Maxcanu at the time (Roys, 1941, doc. 46).

of their evidence was that the three Xius were the legitimate children of Don Alonso and the grandchildren of Don Pedro Xiu; that the witnesses had personal knowledge that Alonso and Pedro were caciques and natural lords, had never paid tribute or given personal services, but on the contrary had received service and been supported by the town; and finally that they had been told by their forebears that Don Pedro's ancestors had been natural lords of the town ever since the conquest.[8] The testimony regarding Pedro and Alonso was confirmed by the decrees of former Governors of Yucatan, but we find no documentary evidence, such as certificates of baptism, of the legitimacy of Juan and his sisters. It is possible that this was not required, because the protector must have been well acquainted with this prominent Indian family. He was already in office when Don Alonso was confirmed as cacique in 1624 and had petitioned in behalf of the latter's widow in 1632. As far as the ancestry of Don Pedro is concerned, the testimony of these witnesses is extremely vague, but it seems likely that the Mani land treaty and the Xiu family tree[9] accompanied the papers of Alonso and Pedro. On the tree Pedro is shown to be the son of a Francisco, who was the nephew of the Don Francisco de Montejo Xiu mentioned in the treaty and the son of Montejo Xiu's older brother, Don Melchor. Cogolludo expresses a belief that Francisco de Montejo Xiu was not the Tutul Xiu who aided Montejo the Younger at Merida in 1542;[10] and Dr. Morley offers convincing reasons for believing that the latter was the Don Melchor Xiu shown on the tree.[11]

Late in July 1641 the protector, citing the decrees and record of the oral testimony discussed above, petitioned the Governor that the documents be read and approved, and on July 29 the latter issued an order confirming the previous decrees in favor of Don Pedro, Don Alonso, and Don Alonso's widow. The usual acceptance by the town authorities appears on the same page beneath the Governor's order; but it was not executed until April 20, 1643, nearly two years later, and I infer from this that it may have been issued with some reluctance.[12]

Among the cacique documents of Mexico we find many relating to the succession of caciques. Some are orders for an inquiry and others are grants as the result of a satisfactory investigation. These orders and grants are usually by the viceroy, but in later years they were sometimes issued by the archbishop. Inquiries are often directed to be made among the Indian town authorities;

[8] *Ibid.*, doc. 17a, b, c.
[9] *Ibid.*, docs. 1, 3.
[10] Lopez de Cogolludo, 1867–68, bk. 5, ch. 8.
[11] Morley, 1941, ch. 2.
[12] Roys, 1941, docs. 19, 21, 22.

and the points to be investigated are the ancestry of the petitioners, whether there are other older children, what property is attached to the caciqueship, what compensation and services have been customary in the past, and whether the town is still able to give them. The succession is usually from father to son, but sometimes from an uncle or older brother where the deceased cacique left no children.[13]

We have little information on how titles of caciques were first issued in Yucatan, but some of the probanzas of the Mexican caciques go back to the original decrees by Charles V. Two of these have already been mentioned in connection with grants of coats of arms. One was issued in 1523 to Don Diego de Mendoza Austria y Moctezuma, the son of Don Fernando Cortez "Cuactemohc," in recognition of his services "in the entire conquest and pacification of that New Spain of Mexico."[14] A probanza dated 1707 is of particular value, because it contains the proceedings of a judicial inquiry into the succession of a cacique in 1609. Here, by means of wills, extracts from books of baptisms, marriages, and burials and by the testimony of six witnesses, the petitioner, Don Diego Cristobal Cortez, proved that he was the grandson of a certain Don Diego Telles Cortez, natural lord of Xochimilco, and exhibited a grant of arms and confirmation of the latter's caciqueship by Charles V. This document, dated 1534, is quoted in full in the proceedings. The royal grant is of especial interest, for it quotes an earlier document signed by Hernan Cortez and citing the services of a certain lord named "Telles Maselotzin" who came to the aid of the conqueror, when the latter was threatened by the lords and principals of Xochimilco. This man was baptized Diego Telles Cortez, and Hernan Cortez, his godfather, afterward declared him to be a cacique with the title of don, promising to make a more complete report of his deeds and services for the information of the Emperor.[15]

Returning to the judicial inquiry into the Xiu succession, I note that the Governor's decree of 1641 grants the status of caciques not only to Don Juan, the head of the family, but also to his two sisters, Maria and Petrona. Apparently as the result of this, in 1659 we find Don Juan petitioning that Petrona's son, Bonifacio Uc, be confirmed in the rights and privileges of the Xiu family. No objection seems to have been raised, and the judge receptor, who acted instead of the Governor in this case, included Don Juan's nephew in his decree.[16]

---

[13] AGM, Indios, vol. 2, nos. 261, 958; vol. 3, nos. 61, 270, 950; vol. 4, no. 640; vol. 25, no. 60; vol. 35, no. 126; vol. 55, no. 339.

[14] AGM, Vinculos, vol. 80 (1721).

[15] *Ibid.*, vol. 240, exp. 10 (1707). The copy of the document signed by Hernan Cortez gives its date as Dec. 19, 1519, which is evidently a clerical error, as it is also signed by his secretary, Alonso Valiente, who was not yet in Mexico at that time, and Cortez refers to himself as Captain General and Governor.

[16] Roys, 1941, docs. 31, 32, 33.

Bonifacio Uc is declared to be a natural lord in a judge receptor's decree and the town's acknowledgment in 1676 and again included in the petitions of Don Juan and the protector in 1688; indeed, in the last two documents exemption from tribute was also claimed for Bonifacio's wife, Maria Tec.[17] By 1752 lists of Xiu women begin to appear in the petitions of the heads of the family,[18] but nowhere do we find the privileges of nobility extended to any of their children.

The headship of the family descended regularly from father to oldest surviving son until the death of Don Juan's great grandson, Salvador, some time between 1759 and 1761. From then on, the probanzas do not state the relationship of the succeeding heads of the family. Salvador was followed by a Lorenzo, who is referred to as an old man in 1764, so we seem justified in assuming that they were brothers.[19] The Xiu succession in colonial times appears to be in accordance with pre-Spanish custom. Landa tells us that if, when a lord died, he had no son old enough to govern, a brother of the deceased succeeded and held the position for life, before the son of the first took his place.[20]

[17] *Ibid.*, docs. 47, 48, 55, 56.
[18] *Ibid.*, doc. 91.
[19] *Ibid.*, docs. 95, 99, 103.
[20] Landa, 1941, p. 100.

Chapter 21. Women Caciques

IN MEXICO, however, when there was no surviving son or brother, a woman could succeed to the caciqueship and was called a *cacica*. This was evidently an old established custom. In two early accounts of the line of Aztec rulers at Tenochtitlan we are told that when the elder Montezuma died, his only son was not by a "legitimate wife," meaning perhaps that she was not of noble lineage. Accordingly, the succession is said to have passed through a daughter to his grandson, Axayacatl.[1] Other accounts make Axayacatl the son of Montezuma,[2] but whatever the actual facts were, this tradition would indicate that such a procedure was not contrary to Mexican custom.

In the cacique documents of Mexico we find occasional mention of cacicas, some of whom are also called *señoras naturales*. Most of these were daughters of caciques, but sometimes it was the daughter of a cacica who had left no son.[3] Naturally a son would inherit, if there was one. Such cacicas not only inherited the property attached to the caciqueship but were also granted the usual compensation of a cacique, such as a salary, the products of a field, domestic service, and the repair of her house when needed.[4] On one occasion in 1582 a cacica of Xaltepec was permitted to receive from the people of her town a bale of spun cotton for her daughter's dowry. It is stated that this was customary and the townspeople were entirely willing to make this contribution.[5] In the cases I have cited the cacica acted in her own behalf, but in the eighteenth century we find the husband acting for her as *"marido y conjunta persona."*[6]

[1] Relación de la genealogía y linaje de los señores que han señoreado esta tierra de la Nueva España. 1891, p. 278; Origen de los Mexicanos, 1891, p. 302.
[2] Historia de los Mexicanos por sus pinturas, 1920, p. 66; Codex Ramirez, 1920, p. 113.
[3] AGM, Indios, vol. 1, no. 255 (1580).
[4] *Ibid.*, vol. 1, no. 238; vol. 2, no. 654; vol. 3, nos. 274, 268; vol. 4, nos. 184, 203; vol. 11, no. 72.
[5] *Ibid.*, vol. 2, no. 41.
[6] AGM, Vinculos, vol. 257, exp. 5; Indios, vol. 45, no. 75.

Chapter 22. Indian Nobles and the Native Militia of Yucatan

DON JUAN XIU'S commissions as captain, first in the Oxkutzcab native militia and later at Maxcanu, are of considerable interest. According to Molina Solis, Merida had in the seventeenth century half a dozen Spanish militia companies, one of mulattoes and four of Indian archers and pikemen.[1] The last were probably drawn from the Indian barrios of the city itself; if there were contingents at Oxkutzcab and Maxcanu, there must have been companies also at other larger towns in the jurisdiction of Merida, especially as there were eight native companies in the Campeche district.

Captain Don Fernando Camal, governor of Yaxakumche in 1624, would appear from his title to have commanded the Oxkutzcab company at that time. Three years later, when he is stated to have been governor of Oxkutzcab, he headed a contingent of Indians from this town and captured some of the leaders of an uprising which had occurred in 1624 at Sacalum in southern Yucatan. In this year an expedition, headed by Captain Francisco Mirones, to organize this district and proceed further against the Itza was overwhelmed and massacred by the local Indians, many of whom were fugitive apostates from northern Yucatan whereas others had never been converted. Don Juan Xiu later claimed that some of his lineage accompanied the punitive expedition, but we do not find any of the Xiu in the list of soldiers under Captain Camal's command.[2] These native militia companies were active not only in policing the interior of the country but also in repelling pirates on the coast. One of the Maya manuscripts tells of a number of Oxkutzcab Indians who took part in an expedition against some English buccaneers and Lorencillo in 1789. The latter was the popular name for the Dutchman, Laurent de Graff, who was a scourge of the Yucatecan coast for many years.[3]

In Don Juan's first commission in 1664 no particular company is mentioned; his command is said to consist of "all the militia and soldiers of the said town of Oxkutzcab." As captain he was granted certain unspecified honors and

---

[1] Molina Solis, 1904–13, 2: 427.

[2] Roys, 1941, docs. 35, 36; Scholes and Adams, 1936, pp. 160, 274.

[3] Codex Perez, p. 166; Molina Solis, 1904–13, 2: 272, 312; Exquemelin, 1898, p. xxii. De Graff burned Champoton and the shipyard at Campeche in 1672, and in 1685 or 1686 he and Grammont succeeded in burning and sacking the latter town, and even plundered the surrounding countryside for a distance of 3 or 4 leagues.

exemptions, but he was forbidden to engage his men in cultivating cornfields or in any other occupation to his own profit. From the last I infer that some militia captains had been accustomed to take an undue advantage of their position.[4] At Maxcanu in 1667 he was made captain of forty Indian archers and was to serve under Captain Don Geronimo Medrano, governor and commander of the companies of free negroes *(morenos)* and mulattoes *(pardos)* and of Indians. Apparently these formed a separate division from the companies of Spanish militia.[5]

The next captain to appear in the Xiu probanzas was Don Juan's great-grandson in 1759. This was Don Salvador, who was head of the family and a man of sixty-two at the time.[6] Molina Solis tells us that Indians were exempted from all military service during the eighteenth century;[7] but this rule evidently did not apply to the native nobility, for in a detailed report of conditions in Yucatan in 1766 it is stated that numerous hidalgos were enrolled in the militia. This is further confirmed in the Xiu probanzas, where Don Lorenzo appears as *alférez* in 1761, Don Pablo as sergeant in 1779, and a Don Manuel as deserter in 1793.[8] If we no longer find Indian militia companies of archers and pikemen in the eighteenth century, as noted by Molina Solis, it may have been because their weapons had become obsolete with the improvement and increased use of the flintlock. It is well known that the Spaniards continued to be unwilling to trust the natives with guns, but it is evident from the later Xiu probanzas that this mistrust did not extend to the Indian hidalgos.[9] It must be admitted, however, that at the outbreak of the Cisteil uprising in 1761 many Indians had guns and were allowed to buy powder and lead, although it is probable that their firearms were not very effective for actual fighting. After the revolt was quelled, Indians were forbidden under penalty of death to have guns even for hunting, but I do not know how long this restriction was enforced.[10]

[4] Roys, 1941, doc. 40.
[5] *Ibid.,* doc. 43.
[6] *Ibid.,* doc. 95.
[7] Molina Solis, 1904–13, 3: 542.
[8] Scholes et al., 1938a, p. 10; Roys, 1941, docs. 99, 111, 128.
[9] Cf. Roys, 1939, p. 64.
[10] Molina Solis, 1904–13, 3: 240–44.

Chapter 23. The Governor Compared with the pre-Spanish Batab

AMONG THE PROBANZAS we find two commissions by successive Governors of Yucatan issued to Don Juan Xiu as governor of Oxkutzcab in 1665 and of Maxcanu in 1667. These two documents, especially the first, furnish many details regarding the duties of an Indian governor. The functions enumerated here remind us of those of the preconquest batab as described in the accounts by the early Spanish settlers in Yucatan. The batab held his position for life and was usually, though not necessarily, succeeded by his son. He was the executive, judicial, and military head of the town, although his powers were often limited by the town council, over which he presided, and by the halach uinic. He acted as judge in both civil and criminal cases, but some matters were referred to the halach uinic for decision in those states where there was a territorial ruler. He supervised the activities of his people closely, seeing to it that they kept their homes and the municipal buildings in good repair and that they cut, burned, and sowed their fields at the proper season as declared by the local priests, who kept track of the calendar. In war he was in charge of all the soldiers from his town, although there was a war chief under him, who directed military operations. His needs were supplied by the townspeople "from what they manufactured and sowed."[1]

Don Juan's commission to govern Oxkutzcab was for one year, but at Maxcanu, where he was sent to replace a predecessor who had been remiss in compelling the people to fulfill their religious duties, his appointment was during the pleasure of the Governor of Yucatan and his successors.[2] Which of these two arrangements was the more usual at this time is uncertain. At Ebtun we know that a number of Indian governors held tenure for several years each; and at Yaxakumche Don Antonio Canche appears as governor in 1684, 1688, and 1693 and a Don Francisco Canche held the position in 1722 and 1727. I do not know, however, whether they were commissioned for several years or were re-elected each year.[3]

Among the duties enumerated in the Oxkutzcab commission, the governor

---

[1] Roys, 1933, app. E; 1939, p. 43; RY, 2: 103.
[2] Roys, 1941, docs. 41, 42.
[3] Roys, 1939, p. 47; AGI, Escribanía de Cámara 321A, pza. 1, 1684; *ibid.,* 321B, pza. 1, 1688; Roys, 1941, docs. 79, 85.

is to administer justice to litigants according to the royal ordinances, protecting widows, plebeians, and the poor, but he must refer such matters as lie outside his jurisdiction to the Spanish government. He must enforce attendance at church, prevent idleness and vice, and see to it that each family lives in a separate house kept in good repair. The church, well-wheels, and government buildings must be kept in repair. Indians from elsewhere may live in the town only if married to residents, but fugitives must be searched for and returned to their homes. A cornfield is to be tilled by the community for the purpose of defraying municipal expenses, and people are to be compelled if necessary to cultivate their own fields and gardens. The governor is to see to it that his people spin and weave tribute mantles for the encomendero and attend to the payment of these and other things required as tribute. Spaniards, mestizos, and mulattoes must not remain in the town for more than a day and a night. The governor is forbidden to engage in business during his term of office but shall receive as compensation the products of a field of sixty mecates, about six acres. The Maxcanu commission is very similar but contains less details. These duties appear to be based largely on the ordinances of the oidor, Diego Garcia de Palacio, who came to Yucatan in 1583. A Maya translation of these ordinances has been found in the archives of the town of Cacalchen.[4] If we compare these duties with the functions which the early reports ascribe to the pre-Spanish batab, they appear to be in remarkably close accord, considering all that had occurred during the intervening period.

[4] Tozzer, 1921, p. 204; Roys, 1941, doc. 41; AGI, Indiferente General, 2987; Libro de Cacalchen, legible portion of these ordinances, pp. 39–46.

Chapter 24. Conclusions

FROM THE EVIDENCE available at the present time I conclude that although the hereditary cacique was legally and socially the heir of the old batab, functionally the town governor became the real successor of the latter. The growing use of the terms batab and cacique as applied to the governor appears to indicate a popular acceptance of this state of affairs, both among the Indian and the Spanish population of Yucatan. It would be no more than the logical consequence of such a condition that in the eighteenth century we find the Xiu reduced to the standing of the lesser Indian nobility and enjoying the status only of hidalgos, which was comparable with that of the hereditary *principales* of Mexico. In the latter country, as we have already noted, the hereditary cacique, in a number of cases at least, retained his title and prestige during the eighteenth century.

In the Titles of Ebtun, which is a record of native land tenure in colonial times, there are occasional references to Indian nobility down to the second decade of the nineteenth century;[1] and we are given the impression that this institution was an important feature in the life of the people who appear in the documents. In the Xiu probanzas we can trace to some extent the history of this native aristocracy during the same period. We have no family papers of other Yucatecan caciques or hidalgos, but it seems evident that the Xiu were representative of their class.

We know little of pueblo government and the functions of the various offices, and an attempt is made here to explore one aspect of the question on the basis of inadequate evidence. A similar study of families that maintained their caciqueship in Mexico would be of value for purposes of comparison and go far to clear up the situation. It is a problem which needs intensive study, and such tentative conclusions as are reached here may be subject to revision later.

[1] Roys, 1939, pp. 50, 367.

Appendix--The Land Treaty of Mani

INTRODUCTION

THE RECORD of the Mani land treaty of 1557 is the earliest authentic example of the Maya language written in European script which has come down to us.[1] Dated only fifteen years after the Spanish conquest of Yucatan, it presents the language as it was before it could have been much influenced by contact with Europeans; and it offers a standard by which to appraise such changes as have subsequently taken place. It is also of considerable historical significance. Not only does it furnish a geographical description of the Province, or *Cacicazgo,* of Mani, one of the most important of the native states into which northern Yucatan was divided at the time of the conquest, but also it gives us a picture of the relations of the Indian towns with one another, especially in regard to their lands.

The Tutul Xiu rulers of Mani were descended from a Mexican family who had apparently come from Tabasco with a band of followers. The Mani chronicle states that they originally departed from Nonoual, or Nonoualco as the Aztec called it, "the place where the language changes," which was a name applied to Tabasco.[2] There is, however, another possible explanation, for Tulapan is also mentioned as the place of their origin. We are reminded of Tula and a neighboring hill called Nonohual north of Mexico City, which were closely associated with the Quetzalcoatl legend, and it is significant that the sculptures uncovered at Tula bear a remarkable resemblance to those of the Mexican period in Yucatan, especially at Chichen Itza.[3]

When they came to Yucatan the first Xiu ruler is said to have been Hun Uitzil Chac Tutul Xiu, whose title probably means "ruler of the hill country." The Xiu first established themselves at Uxmal, but the remains of that city, unlike Chichen Itza and Mayapan, show few traces of a Mexican occupation, and it would appear either that this group of foreigners was not numerous, or that they did not remain very long in Uxmal. They are said to have made friends and intermarried with the Yucatecans, and they increased their influence and power "more by strategy than by force," until they became a part of the joint government at Mayapan, second only to the Cocom among the chiefs who resided at the capital. In spite of their own alleged descent from the Mexican culture hero, Quetzalcoatl, the Cocom considered themselves the "natural

---

[1] We do not know just when Maya was first written in European script. Juan de Herrera, it is believed, was probably the first to teach the Maya language written in Spanish characters (Tozzer, 1921, p. 140).

[2] Brinton, 1882, p. 11: ch. 13, *supra.*

[3] Brinton, 1882, p. 110.

lords" of the country and called the Xiu foreigners. About the middle of the fifteenth century the latter instigated a revolution, as a result of which all but one of the Cocom leaders were killed, Mayapan was destroyed, and northern Yucatan was divided into a number of independent states. The Xiu now established themselves at Mani, from which they ruled the large and prosperous province of that name. During the first unsuccessful Spanish invasions they appear to have maintained a benevolent neutrality, but their halach uinic finally came to the aid of the Spaniards, when the latter were attempting to establish themselves at Merida early in 1542. This ruler died within the next few years and was succeeded by Kukum Xiu, probably a younger brother, who was baptized Francisco de Montejo Xiu about nine years prior to the date of the Mani land treaty.[4]

The Province of Mani was divided diagonally by a range of low mountains, which the Spaniards called the sierra and the Maya, the *puuc*. It extends in a southeasterly direction from Muna to a point south of Tzuccacab. Northeast of this range is a lowland plain covered by dry forest where it is not in cultivation. Much of it is rolling; low limestone ridges constantly alternate with thin pockets of soil. Here the Spaniards found many towns and villages and it was considered a rich and populous region, although today the land does not seem to be very fertile except for a long narrow belt extending along the base of the sierra. Besides the famous remains of Mayapan to the north,[5] ruined substructures are to be seen at Ticul, Dzan, Chapab and near Oxkutzcab and Tekax; and others are encountered throughout the area. Most of these were probably once surmounted by vaulted stone superstructures, but the latter are usually so completely in ruins that it is difficult to form any idea of their architectural style. It is my belief that few, if indeed any, vaulted buildings were still in use in this region at the time of the conquest, but that temples and government buildings alike were thatched structures.[6] Some of them may have had stone walls, however.

There are no surface streams, and the water of the few ponds is not potable. Cenotes are not actually rare, but they are not so numerous as in some other parts of Yucatan and do not exist at many of the Xiu towns. Since the water table lies about 27–30 m. below the surface and since the natural depressions which would facilitate digging down to water are not frequent, I conclude that many of the people ordinarily depended on artificial cisterns for their water supply. Remains of pre-Spanish cisterns or reservoirs in this region,

[4] Roys, 1933, p. 194; RY, 1: 288; ch. 9, *supra;* Morley, 1938, pp. 550–60.
[5] Morley, 1938a, p. 5.
[6] Cf. Bienvenida, 1548, *apud* Brinton, 1882, p. 243.

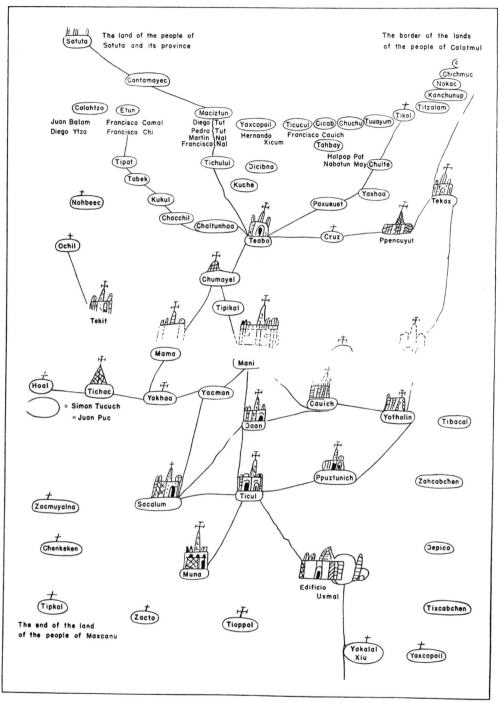

The land of the people of
Sotuta and its province

The border of the lands
of the people of Calotmul

Sotuta

Cantamayec

Chichmuc
Nokac
Kanchunup
Titzalam

Calahtzo   Etun   Maciztun
Juan Balam   Francisco Camal   Diego Tut   Yaxcopoil   Ticucul Cicab Chuchu Tuuayum Tikal
Diego Ytza   Francisco Chi   Pedro Tut   Hernando   Francisco Cauich
                                Martin Nal   Xicum
                                Francisco Nal   Tahbay

Tipat   Tichulul   Holpop Pot
Tabek   Nabatun May Chulte
                                        Jicibna
Nohbeec   Kukul   Kuche   Yaxhaa
                Chacchil   Tekax
Ochil   Chaltunhaa   Paxueuet
                              Teabo   Cruz   Ppencuyut

Tekit   Chumayel

                     Tipikal

              Mama

Hoal   Tichac   Yacman   Mani
          = Simon Tucuch   Yokhaa   Cauich
          = Juan Puc   Yotholin   Tibacal
                                        Oaan
                                                        Ppuztunich   Zahcabchen
Zacmuyalna
                              Sacalum   Ticul

Chenkeken   Jepico

Tipkal   Zacto   Edificio
The end of the land   Tioppol   Uxmal   Tixcabchen
of the people of Maxcanu

                                              Yakala!   Yaxcopoil
                                               Xiu

MAP 5—TRANSLATION OF MAP OF PROVINCE OF MANI IN XIU CHRONICLE
(SEE FIGS. 19 AND 20)

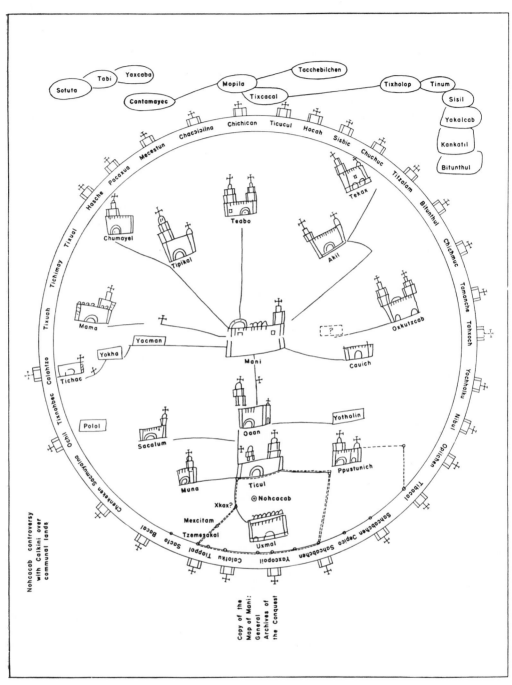

however, are not known to me. A few early Spanish cisterns did exist, and in course of time, with the introduction of steel and iron tools, many wells were dug.

Southwest of the sierra conditions are very different. There are many detached hills called *uitz*. The soil is deeper, more fertile, and more widely extended between the exposed limestone ledges. As there are no cenotes and the water table is much farther beneath the surface, the former inhabitants must have depended on the few deep caves and the artificial cisterns and surface ponds. The last are fairly numerous, and the water of the ponds is frequently drinkable in this region. Although the small towns of Xul and Nohcacab (the modern Santa Elena) seem to have been the only two inhabited settlements in this area at the time of the conquest, nevertheless many people living northeast of the range still cultivated the land there and carried its products to their homes, as they do today.

Here we find the remains of numerous ancient cities; many of their buildings are still in an excellent state of preservation. In a Maya chronicle is an account of the Xiu establishing themselves at Uxmal some centuries before the Spanish conquest and a vague reference to Kabah occurs in another native manuscript;[7] but I do not know of even a legend concerning the other ruined sites in this district. The fact that one of the handsomest of these cities is known today as Labna, meaning ruined house, and others are called Xlabpak (ruined wall), Chacmultun (red mound), Xethpol (fragment of a head), and Cabalpak (low wall), strongly suggests an abrupt break in historical tradition. It seems possible that such tradition as we know goes back only to the advent of certain Mexican intruders like the Xiu. At both Uxmal and Kabah we find a few sculptured figures or symbols that appear to be Mexican in character, although the architecture, generally speaking, is typically Maya. Regarding the depopulation of the region, we can only surmise that some of the townsfolk to the northeast of the range, who still own and farm the lands across the puuc, are descended from the former inhabitants of these ancient cities.

It is difficult to offer a reason for their moving away from this fertile region. It is true that the land may have become exhausted, but less fertile regions near large ruined sites like Merida, Ake, and Uci have been cultivated by Yucatecan methods for the past five centuries. Today the country behind the puuc is unhealthy, but if malaria was introduced by Europeans this was hardly the case in pre-Spanish times. A possible suggestion may be found in the Book of Chilam Balam of Mani, in which some of the oldest prophecies refer to people going

---

[7] Morley, 1920, p. 499; Roys, 1933, p. 82.

about begging for water to drink in time of drought.[8] These may go back to a time when they lived beyond the sierra, for northeast of the range there are few places that are not within fairly easy walking distance of a cenote with its never-failing supply of good water.

When the Spaniards arrived in Yucatan, they found certain of the native states almost constantly at war with one another, one of the most frequent causes of such dissensions being boundary disputes. Maya agricultural methods necessitate letting the land lie fallow for many years at a time, and along the borders there was the constant temptation for the people from one side to seize and cultivate a tract of land belonging to the neighboring state, which had been left unoccupied for a considerable time.[9] However useful such dissensions may have been to the Spaniards during the conquest, they became objectionable once the country was subdued; and measures were taken to induce the people to regulate their boundaries and live in harmony with one another, both to their own advantage and that of their new masters.

The convention at Mani was the result of this policy, although it was not the first attempt after the conquest to establish the boundaries of a native state. As early as 1545 Nachi Cocom, the ruler of the Province of Sotuta, with his principal chiefs surveyed the limits of his domain,[10] but the territory so included covered a fringe of land later claimed by his Xiu neighbors on the west and by the Cupul to the east. The Xiu and Cocom had been bitter enemies ever since the former had driven the latter out of Mayapan about the middle of the fifteenth century, and as late as 1536 Nachi Cocom violated a truce and murdered the Xiu ruler at Otzmal, a town near Sotuta. In 1557, however, the chiefs of the principal Xiu towns and those of the neighboring states were induced to meet together at Mani, the Xiu capital, and fix their boundaries. Nachi Cocom prudently sent word that he was ill and could not come, but the other chiefs appeared. Good feeling was promoted by dispensing wine and valuable gifts, and the treaty is a record of the settlement reached at this conference.

The original report of the proceedings has not come down to us, although it is possible that this was the document which Stephens saw in the archives at Mani in 1842. He gives a translation of a portion of it, and although it furnishes no information not contained in one or another of the documents noted in this study, it appears to be a slightly different version from any of them. Stephens also reports seeing another document dated August 10, 1556, and telling of a similar conference, but the latter has not been found.[11]

[8] Codex Perez, p. 102.   [9] Redfield and Villa, 1934, p. 22.
[10] Documentos de tierras de Sotuta, 1939, pp. 424–27.   [11] Stephens, 1843, 2: 265–68.

The document and map in the volume of the Xiu probanzas may well be a contemporary copy made for the town of Yaxakumche, now a part of Oxkutzcab; it contains a special account of the lands of Oxkutzcab, Yaxa, and Ticul.[12]

The Middle American Research Institute at Tulane University possesses a transcript of the original dated July 10, 1596, and accompanied by a copy of the map. With these papers is a Spanish translation made during the fifth decade of the seventeenth century.[13] Photographs of all these documents were kindly furnished by Tulane.[14]

There exists a third version of the Mani treaty, which has been named the Calotmul document because of the prominence it gives to this town. Cogolludo mentions the town[15] as being 5 leagues from Tekax on the road to Chunhuhub and Bacalar, but no settlement of this name could be found within the Xiu area.[16] It was finally located by Sr. Hermilo Lara Ancona, director of Catmis Hacienda, who had found a site of this name marked by a ruined colonial church near Ermita, about 10 km. south of Tzuccacab. The document was copied by Pio Perez in his Codex Perez, possibly at the time when he was *jefe politico* (a local administrative official) of Peto.[17] There is no map accompanying it.

Each of the three documents contains information not found in the other two. The Tulane version, known as the Mani document, gives the important information that Don Juan Cocom, or Nachi Cocom, of Sotuta alleged sickness and did not attend the convention in person, but sent representatives instead. Here also we read that the Spanish judge, Felipe Manrique, accompanied by his interpreter, Gaspar Antonio Chi, went to Uxmal to confirm a portion of the boundary. This document includes a summary of the 1557 treaty not found elsewhere and a supplementary agreement made in 1588 by the towns of Ticul and Ppustunich regarding certain lands in the region of Uxmal. The map accompanying these papers is very similar to one published by Stephens, but it omits the town of Ppencuyut which appears on the Stephens reproduction.[18]

The first part of the Calotmul document agrees with the Yaxakumche and Mani versions, but the part of the geographical description translated here also

---

[12] Most of these lands apparently lay southwest of the sierra, some of them possibly 80 km. distant from the towns. Of the sites mentioned I can recognize only Tanamche and Nibul, which appear on the border of the province in the Mani map.

[13] Crónica de Mani; the date of the Spanish translation is partly obliterated.

[14] The map has been reproduced and the documents described by Gropp (1934, pp. 260–62).

[15] Lopez de Cogolludo, 1867–68, bk. 9, ch. 5.

[16] There are several towns of this name, which means "twin mounds." The so-called Calotmul de Peto is east of the modern Dzonotchel and lies outside the Xiu area.

[17] Stephens, 1843, 2: 277.

[18] *Ibid.*, 2: 264.

covers the lands belonging to the towns of Calotmul, Tzuccacab, and Peto, which are not included in the texts and maps of the other two documents. This territory was closely associated with the Province of Mani; but it seems to have been regarded as an outlying area, as the agreement with the chiefs of these three towns forms a separate treaty. Don Juan Montejo Xiu, governor of Calotmul, was the father-in-law of Don Francisco de Montejo Xiu according to the Xiu family tree.[19] This is surprising, for although they were only distantly related, it was contrary to Maya custom, which forbade the marriage of two persons of the same patronymic.[20]

In all the documents the survey of the frontier of the province begins at a well, named Hoal, a short distance north of Tichac, the modern Telchaquillo.[21] The area includes the ruins of Mayapan, the former capital. As the descendants of those noble families, which were said to have lived within a certain walled enclosure at Mayapan, still kept a record of the location of their old homes there,[22] the possession of this site must have conferred a certain prestige on the halach uinic of Mani, whose family had once reigned there jointly with the Cocom.[23]

From Hoal the boundary is traced northward to Sacmuyalna, about 5 km. south of Tecoh, a town in the Province of Chakan. From there it continues in a southwesterly direction through Chenkeken to Acansip. Somewhere between these two sites the south border of Chakan ended, for the line turns south to Tipikal, which is said to be the end of the lands of the towns of Maxcanu and Becal in the Province of Ah Canul to the west.[24] It continues south passing the aguadas, or ponds, named Tzimezakal and Tioppol, the latter being the end of the lands of Becal and Calkini.

For a considerable distance south of Tioppol I am unable to locate the border sites mentioned in the treaty; but we find on the map accompanying the Mani document at the southwest border of the province four places named "Sahcabchen," "Tibacal," "Opilchen," and "Nibul." I cannot identify Tibacal but believe that the other three are the modern villages of Sahcabchen and Hopelchen and the aguada called Nibul which lies 8 km. southeast of Hopelchen. The location of these sites corresponds to their position on the Mani map.[25]

Unlike the Province of Mani, it seems doubtful that either Chakan or Ah

[19] Crónica de Oxkutzcab; Morley, 1941. Cf. Morley, 1920, pp. 470, 485.
[20] Landa, 1941, p. 100.
[21] Stephens, 1843, 2: 267.
[22] Lopez de Cogolludo, 1867–68, bk. 4, ch. 3.
[23] Ciudad Real, 1873, 2: 470; Noyes, 1932, p. 354.
[24] After the fall of Mayapan the Ah Canul allies of the Cocom were allowed to settle on the west coast of Yucatan (Landa, 1941, p. 39).
[25] Sahcabchen and Hopelchen appear on modern maps of the state of Campeche. Nibul was located through inquiries made at Bolonchenticul by J. I. Rubio Mañé.

Canul had a single territorial ruler, or halach uinic; they consisted apparently of groups of federated independent towns. Chakan was named for the savannas said to have abounded in that region, and its most important towns were Caucel, Uman, Acanceh, and Tecoh. Ah Canul was named for a group of people headed by the Canul family. Landa states that they were mercenaries brought from Mexico and in the service of the Cocom at Mayapan. He tells us that they were not allowed to intermarry with the Maya population, but we hear nothing of this prohibition elsewhere.[26] As already noted, they seem to have formed a loose confederation of towns, among which were Maxcanu, Halacho, Becal, Calkini, Numkini, Dzitbalche, and Hecelchakan.

The names of points along the border were not often those of towns, although in some cases villages or haciendas have since grown up at these places. Usually they were cenotes, wells, caves containing springs, ponds, and natural rock tanks. These would naturally be of importance in a country where the drainage is subterranean and there are no surface streams. Some were the sites of ancient ruins, probably abandoned before the conquest.

Following the delimitation of the western border, the description of the line begins again at Hoal near Telchaquillo; but this time it runs east and south. We follow it eastward to Ochil,[27] Tikanbul (Kambul), Cadzockal (probably the modern Hascocal), Tichuum and Ticalahtzo, where guards were stationed. Immediately to the north was the Province of Hocaba, called "Hocabaihumun" by Landa.[28] At the time of the conquest it was ruled by the warlike Nadzul Iuit[29] of Hocaba, noted for his slave raids into his neighbors' territories.

At Ticalahtzo, which can be located from the tax-office records at Merida,[30] the line leaves the border of the Province of Hocaba and extends south along the boundary of the Province of Sotuta. It passes through Mecestun, an unidentified site lying between the modern towns of Cholul and Cantamayec. Guards were set at intervals along this frontier, which is not surprising. Not only had the two provinces long been enemies, but on the native map of Sotuta at Tulane University[31] this province extends some distance west of the 1557 line. The latter boundary passes so close to the towns of Sotuta and Cantamayec and so far from the nearest Xiu towns that we suspect the Xiu of taking advantage of the favor they enjoyed with the Spaniards to encroach on the lands of their neighbors to the east.

[26] Landa, 1941, p. 39.
[27] Reported in 1588 as the former site of a town. Ciudad Real, 1873, 2: 473; Noyes, 1932, p. 356.
[28] Named for its two principal towns, Hocaba and Homun. Landa, 1941, p. 18 and note.
[29] RY, 1: 89; Roys, 1940, pp. 36, 43. In the Spanish report it is written "Naculybit" and has been reconstructed by me.
[30] Libro de Catastral, p. 545, Merida.
[31] Roys, 1939, p. 9, fig. 2.

Continuing in a southerly direction through Cucul and Hocah, located roughly from inquiries made at Teabo and Cantamayec, at the unidentified site of Tizizbic the line leaves the Sotuta border and follows that of the lands of Hunacti.

Hunacti, which is mentioned in the Book of Chilam Balam of Chumayel and played a considerable part in Landa's inquisition of 1562, seems to disappear from history after this time.[32] It lies 6 km. northeast of Tixmeuac, but the site is generally known as the ruins of Sisbic, the name of the hacienda on which it is located, though not the border site mentioned above. Only the Indian farmers on the actual site still call it Hunacti. Here are about fifteen platforms and pyramids, two of them possibly over 25 m. in height. No superstructures remain standing, but dressed stone and a few small sculptures are still to be seen; and on several of the old platforms are the walls of colonial buildings, apparently constructed from the debris of ancient Maya structures. At the foot of the largest pyramid is the vaulted chancel of a church and built into another mound is a cistern of Spanish masonry. The farmers report long lines of fallen stone fences defining the former streets, so it was evidently a town of some local importance in early colonial times.

From the Sotuta frontier the line follows the northwestern and western edge of the Hunacti area. It passes through what is now the hamlet of San Isidro Buleb, a short distance south of the town of Kini and said at Tixmeuac to be the site of ruins of some importance, and on through Tihaas, now known as Haasil, where a ruined pyramid with debris of dressed stone lies on the side of the highway from Tekax to Tixmeuac. Continuing through Kanchunup hacienda, it goes on to Nocac. Here are the ruins of a colonial hacienda and two Maya substructures into the terraces of which vaulted chambers are set. A guard was placed at this site, so it was probably the end of the Hunacti lands and the beginning of those of Peto, Tzuccacab, and Calotmul. In the descriptions of the Province of Mani proper the line is stated to continue to Bitunthul, the modern Thul near the railroad. It probably passed through Dzoyola, which can be seen from Nocac and lies 2 km. to the southeast. South of Thul we know from the Calotmul document that the line passed through what is now Sabachalal hacienda. From this point I am unable to identify the border sites, but I believe that the boundary of the Province of Mani continued south to the unidentified site of Tinaac, where it turned west toward Nibul and what is now Hopelchen.

The Calotmul document, as already noted, describes an outlying Xiu district belonging to the towns of Calotmul, Tzuccacab, and Peto. The last two are

---

[32] Roys, 1933, pp. 72, 142; Scholes and Adams, 1938, 1: 35, 166, 179, and 2: 75, *passim*.

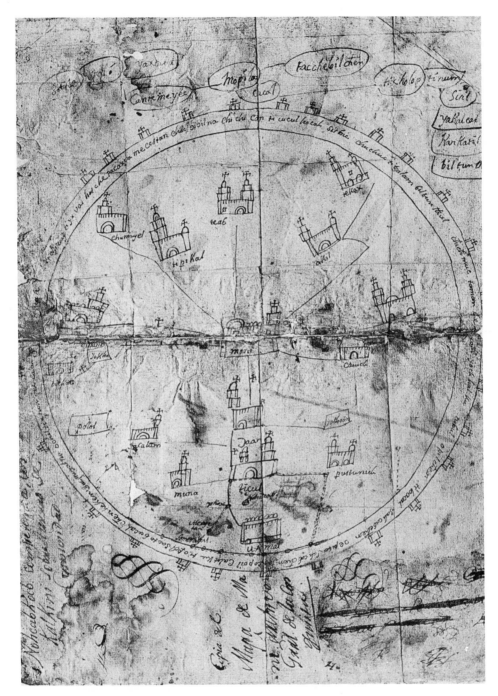

FIGURE 18—PROVINCE OF MANI, CRONICA DE MANI

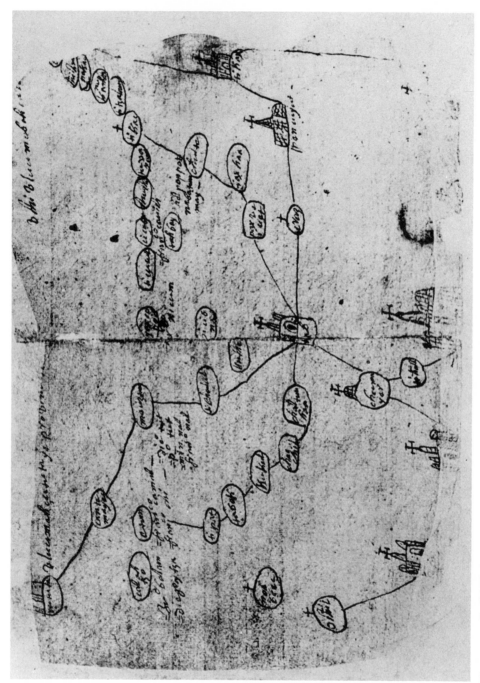

FIGURE 19—EAST HALF OF PROVINCE OF MANI, XIU CHRONICLE

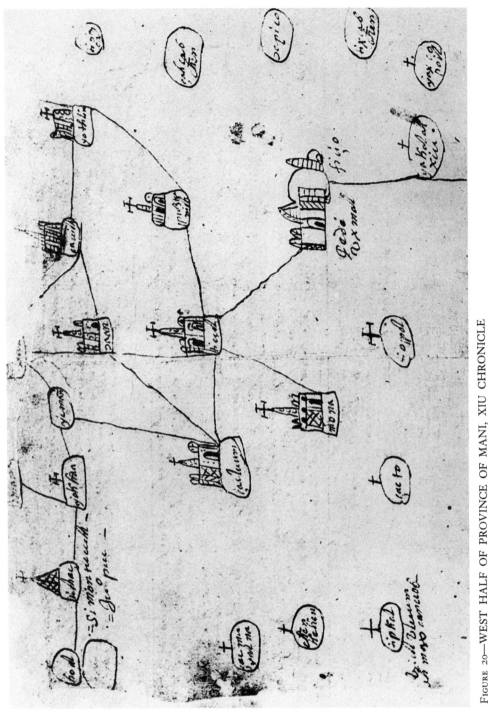

FIGURE 20—WEST HALF OF PROVINCE OF MANI, XIU CHRONICLE

FIGURE 22—WATTLE HOUSE, VALLADOLID (AFTER WAUCHOPE)

FIGURE 21—HOUSE WITH STOCKADE WALLS, CHAN KOM
(AFTER WAUCHOPE)

FIGURE 23—HOUSE INTERIOR, TIZIMIN (AFTER WAUCHOPE)

still towns of some importance, but I have been unable to find any historical reference to Calotmul since that by Cogolludo about the middle of the seventeenth century.[33] Approximately 5 leagues southeast of Tekax, the distance I have noted, is a deserted site named Calotmul. Here are a number of large mounds and platforms indicating that in ancient times it was a town of considerable size. The high vaulted chancel and thick walls of a large Spanish church are still standing. This and another structure among the mounds are the only buildings that appear to date from colonial times. A cylindrical cistern of Spanish masonry is set into the slope of one of the mounds a short distance northwest of the church.

It seems strange that this large district was not considered part of the Province of Mani proper. The town of Tahdziu, a short distance north of Peto, paid tribute and furnished soldiers in time of war to the ruler of Mani,[34] and the same was probably true of the entire district.

The portion of the Calotmul document presented here is devoted to a description of the borders of the lands of Calotmul, Tzuccacab, and Peto. This line begins at Bitunthul, and extends north to Dzoyola and probably to Nocac, following the boundary of the Province of Mani already described. From here it runs along the south and east border of the Hunacti district, through what are now the haciendas of Balche, Panaba, Texan, and Huntulchac, to the site of the modern village of Nenela, which was on the frontier of the Province of Sotuta. Turning sharply to the southeast the line can be traced through Sisbic,[35] the third site of this name encountered in this study, to Tisibak, where the Province of Sotuta ended and that of Cochuah began.

From Tisibak the line followed the Cochuah frontier southward through Dzonotchel to a site named Xayha on the west shore of Lake Chichankanab. There it turned west to Bolonnicib, said by chicle gatherers at Peto to be 6 km. from the lake and on the old road from Peto to Bacalar. Beyond this point I am unable to identify the sites mentioned. It would seem probable that the line continued in a westerly direction to the unidentified site of Tinaac, which was on the border of the Province of Mani, and thence north to Sabachalal. From here it ran north to Bitunthul, where the survey of this outlying district began.

Cogolludo describes the journey of Fuensalida and Orbita across this region in 1618. From Calotmul southeast to Chunhuhub the country was largely uninhabited. "Some sections of the road are open land without trees, which they

[33] Lopez de Cogolludo, 1867–68, bk. 9, ch. 5.
[34] RY, 1: 187.
[35] The word means vanilla. Cf. Roys, 1935, p. 9.

call savannas here, and some are difficult to pass over. By certain lakes are huts and stopping places, where Spaniards and Indians rest and sleep at night, although there are no people who live there. To all these sites, huts, lakes, savannas and marshes the Indians have given names in their language by which they know them, for in this they are very curious and pay much attention to it."[36]

Of all the lands adjoining those of the various Xiu districts described in these documents, only the territory of Campeche, which lay to the south, is left unmentioned. We do not know how far to the east the lands claimed by the people of Campeche extended, but it seems doubtful that they stretched very far inland from the coast. I am inclined to believe that an unoccupied belt of forest separated the Province of Mani from that of Campeche. In the 1766 Plano de la Provincia de Yucatán by Juan de Dios Gonzalez[37] roads are shown connecting Hopelchen and Bolonchen with Hecelchakan, but none appears leading to Campeche.

The maps accompanying the Oxkutzcab and Mani documents are of especial interest. In both of these the top is to the east. The former gives the most topographical information, as its style is more or less that of a European map. The latter, however, is like nothing I know outside of Yucatan. It is highly conventionalized, the boundary being drawn so as to form a perfect double circle, on which the border sites are set at approximately regular intervals. It is very similar to the Map of Sotuta at Tulane University, and I believe that these two examples are peculiar to the Maya area. Both resemble in some respects Melchor Alfaro's map of Tabasco and the circular map of Yucatan in the Book of Chilam Balam of Chumayel,[38] although the last is much cruder and more inaccurate.

These maps resemble the calendrical wheels found in the Books of Chilam Balam, in which the time period ascribed to the east is also at the top. The only literary reference to these circular maps, as far as I know, is found in the Maya translation of an order by Governor Fernandez de Velasco issued in 1600.[39] In the Spanish original they are simply called *"pinturas,"* but the Maya version refers to them as *"pepet ɔibil,"* which means circular paintings or writings. I am inclined to believe that this circular form of map with the top toward the east was a genuine Maya convention and dated from pre-Spanish times.[40]

[36] Lopez de Cogolludo, 1867–68, bk. 9, ch. 5.
[37] Ms. in the British Museum (numbered 17654a). Photoprint by F. V. Scholes.
[38] Roys, 1939, p. 9; RY, 1: map; Roys, 1933, p. 125. The top of the Alfaro map is to the south, and no border sites are shown.
[39] Bowditch, 1910, pp. 324–31; Documentos de tierras de Sotuta, 1939, p. 423.
[40] The only circular European maps known to me are those of a hemisphere or of the world, in which the subject matter naturally called for this form.

This study of the Mani land treaty has been made from photographs of the Tulane manuscript entitled Crónica de Mani and of an extract from the Codex Perez. In the names in the translation of the Maya text I have retained the character ɔ, which both Spanish and native colonial writers employed to indicate a glottalized or fortis ts sound; but elsewhere I have followed as far as possible the official Mexican spelling, in which ɔ is replaced by dz. A glottalized ´tš sound is indicated by čh in colonial Maya manuscripts.[41]

THE MANI DOCUMENT

LAND TREATY OF MANI, 1557

At the town of Mani on the fifteenth day of the month of August in the year 1557 there assembled the halach uinic Don Francisco de Montejo Xiu, governor here in the town and district of the Tutul Xiu, and the noble Don Francisco Che, governor of Ticul with his principal men, also Don Francisco Pacab, governor of the town of San Francisco Oxkutzcab, Don Diego Uz, governor of the town of San Juan Tekax, Don Alonso Pacab, governor of the town of Muna, Don Juan Che, governor of the town of Mama, Don Alonso Xiu, governor of the town of San Andres Tekit, also the other governors in the Mani district with their regidors. There they assembled and deliberated as to the advisability, they said, of marking off [the boundaries], fixing the corners and placing crosses at the borders of the fields of the towns of their subjects, for each [town] separately. This, then, was the occasion of their marking the limits of the lands of the Ah Canul, the people of Maxcanu, of Uman, of Acanceh, of Tecoh, Cuzama, Homun,[42] Sotuta and Tixcacal[tuyu],[43] also the districts of the people of Peto, Calotmul, Hunacti and Tzuccacab.[44] After they had deliberated together, they said it was advisable to bring in the governors of the towns. We answered that they should come here to the center of the town of Mani and that they should each bring two regidors with them to witness the marking off of the borders of the forests, the borders of the lands.

These are the names of the nobles who arrived here at the town: Don Juan Canul, governor of Numkini, with Don Francisco Ci, his associate,[45] also the batab of Maxcanu, Don Juan Cocom of Tecoh, Don Gaspar Tun, governor of

---

[41] Pp indicates an explosive p, th an explosive t, k is glottalized, and c is always hard. Cf. Beltran de Santa Rosa, 1859, pp. 4–5; Tozzer, 1921, pp. 17–29; Roys, 1933, p. 10.

[42] Cuzama and Homun were in the Province of Hocaba.

[43] Sotuta was the capital of the province of that name and Tixcacal, now known as Tixcacaltuyu, another important town in the same province.

[44] Hunacti was one district, and the lands of Peto, Tzuccacab and Calotmul constituted another; but both were associated with Mani.

[45] Francisco Ci was governor of Calkini.

Homun, Don Juan Cocom,[46] governor of the town of Sotuta, Don Gonzalo Tuyu, governor of the town of Tixcacal[tuyu], Don Juan Hau, governor of the town of Yaxcaba.[47] These were the governors of the towns who received the gifts of five four-hundred-piece lots [of cacao] each and five cotton mantles of four breadths each, also a string of red beads as long as one's arm and one score each of green stones, the gifts presented to each of the principal men of the towns, as they were presented by Juan Nic, Diego Camal, Pedro Coba and Pedro Maz, the ah kulels. They were assembled at the audiencia, here at the exalted house of the ruler, while they confirmed and ratified their deliberations as to how it was proper to serve our Lord God, the ruler, and in order that we may fulfill the command of our great ruler, his Majesty. When the governors had completed their deliberations here at the audiencia at Mani, they were con- ducted to the house of Don Francisco de Montejo Xiu, the governor, where they ate. Three arrobas of wine were consumed while they conversed. But Don Juan Cocom,[48] governor of Sotuta, was sick, having fallen ill, and did not come. Melchor Canche and Pedro Ucan came as his messengers. They received the gifts for the nobles, after they conferred here at the great town of Mani.

[This is a copy made][49] by me, the clerk, just as it was written in [the orig- inal] document. I testified to its truth, just as it stands [in the original.] It is because two towns, the people of Ticul [being one of them, agreed that there should also be two] documents regarding the marking off of the borders of the forest lands, [and that these shall be the titles for their lands and for those of] the other governors who came from each [town, that their children may see it] in time to come. On the tenth [day of the month of July, in the year one thousand five hundred] ninety-six.

[FRANCISCO CAB, clerk.]

This is the beginning of the marking off of the limits of the forest lands of the people of Acanceh, Tecoh, Cuzama, Homun, Sotuta, Calotmul, Calkini and Maxcanu there to the west.[50] It is there at Hoal; this is the name of the well which is on the road to Tihoo (Merida) to the north of Tichac and where

[46] We find the name Cocom in many parts of Yucatan, and there appears to be no reason to believe that there was any other connection between the governors of Tecoh and Sotuta than that they were of the same large lineage group. Cf. Roys, 1940, p. 36.

[47] Yaxcaba was the easternmost town of importance in the Province of Sotuta.

[48] Alternative translation "having fallen ill, was dying." Don Juan Cocom was the Christian name of Nachi Cocom, who in 1536 murdered the former Xiu halach uinic and his retinue, while they were pass- ing through his territory on a pilgrimage to Chichen Itza. Possibly he now considered it imprudent to visit the Xiu capital. His death occurred about four years later in 1561 (Scholes and Adams, 1938, 1: 73).

[49] The page is torn, and the missing portion is supplied here from the seventeenth-century Spanish translation (Crónica de Mani, ff. 3–5). Cf. Gropp, 1934, p. 262.

[50] Only Calkini and Maxcanu lie to the west.

a cross was placed. Next is Zacmuyalna where a cross was placed at the edge
of the lands of the people of Tecoh. The next is Kochilhaa where a cross was
placed. The next is Cheenkeken where there is a cross. The division of the
borders of the forest lands is to be followed[51] by Don Francisco de Montejo
Xiu, halach uinic there at Mani, before the principal men of the towns, the
governors from each town. Here are the names of the boundary mounds and
the crosses set in mounds:[52]

Cizinil.

Ɔoyola.

Tichulul.

Iza.

Acanzip.

Tippkat. There is a cross at the limits of the lands of the people of Maxcanu
and Becal, the Ah Canuls.

Kaxabceh.

Chacnocac.

Ticalam.

Zacto. There is a cross there.

Tzimezakal.

Tioppol. A cross is there at the limits of the lands of the people of Calkini
and Becal.

Tiyaaxche.

Zucila.

Tixcabcħen.

Ɔepico.

Zahcabcħen.

Tibacal.

Tiopilcħen. A cross was placed there.[53]

Boundary between Nohcacab and Calkini.[54]

Here are written down the boundary mounds which were set up a second
time and confirmed by Judge Felipe Manrique, specially commissioned by the
Sr. Governor, when he arrived at Uxmal with his interpreter, Gaspar Antonio.
The halach uinic, Don Francisco de Montejo Xiu, governor of Mani and the

[51] Maya, *manebal;* literally "passed over" or "traveled over."

[52] This would indicate that the Xiu ruler was to inspect the survey in person after the border points
had been agreed upon.

[53] Chenkeken, Acansip, and Tipihal appear on the modern maps of Yucatan. Tzemezakal, literally
"centipede pond," is an aguada 3 km. north of the present road from Uxmal to Becal. Stephens, who
passed by another trail and noted a ruin near this pond, calls it "Senuisacal" (Stephens, 1843, 1: 188;
Roys, 1937, p. 24). Tioppol is another pond lying east of Calkini.

[54] Gloss, written in Spanish.

entire province, confirmed this, placed the corners and placed the boundary mounds. I, Francisco Cab, the clerk, witnessed this.

Then began the count [of the boundary mounds] for the people of Mani, Mama, Tekit, Teabo, and for the people of Sotuta as follows:

Haba, the name of a well [belonging to] Mani, to the north of Tixchobenal [belonging to] Mani.

Ochil, where a cross was placed.

Tikanbul.

Caɔockal.

Yaalahau.

Tichuum.

Tituk.

Tixnohbec, where [a cross] was placed.

[Ticaa.]

[Tixconilchen.]

[Ticalaytzo, where a cross was placed.] There Diego Itza and Juan Balam were placed as guardians at the borders of the lands of the people of Cuzama and Homun. These guardians of the borders of the forest lands are men of Tekit.[55]

Tichulul.

Tixuah.

Tixkinxac.

Ebtun, the border of the lands of the people of Mani, where a cross was set. Francisco Camal and Francisco Chi were the guardians of the forest lands at the border of the lands of the people of Sotuta. These guardians of the borders of the forest lands were Mani men.

Tichimiy.

Pacaxua, beside the well of Batab Tucuch.

Tinicte.

Haazche.

Tahmiciztun, the border for the people of Mani and Teabo. There a cross was set and Diego Tut and Pedro Tut were placed by the halach uinic, Don Francisco de Montejo Xiu, as guardians of the limits of the forest lands.

Yaxcopoil. Ah Ceh Xicum was set here to guard it.

Ticucul.

---

[55] Ochil appears on the modern maps; Kambul is part of the same hacienda; and Tichum is said to be an aguada east of the latter (communication from J. I. Rubio Mañé). Ticalaytzo is evidently the modern Calaptzo situated 1 km. south of the town of Zavala. Words in brackets are supplied from the Spanish translation.

Hocah. Francisco Cauich of Mani was the guardian of the border of the forest
  lands. A cross was placed there.[56]

Tizizbic, where a cross was set and guardians placed by Don Gonzalo Tuyu
  and Don Juan Xiu. Diego Cauich and Diego Mo were guardians of the
  forest borders of the people of Tixcacal[tuyu] and Hunacti.

Chuchu.

  ɔonot.

[Tuuayin.]

[Tahbuleb.]

[Tikom.]

[Titzalam.]

[Tikanchunup.]

[Tinocac.]

[Tichichmuc.]

[Bitunthul, where a cross was placed. Juan Uitz was the name of the guardian
  of the border of the forest lands for the people of Tzuccacab and Tekax.][57]

Tiyochhaalku.

Tahxoch.

Titamanche.

Xixomkuch.

Tinaac, where a cross was placed at the border of the forest lands of the people
  of Calotmul.

The border of the forest lands of the people of Mani and Ppencuyut was confirmed and marked off by Judge Francisco de Magaña. These are the border
  mounds and crosses which were set up by the halach uinic, Don Francisco de
  Montejo Xiu, governor there at Mani:

Tixbecanzahcab.

Tahmulox.

Tahpacab.

Tixkomxan.

Tziuek.

Zikax.

Tahcoh.

---

[56] Tahmicistun, or Mecestun, which might be translated as "twisted or curved rock," is shown on the
map accompanying the Oxkutzcab version of the treaty as lying on a road between Cholul and Cantamayec. Yaxcopoil, Ticucul, and Hocah were located from inquiries by J. I. Rubio Mañé and myself at
Cantamayec and Teabo as lying in an irregular line almost due south of Cantamayec.

[57] Titzalam, the modern Tzalmil, is 14 km. from Tekax and said at Tixmeuac to lie halfway between the latter and Xaya. Cf. Libro del Catastral, p. 505. Tihaas, which appears in the Calotmul document as a border site, is the modern Haasil, a ruined site on the highway to Tixmeuac. Tahbuleb is written
Tahbulev in the Spanish translation and Tahbuleu in the Maya text.

Tahxaya.
Tichulte.
Tikom.
Tahbuleb a second time.[58]

AGREEMENT BETWEEN TICUL AND PPUSTUNICH, 1588

In this year of one thousand five hundred 88 there assembled the nobles: Don Melchor Coba with his principal officials and Don Alonso Xiu from Ppuztunich with his principal officials. They assembled beside the pond of Yiba[59] and deliberated as to where the borders of their lands, the borders of their forests, were for each [town] separately. Then Don Alonso Xiu and his principal officials said [that they were as follows:] Tahxyat, Tahcib, Tzucox, Yiba, which is a pond, Canalzahcab, Calppul,[60] [Pet]enya, [Mizc]it; these are the limits of the cornfields of the towns, they said. These are the limits [of their fields, the people of Ticul] also said, and they said that no one should [say anything to the contrary, nor shall] our sons in time to come. [This is the truth. We have signed] our names that it may be known to be true.

[Don Melchor Coba, governor of Ticul.]   Don Alonso Xiu from Ppuztunich.
... [chunthan alcalde.]   ... chunthan.
[Francisco Cua, chunthan alcalde.]   ... [Chuc], chunthan.
... [chunthan regidor.]   ... chunthan.
[Gaspar Itza] ...   ... chunthan.
                              ... clerk.

RECAPITULATION OF THE TREATY OF 1557

At the town of San Miguel Mani in the Province of Yucatan on the tenth day of the month of July in the year 1596.[61] There assembled the governors, alcaldes and regidors at the cabildo, here at the audiencia of the great town of Mani, before the halach uinic, Don Francisco de Montejo Xiu, governor here at the capital, at the great town of Mani. Then they considered together that it was advantageous to confirm their deliberations and the orders set down in their titles, when the limits of our forest lands were marked off, with the batabs of the towns, who came from

---

[58] Tixbecanzahcab is said to lie a short distance east of Ppencuyut. The line evidently continued eastward through the site of the modern town of Xaya to what is now San Isidro Buleb.

[59] Yiba, a fair-sized pond 4 km. south of the ruins of Uxmal, is still a well-known watering place on one of the main highways of the region. A ruin has recently been reported from this site.

[60] Calppul is said at Uxmal to be a pond 3 km. southeast of the hacienda.

[61] As we have seen, July 10, 1596, was the date of this transcript. What follows relates to the treaty of 1557.

the east, who came from the north, who came from the west, who came from the south.[62] This was determined by all the governors from the Province of Mani. These are their names: Don Francisco de Montejo Xiu, governor here at the great town of Mani, with all his principal officials, Don Francisco Che, governor of Ticul, with all his principal officials, Don Francisco Pacab, governor of the town of San Francisco Oxkutzcab, with all his principal officials, Don Diego Uz, governor of the town of San Juan Tekax, with all his principal officials, Don Alonso Pacab, governor of the town of San Juan Muna, with all his principal officials, Don Juan Che, governor of the town of Mama, with all his principal officials, Don Alonso Xiu, governor of the town of San Andres Tekit, with all his principal officials, Don Juan Canul,[63] governor of Numkini, with all his principal officials, Don Francisco Ci, governor of Calkini with the batab of Maxcanu and all his principal officials, Don Juan Cocom, governor of Tecoh, with all his principal officials, Don Gaspar Tun, governor of the town of Homun, with all his principal officials, Don Juan Cocom,[64] governor of the town of Sotuta, with all his principal officials, Don Gonzalo Tuyu, governor of the town of Tixcacal[tuyu], with all his principal officials, and Don Juan Hau, governor of the town of Yaxcaba, with all his principal officials. These are the names of the governors in the Province of Mani,[65] in the jurisdiction of the halach uinic, Don Francisco de Montejo Xiu, governor here at the great town of Mani.

This is the truth as to what they determined by common assent and as to how they placed boundary mounds and set up crosses at the borders of our forest lands. These are the nobles from each province, in order that it may be known by our halach uinic, our lords Governors,[66] in the future in time to come; the same regarding the judges who shall be sent to see us in the service of our lord, the great ruler, his Majesty the King, and in the service of our great Lord God, the ruler. This is in order that proper attention may be given to the tribute for our lord, our great ruler, the King, also that attention may be given to the tribute for the encomenderos who are in each town. This is the reason that they determined these things together, the governors and the principal men from each town. So let there be no persons among [our] descendants in female or male line who shall state the contrary in time to come. This is the reason for completing the document, the *auto,* by the chief officials of all the

[62] The four directions cited here are given in the same order in which they occur in the Maya rituals.

[63] Here begin the names of the governors from outside the Province of Mani.

[64] As we have previously noted, Don Juan Cocom, or Nachi Cocom, was represented by proxy at this convention.

[65] This statement is obviously inaccurate. The towns listed from Numkini on lie outside the Province of Mani.

[66] This refers to the Spanish Governors, to whom the title halach uinic was applied in colonial times.

towns, the governors, and by Don Francisco de Montejo Xiu, governor here at the great town of Mani, in order that it may be known truly and accurately how the borders of our forest lands were marked off for us, the men of Mani. Since it is true, they appended their names before me, the clerk.

Don Francisco de Montejo Xiu, governor of Mani.

Don Francisco Che, governor of Ticul.

Don Francisco Pacab, governor of Oxkutzcab.

Don Diego Uz, governor of Tekax.

Don Alonso Pacab, governor of Muna.

Don Juan Che, governor of Mama.

Don Alonso Xiu, governor of Tekit.

Don Juan Canul, governor of [Numkini.]

Don Francisco Ci, governor of Calkini.

Don Juan Cocom, governor of Tecoh.

Don Gaspar Tun, governor of Homun.

Don Juan Cocom, governor of Sotuta.

[Don Gonzalo Tuyu, governor of Tixcacal.]

[Don Juan Hau, governor of Yaxcaba.]

THE CALOTMUL DOCUMENT[67]

The following are the lands of the noble governors and regidors, Don Juan Xiu, Ah Kukil Xiu, there at Calotmul, Don Pablo Camal, governor of Peto and Don Juan Xiu, governor of Tzuccacab, with their alcaldes, regidors, ah kulels, clerk and the principal men of the towns here in the land. Herewith we declare our true testimony of how this land is not slave which we leave to them, in order that the nobles may sustain themselves, in order that they may farm it in time to come.[68] This is our true testimony; no one shall discuss it, because [the land] was given to them by our Lord God, the ruler, and we have given our testimony to that effect. Governor Don Francisco de Montejo Xiu, here in the town and district of the Tutul Xiu and the [following] nobles: Don Francisco Che, governor of Ticul, Don Francisco Pacab, governor of Oxkutzcab, Don Diego Uz, governor of Tekax, governor Don Alonso Pacab of ɔan-Muna, Don Juan Che, governor of Mama, Don Alonso Xiu, governor of Tekit, and the other governors in the district of Mani with their principal officials, alcaldes and clerk. This we decided together,[69] with my grandfathers, Don Francisco Xiu, Ah Kukil Xiu, Ah Misib Xiu there at Calotmul, and Don

---

[67] Codex Perez, pp. 82–84. The following is an extract from the Calotmul version of the Mani treaty defining the lands of Calotmul, Peto, and Tzuccacab and is not found in either the Mani or the Oxkutzcab document. The remainder of the Calotmul document is substantially the same as that contained in the Mani version.

[68] This is an important statement, since it implies that the ruling class considered the town lands to be their property.

[69] Maya *tumtah*, "to deliberate together and make a decision in conference."

Pablo Camal of Peto, also Don Juan Xiu,[70] governor of Tzuccacab. We, the nobles of the district of Calotmul, deliberated upon this, and accordingly we declare our true testimony, how this forest and their lands are not slave.[71] Accordingly we declare this with my maternal grandfather,[72] that the limits of the forest land be marked off for my maternal grandfather and his subject towns, in order that no one may take them from them, because we decided upon this together, that it may be known in time to come. When it shall be disputed with them, let them display our true testimony if anyone shall bring the matter up.

The beginning[73] is at Bitunthul. Ɔoyola, Tibalche, Tipanaba, Cetbolonua, Titzuctun, Tixan, where a cross was set up. Panabchen, Sabacche , Yaxcopoil, Tihuntulchac, Nenela, Sisbic, where a cross was set up. Tinicte, Tiyubak, Tituk, Tisibak.[74] It comes from Tzuccehche to the north of Ɔonotchel. In the middle of the entrance to Ɔonotchel there is a cross at the limits of the land of Cochuah.[75] Then having passed to the south of the cenote, it will come out at Ticatzim, where there is a cross. Then it goes to Holca, Keken, Tzitzila.[76] Then it will go south to the Kaknab,[77] the survey passes to the middle of the Kaknab, to Xaya, where there is a stone mound at the survey corner. Then it turns back and comes out at Tixbolonnicib, where there is a stone mound on the road.[78] Tiyochhalku, Tacchoh, Titanamche, Xixomkuch, Tinac, where a cross was set at the corner of the land.[79] Then it will come out at Nohakal, Sabachalal; and it will come to Chanchan, Palul,[80] Tiek, Yokakal; and it will

[70] The governor of Tzuccacab is elsewhere in this document stated to be a Don Juan Tzuc.

[71] Maya, *ppentac*. The term is usually applied to a person and means slave or captive, or, as a verb, to enslave. It might mean that they considered it the land of a free people, or possibly that they had not captured it from a neighboring state.

[72] Maya, *mam*. The term could also mean mother's sister's son or father's brother's son (Eggan, 1934, p. 190). I surmise that here it means that the clerk was a maternal grandson of Don Juan Xiu of Calotmul.

[73] Here begins the description of the borders of the lands of Calotmul, Peto, and Tzuccacab, which lay outside the area included by the Oxkutzcab and Mani maps.

[74] Huntulchac, Nenela, and Dzibac are shown on the published maps of Yucatan. Balche, Panaba, and Tixan are haciendas, which appear on the Plano del Departamento de Tekax or that of Peto. Panabchen, Sabacche, and Chab were located by Don Pedro Morales, proprietor of Huntulchac hacienda, who made a trip to verify these sites. Sisbic, not to be confused with the two sites of this name already mentioned, is well known to a number of people at Tadziu, where I made inquiries.

[75] This was the large Province of Cochuah, which lay to the east (RY, 1: 147; 2: 94, 116). Dzonotchel appears on most modern maps and is described by Shattuck (1933, p. 172).

[76] Chicle gatherers at Peto reported that Catzim is 12 km. due south from Dzonotchel and that Holca is 4 km. south by west from Catzim. Tzitzila was said to be a little farther south and about 26 km. from Peto.

[77] Literally, "the sea." It is a good-sized lake now known as Chichankanab, which means "little sea."

[78] Xayha was reported by the same informants as being the site of ruins, halfway down Chichankanab and beside the lake. Bolonnicib is 6 km. west of the lake on the old road to Bacalar. There were formerly houses there, but only the wooden pillars remain.

[79] Yochhaltun, a variant of Yochhalku according to the Stephens map, and Tanamche are known vaguely to exist, but nothing could be learned of Tinac. Evidently the line turned north at this point.

[80] Sabachalal is shown as a hacienda 16 km. south by west from Tzuccacab on the Plano del Departamento de Peto. Palul has been reported to be between 6 and 12 km. south of the railroad. Cf. Scholes and Adams, 1938, 1: 64.

come out at Bitunthul. It is for our nobles in order that they may sustain themselves in time to come. Below are our signatures, our true testimony, of us who are chiefs here in the land of Yucatan. At the house of Ah Mochan Xiu and Nacab Chi and Ah Mochan Xiu and Nacab Xiu of Tekax. He [Mochan Xiu?] was the father of Ah Nacab Xiu, the son of Ah Cot Xiu of Panabchen. Also Ah Cot Xiu and Ah Kukil Xiu of Calotmul. This is our true testimony. No one shall deny this statement. The document is given herewith to the alcaldes of Calotmul, the regidors and principal men; also to the alcaldes and regidors of Tzuccacab; also to the people of Peto: the batabs and alcaldes written below. On this day of the month of August in the year 1557.

Don Juan Cocom, Don Francisco de Montejo Xiu of Mani, Kukil Xiu of Calotmul, Don Francisco Cuat[81] Cocom of Sotuta, Don Juan Tzuc, governor of Tzuccacab, Andres Che, Don Pablo Camal, [governor of Peto,] Melchor Mo, his alcaldes, his principal officials, Gaspar Che, Francisco Kuk, his principal official, governor Don Diego Uz [of Tekax], governor Don Mateo Couoh, Antonio Pot, Juan May, Juan Chuc, Pedro Chable, Francisco Coyi, Andres Pol, the regidors of Calotmul. Don Juan Tzuc, governor [of Tzuccacab], with Pedro Bak, Luis Montejo Xiu, Pascual Mian, Andres Uc, Pedro Coba, his alcaldes. . . .[82] Nachi Xiu of Panabchen, Nacab Xiu of Tekax, the father of Nachi Xiu. Herewith I append my signature, as written above.

[81] Written Cual in the text. There was an Ah Cuat Cocom, who was implicated in the blinding of Montejo's messengers at the time of the conquest, and Nachi Cocom had a son Francisco, although we know that these were two different persons. Cf. Brinton, 1882, p. 237, and Roys, 1939, p. 7.

[82] I am unable to translate the words *"ah xul canche uinicob lae."* They might mean that the halach uinics were at the end of the bench or table. The phrase was first written *ah xulcumche* and corrected to *ah xul canche.*

Glossary

[The definitions given here apply only to the use of the terms in this study, and in some cases they are oversimplified.]

aguada (Span.): surface pond.

Ahau (Maya): a certain day name; sometimes the title prefixed to the patronymic of a *halach uinic*; *ahau* means ruler.

ah cuchcab (Maya): a member of the town council; the head of a subdivision of a town.

ah kin (Maya): priest.

Ah Kul (Maya): the title prefixed to the patronymic of an *ah kulel* and treated as a part of his personal name.

ah kulel (Maya): a deputy or assistant of the *batab*.

alcalde (Span.): in a Spanish town an official having limited executive and judicial functions within the jurisdiction of the town; in an Indian town he was under the governor and apparently had certain police duties as well.

alcalde meson (Span.): an alcalde in charge of the local rest house.

alférez (Span.): a military officer roughly corresponding to the English ensign or sub-lieutenant.

alguacil (Span.): a minor peace officer.

almehen (Maya): noble; the term apparently implies a known descent in both the male and female line.

arroba (Span.): a wine measure varying from 4.11 to 8.04 gals. according to the locality; also a weight of approximately 25 lbs.

audiencia (Span.): a certain superior court and administrative commission; the term is also applied to the council room in the *casa real*.

auto (Span.): a judicial decree or edict.

ayuntamiento (Span.): a municipal government.

batab (Maya): in pre-Spanish times the civil and military head of a town; during the colonial period the cacique and later also the governor of an Indian town.

bonete (Span.): *Leucopremna mexicana* Standl.

cabecera (Span.): the capital or principal town of a country or district; here the term is usually applied to the local missionary headquarters.

cabildo (Span.): a town corporation.

cacica (Span.): a woman cacique.

cacicazgo (Span.): the dignity or office of a cacique and his territory.

cacique (Span.): an Indian chief; in colonial times the holder of a certain hereditary position, and later the governor of an Indian town.

can (Maya): a gift presented to a judge by a litigant; a serpent.

casa (Span.): house; a line or branch of a family.

casa real (Span.): the administrative building of a town.

catastral (Span.): tax office.

cenote (from Maya *ɔonot*): a natural cistern or water hole peculiar to the Yucatecan peninsula.

chunthan (Maya): one of the principal officials of a town, sometimes translated as regidor.

corregidor (Span.): a certain magistrate.

cuchcabal (Maya): district, province or jurisdiction.

cuchillo del monte (Span.): a large hunting knife sometimes attached to a gun like a bayonet.

de color (Span.): a person with some admixture of negro blood; possibly also a negro.

doctrina (Span.): Christian instruction; a town or village of Christian Indians, where a regular parish has not been established.

encomendero (Span.): the holder of a grant called an encomienda, or the right to receive services and tribute from certain specified Indians.

ex (Maya): a loincloth; in colonial times the cotton drawers worn by Indians.

fanega (Span.): a dry measure variously defined as 1.60 and 2 bu. in Spain and 2.56 bu. in Mexico.

fuero (Span.): privilege or exemption.

gente vil (Span.): low-class people.

gobernador (Span.): governor, a term applied to the Governor of Yucatan and also to the local executive of an Indian town.

gobernación y guerra (Span.): government and war; apparently the chief administrative department of the Province of Yucatan.

halach uinic (Maya): a head chief or territorial ruler of an independent Maya state.

hidalgo (Span.): a noble.

holpop (Maya): the holder of a position or office of undetermined character, sometimes called a cacique.

honra (Span.): honor.

indio (Span.): Indian; a person with an Indian surname.

intendente (Span.): intendant, a provincial administrator.

Ix (Maya): a certain day name.

jefe politico (Span.): the political head of a district.

judge receptor (Span. *juez receptor*): apparently a court clerk acting as delegate judge.

juez ordinario (Span.): a judge of the lower court.

kaan (Maya): see *mecate*.

kan (Maya): a red shell bead.

kantixal, or *kanthixal* (Maya): a breast ornament of precious stone, possibly also of shell.

katun (Maya): a time period of 7200 days.

macehual, macegual, mazeual (Nahuatl): a common Indian, not a noble.

maestre de campo (Span.): a certain military officer of high rank.

mam (Maya): mother's father, daughter's son.

mandamiento (Span.): mandate, order.

mariscal de campo (Span.): field marshal.

mat, or *matun* (Maya): a nose bead.

matricula (Span.): a tax list.

mayor domo (Span.): a town steward.

mecate (Span.; Nahuatl *mecatl*): a surface measure 20 m. square, or approximately one tenth of an acre; a linear measure of approximately 20 m.

mestizo (Span.): a man of mixed Spanish and Indian blood.

moreno (Span.): brown or swarthy; a negro.

nacom (Maya): a war chief.

natural (Span.): native; natural.

nombre (Span.): name, reputation, credit.

nucteil uinicob (Maya): the elders or principal men of a town.

pati (Maya): a tribute mantle consisting of four breadths of cotton cloth.

parcialidad (Span.): a ward or subdivision of a town.

pardo (Span.): brown; apparently a term applied to a mulatto.

pintura (Span.): painting; a native land map, probably painted.

política (Span.): the art and science of government.

preeminencia (Span.): preference.

principal (Span.): an Indian of recognized noble status; the head of a subdivision of a town.

probanza (Span.): proof; an official record of merits and services; a documentary proof of the nobility of a native family.

puuc (Maya): a range of high hills in Yucatan.

regidor (Span.): a member of the town council.

registro, or *registro civil* (Span.): a municipal record of vital statistics and local census.

relación (Span.): an account or report.

residencia (Span.): an accounting required of the holder of a public office.

señor (Span.): lord.

señor natural (Span.): a natural lord; a term here applied to native rulers and their descendants.

señora natural (Span.): a woman having the status of a natural lord.

sierra (Span.): see *puuc.*

síndico procurador (Span): municipal attorney.

teniente (Span.): lieutenant; a municipal officer ranking next to the governor of an Indian town.

tierra de guerra (Span.): a region threatened by enemies or continually at war.

tilma (Span.; Nahuatl *tilmatli*): mantle.
topil, or *tupil* (Nahuatl): see *alguacil.*
tun (Maya): a green stone bead; a time period of 360 days.

u (Maya): necklace; moon; month.
uinal (Maya): a time period of 20 days.
uinic (Maya): man; a surface measure said to contain 20 mecates.
uitz (Maya): a detached hill.

vecino (Span.): a citizen or householder of a town; later, a person with a Spanish name as distinguished from an Indian.
villa (Span.): a town enjoying certain privileges; in Yucatan, Campeche, Valladolid, and Bacalar were villas.
visita (Span.): here the term is applied to a town with a church but no resident clergy.

xanab (Maya): sandal.
xicul (Maya): a sleeveless shirt or jacket.

References

ACOSTA, JOSE DE
  1880   The natural and moral history of the Indies. . . . Reprinted from the English translated edition of Edward Grimston, 1604. (Works issued by the Hakluyt Society, nos. LX–LXI.) London.

ALTOLAGUIRRE Y DUVALE, ANGEL DE, ed.
  1928   Gobernación espiritual y temporal de las Indias. *In* Colección de documentos inéditos relativos al descubrimiento, conquista y organización de las antiguas posesiones Españoles de ultramar. 2a ser., vol. 21. Madrid.

ANDRADE, M. J.
  1931   Linguistic research in the Maya field. *Carnegie Inst. Wash.*, Year Book 30, pp. 126–28. Washington.

ANGHIERA, PIETRO MARTIRE D'
  1912   De orbe novo, the eight decades of Peter Martyr d'Anghiera. Translated from the Latin with notes and introduction, by Francis Augustus MacNutt. . . . New York and London.

ARCHAEOLOGICAL SITES IN THE MAYA AREA
  1940   Prepared by Middle American Research Institute under a grant from Carnegie Inst. Wash. G. Kramer, delineator; research by S. K. Lowe. New Orleans.

ARCHIVO GENERAL DE INDIAS, SEVILLE
  Documents from the following legajos: Contaduría 920; Escribanía de Cámara 305A, 308A, 315A, 319C, 321A, 321B; Indiferente General 1206, 2987; Justicia 195, 245, 247; México 104, 138, 367, 369. See notes for detailed citations.

ARCHIVO GENERAL DE LA NACIÓN, MEXICO
  Documents from the following volumes: Indios 1–4, 6, 7, 9, 11, 15–17, 25, 30, 35, 45, 50, 55; Mercedes 1–3; Vínculos 80, 240, 257, 272; Tierras 2809. See notes for detailed citations.

AVENDAÑO Y LOYOLA, ANDRES DE
  1696   Relación de las dos entradas que hize a la conversión de los gentiles Ytzaex. MS. reproduced by Gates. (MS. translation by C. P. Bowditch in Peabody Museum.) *See* Means, 1917.

BACABS, RITUAL OF THE
  Medical incantations and prescriptions. MS. Gates reproduction.

BANCROFT, H. H.
  1883   The native races. 5 vols. San Francisco.

BARTLETT, H. H.
  1935   A method of procedure for field work in tropical American phytogeography. . . . In *Carnegie Inst. Wash.*, Pub. 461, pp. 1–25. Washington.

BELTRAN DE SANTA ROSA, PEDRO
  1859   Arte del idioma Maya reducido a succintos reglas y semilexicón Yucateca. Merida. (Originally published in 1746, Mexico.)

BENEDICT, F. G., AND M. STEGGERDA

1936   The food of the present-day Maya Indians of Yucatan. *Carnegie Inst. Wash.,* Pub. 456, Contrib. 18. Washington.

BLOM, F.

1928   Gaspar Antonio Chi, interpreter. *Amer. Anthropol.,* n.s., 30: 250–62. Menasha.

1932   Commerce, trade and monetary units of the Maya. *Middle Amer. Research Ser.,* Pub. 4, pp. 531–56. New Orleans.

——, AND O. LA FARGE

1926–27   Tribes and temples. A record of the expedition to Middle America conducted by Tulane University of Louisiana in 1925. 2 vols. New Orleans.

BOEKELMAN, H. J.

1935   Ethno- and archeo-conchological notes on four Middle American shells. *Maya Research,* 2: 255–77. New Orleans.

BOWDITCH, C. P.

1910   The numeration, calendar systems and astronomical knowledge of the Mayas. Cambridge.

BRINTON, D. G.

1882   The Maya chronicles. *Library of Aboriginal American Literature,* no. 1. Philadelphia.

1890   Essays of an Americanist. Philadelphia.

1896   The battle and ruins of Cintla. *Amer. Antiquarian,* 18: 259–67. Worcester.

BUTLER, R. L.

1937   A check list of manuscripts in the Edward E. Ayer collection. *Newberry Library.* Chicago.

CACALCHEN, LIBRO DE

[Collection of wills, statutes, and other legal documents in Maya.] MS. Gates reproduction.

CALKINI, CRÓNICA DE

[Chronicle and geographical description of the Province of Ah Canul in Maya.] MS. Gates reproduction.

CARTA DE DIEZ CACIQUES

1877   *In* Cartas de Indias, p. 367 and facsimile U.

1929   *In* Martinez H., 1929, pp. 57–61.

CARTA GEOGRÁFICA DEL ESTADO DE YUCATÁN

1931   Secretaría de Agricultura y Fomento. [Tacubaya.]

CARTAS DE INDIAS

1877   Publícalas por primera vez el Ministerio de Fomento. Madrid.

CATASTRAL, LIBRO DE

MS. Merida.

CERVANTES DE SALAZAR, FRANCISCO

1914   Crónica de la Nueva España. (Chaps. 25–29 translated in Landa, 1941, pp. 233–39.) Madrid.

CHAMBERLAIN, R. S.

1939   The concept of the *señor natural* as revealed by Castilian law and administrative documents. *Hispanic Amer. Hist. Rev.,* 19: 130–37. Durham.

CHARNAY, C. J. D.
1887   The ancient cities of the New World. . . . New York.
CHI, GASPAR ANTONIO
1941   Relación. *In* Landa, 1941, pp. 230–32.
CHICXULUB, DOCUMENTOS DE TIERRAS DE
       MS. owned by José Rafael de Regil of Merida. Gates reproduction. Photostat
       made for Carnegie Inst. Wash.; copy by Hermann Berendt. Berendt Ling.
       Col., *Univ. Mus.* Philadelphia.
CHUMAYEL, BOOK OF CHILAM BALAM OF
1913   The Book of Chilam Balam of Chumayel, with introduction by G. B. Gordon.
       Univ. Mus., Anthropol. Pub., vol. 5. Philadelphia.
1930   *See* Mediz Bolio, 1930.
1933   *See* Roys, 1933.
[CIUDAD REAL, ANTONIO DE]
1873   Relación breve y verdadera de algunas cosas de las muchas que sucedieron al
       Padre Fray Alonso Ponce en las provincias de la Nueva España. . . . 2 vols.
       Madrid.
1932   *See* Noyes, 1932.
CONTRERAS, JUAN DE
1934   Historia del arte hispánico. Barcelona.
COOKE, C. W.
1931   Why the Mayan cities of the Petén district, Guatemala, were abandoned. *Jour.
       Wash. Acad. Sci.,* 21: 283–87. Washington.
CORONEL, JUAN
1929   Arte en lengua Maya recopilado, y enmendado. . . . *In* Martinez H., 1929.
       (Originally published in 1620, Mexico.)
CORTES, HERNAN
1866   Cartas y relaciones de Hernán Cortés . . . colegidas e ilustradas por Don Pascual
       de Gayangos. Paris.
1916   The fifth letter of Hernando Cortés to the Emperor Charles V, containing an
       account of his expedition to Honduras. (Works issued by the Hakluyt So-
       ciety, 2d ser., vol. 40.) London.
1931   Cartas de relación de Fernando Cortés sobre el descubrimiento y conquista de la
       Nueva España. *Historiadores primitivos de Indias.* Biblioteca de autores
       españoles desde la formación del lenguaje hasta nuestros dias, 22: 1–153.
       Madrid.
CORTESIANUS, CODEX
       See de Rosny, 1883.
DAMPIER, W.
1906   Dampier's voyages. . . . 2 vols. New York.
DIAZ, JUAN
1858   Itinerario. . . . *In* Colección de documentos para la historia de México, 1: 281–308.
       Mexico.
1939   Itinerario de Juan de Grijalva. *Crónicas de la conquista de México.* Biblioteca
       del estudiante universitario, 2: 17–39. Mexico.

DÍAZ DEL CASTILLO, BERNAL

1908–16   The true history of the conquest of New Spain. . . . Translated by A. P. Maudslay. 5 vols. (Works issued by the Hakluyt Society, 2d ser., nos. 23–25, 30, 40.) London.

1933–34   Verdadera y notable relación del descubrimiento y conquista de la Nueva España y Guatemala. 2 vols. Guatemala.

1939   Historia verdadera de la conquista de México. 3 vols. Mexico.

DOCUMENTOS INÉDITOS

1864–84   Colección de documentos inéditos, relativos al descubrimiento, conquista y organización de las antiguas posesiones españolas de América y Oceanía, sacados de los archivos del reino, y muy especialmente del de Indias. 42 vols. Madrid.

DOCUMENTOS PARA LA HISTORIA DE YUCATÁN

   See Scholes et al., 1936–38a.

DRESDEN CODEX

1892   Die Maya-Handschrift der Königlichen Bibliothek zu Dresden. Dresden.

EBTUN, THE TITLES OF

   See Roys, 1939.

EGGAN, F.

1934   The Maya kinship system and cross-cousin marriage. Amer. Anthropol., n.s., 36: 188–202. Menasha.

ESPINOSA, ANTONIO

ca. 1910   Mapa de la península de Yucatán (México) comprendiendo los estados de Yucatán y Campeche y el territorio de Quintana Roo.

ESPINOSA E., MANUEL, AND LUIS H. ESPINOSA S.

1928   Calendario de Espinosa para el año bisiesto 1928. Merida.

EXQUEMELIN, A. O.

1898   The buccaneers of America. . . . London and New York.

FISKE, J.

1892   The discovery of America, with some account of ancient America and the Spanish conquest. . . . 2 vols. Boston and New York.

FUENTES Y GUZMAN, FRANCISCO ANTONIO DE

1932–33   Recordación florida. . . . 3 vols. Guatemala.

GAGE, T.

1928   Thomas Gage, the English-American. A new survey of the West Indies, 1648. London.

GALINDO, J.

1920   Report of the scientific commission appointed to make a survey of the antiquities of Copan. . . . In Morley, 1920, pp. 593–603.

GANN, T. W. F.

1918   The Maya Indians of southern Yucatan and northern British Honduras. Bur. Amer. Ethnol., bull. 64. Washington.

1934   Changes in the Maya censer from the earliest to the latest times. Proc. 24th Int. Cong. Amer., pp. 51–54. Hamburg.

———, AND J. E. S. THOMPSON

1931   The history of the Maya, from the earliest times to the present day. New York.

GATES, W.

1920   The distribution of the several branches of the Mayance linguistic stock. *In*
       Morley, 1920, pp. 605–15.

1931   The thirteen Ahaus in the Kaua manuscript and related Katun wheels in the
       Paris Codex, Landa, Cogolludo, and the Chumayel. *Maya Soc. Quarterly,*
       1: 2–20. Baltimore.

GODOY, DIEGO

1931   Relación hecha por Diego Godoy a Hernando Cortés. . . . *Historiadores primiti-*
       vos de Indias, pp. 465–70. Madrid.

GONZALEZ, JUAN DE DIOS

1766   Plano de la Provincia de Yucatán. MS. in British Museum.

GROPP, A. E.

1933   Manuscripts in the Department of Middle American Research. *Mid. Amer.*
       Research Ser., Pub. 5, pp. 217–97. New Orleans.

HABEL, S.

1878   The sculptures of Santa Lucia Cosumalwhaupa in Guatemala. With an account
       of travels in Central America and on the western coast of South America.
       Smithsonian Contrib. Knowledge, no. 269, vol. 22, art. 3. Washington.

HERRERA Y TORDESILLAS, ANTONIO DE

1725–26   The general history of the vast continent and islands of America, . . . trans-
          lated into English by Capt. John Stevens. London.

1726–27   Historia general de los hechos de los Castellanos en las islas i tierra firme
          del mar océano. 9 parts. (Originally published in 1601–15, Madrid.)

HISTORIA DE LOS MEXICANOS POR SUS PINTURAS

1920   *See* Radin, 1920.

HOLMES, W. H.

1919   Handbook of aboriginal American antiquities. Part I. The lithic industries. *Bur.*
       Amer. Ethnol., bull. 60. Washington.

HOOTON, E. A.

1940   Skeletons from the Cenote of Sacrifice at Chichen Itza. *In* The Maya and their
       Neighbors, pp. 272–80. New York.

HUSSEY, R. D.

1932   Document: text of the laws of Burgos, 1512. . . . *Hisp. Amer. Hist. Rev.,* 12:
       306–21. Durham.

JOHNSON, F.

1940   The linguistic map of Mexico and Central America. *In* The Maya and their
       Neighbors, pp. 88–114. New York.

JUARROS, DOMINGO

1937   Compendio de la historia de la Ciudad de Guatemala. Guatemala.

KAUA, BOOK OF CHILAM BALAM OF

       MS. Gates reproduction.

KEMPTON, J. H.

1935 Preliminary report of the agricultural survey of Yucatan of 1935. (Mimeographed.) Washington.

KIDDER, A. V.

1932 Annual report of the Division of Historical Research. *Carnegie Inst. Wash.,* Year Book 31, pp. 89–91. Washington.

1935 Notes on the ruins of San Agustin Acasaguastlan, Guatemala. *Carnegie Inst. Wash.,* Pub. 456, Contrib. 15. Washington.

1936 Annual report of the Division of Historical Research. *Carnegie Inst. Wash.,* Year Book 35, pp. 111–15. Washington.

1940 Archaeological problems of the highland Maya. *In* The Maya and their Neighbors, pp. 117–25. New York.

——, AND J. E. S. THOMPSON

1938 The correlation of Maya and Christian chronology. In *Carnegie Inst. Wash.,* Pub. 501, pp. 299–328. Washington.

LANDA, DIEGO DE

1938 Relación de las cosas de Yucatán. Ed. Rosado Escalante and Ontiveros with an introduction by Alfredo Barrera Vásquez. *Mus. Archaeol. Hist.* Merida.

1938a Relación de las cosas de Yucatán, por el Fray Diego de Landa, obispo de esa diocesis. Introducción y notas por Héctor Pérez Martínez. Mexico.

1941 Landa's relación de las cosas de Yucatán. A translation edited with notes by Alfred M. Tozzer. *Papers Peabody Mus. Harvard Univ.,* vol. 18. Cambridge.

LEHMANN, W.

1920 Zentral-Amerika. Teil I. 2 vols. Berlin.

LIBRO DEL CONSEJO, EL

1939 Traducción y notas de Georges Raynaud, J. M. González de Mendoza y Miguel Angel Asturias. Mexico.

LINTON, R.

1940 Crops, soils, and culture in America. *In* The Maya and their Neighbors, pp. 32–40. New York.

LIZANA, B. DE

1893 Historia de Yucatán. Devocionario de Ntra. Sra. de Izamal, y conquista espiritual. Mexico. (Originally published in 1633, Valladolid.)

LOPEZ DE COGOLLUDO, DIEGO

1867–68 Historia de Yucatán. 3d ed., 2 vols. Merida. (Originally published in 1688, Madrid.)

LOPEZ DE GOMARA, FRANCISCO

1931 Hispania Victrix. Primera y segunda parte de la historia general de las Indias. *Historiadores primitivos de Indias,* pp. 155–455. Madrid.

LOPEZ MEDEL, TOMAS

1941 Relación. *In* Landa, 1941, pp. 221–29.

LOTHROP, S. K.

1924 Tulum: an archaeological study of the east coast of Yucatan. *Carnegie Inst. Wash.,* Pub. 335. Washington.

1940   South America as seen from Middle America. *In* The Maya and their Neighbors, pp. 417–29. New York.

LUNDELL, C. L.

1933   Archaeological discoveries in the Maya area. *Proc. Amer. Philos. Soc.,* 72: 147–79. Philadelphia.

1934   The agriculture of the Maya. *Southwest Rev.,* 19: 65–77. Dallas.

1934a   Preliminary sketch of the phytogeography of the Yucatan peninsula. *Carnegie Inst. Wash.,* Pub. 436, Contrib. 12. Washington.

1937   The vegetation of Peten. *Carnegie Inst. Wash.,* Pub. 478. Washington.

1938   The 1938 botanical expedition to Yucatan and Quintana Roo, Mexico. *Carnegie Inst. Wash.,* Year Book 37, pp. 143–47. Washington.

MALER, T.

1902   Yukatekische Forschungen. *Globus,* 82: 197–230. Brunswick.

MANI, CRÓNICA DE

1557–1813   MS. at Tulane University.

MARTINEZ HERNANDEZ, JUAN

1913   La creación del mundo según los mayas. Páginas inéditas del manuscrito de Chumayel. *Proc. 18th Int. Cong. Amer.,* pp. 164–71. London.

1926   Crónicas Mayas. Crónica de Yaxkukul. Merida.

1929   Diccionario de Motul: Maya Español. Merida.

MAYA AND THEIR NEIGHBORS, THE

1941   Dedicated to Alfred M. Tozzer. New York.

MEANS, P. A.

1917   History of the Spanish conquest of Yucatan and of the Itzas. *Papers Peabody Mus. Harvard Univ.,* vol. 7. Cambridge.

MEDIZ BOLIO, ANTONIO

1930   Libro de Chilam Balam de Chumayel. Traducción del idioma Maya al Castellano. San Jose, Costa Rica.

MENDIZABAL, MIGUEL O. DE

1930   Influencia de la sal en la distribución geográfica de los grupos indígenas de Mexico. *Proc. 23d Int. Cong. Amer.,* pp. 93–100. New York.

MOLINA, ALONSO DE

1880   Vocabulario de la lengua Mexicana. Leipzig.

MOLINA SOLIS, J. F.

1904–13   Historia de Yucatán durante la dominación española. 3 vols. Merida.

MORLEY, S. G.

1915   An introduction to the study of the Maya hieroglyphs. *Bur. Amer. Ethnol.,* bull. 57. Washington.

1920   The inscriptions at Copan. *Carnegie Inst. Wash.,* Pub. 219. Washington.

1935   Archaeological work in Yucatan. *Carnegie Inst. Wash.,* Year Book 34, pp. 123–24. Washington.

1938   The Maya New Empire. In *Carnegie Inst. Wash.,* Pub. 501, pp. 533–65. Washington.

1938a   Chichen Itza. *Carnegie Inst. Wash.,* Year Book 37, pp. 141–43. Washington.

Morley, S. G. *(continued)*

[1941]   The Xiu chronicle. Part I: The history of the Xiu. MS. in Peabody Museum, Harvard University.

Morris, E. H., Jean Charlot, and A. A. Morris

1931   The Temple of the Warriors at Chichen Itza, Yucatan. *Carnegie Inst. Wash.,* Pub. 406. Washington.

Motul, Diccionario de

See Martinez H., 1929.

Nakuk Pech, Chronicle of

See Brinton, 1882.

Noyes, E., ed. and tr.

1932   Fray Alonso Ponce in Yucatan, 1588. *Middle Amer. Research Ser.,* Pub. 4, pp. 297–372. New Orleans.

Origen de los Mexicanos

1891   *In* Nueva colección de documentos para la historia de México, 3: 281–308. Mexico.

Orozco y Berra, Manuel

1864   Geografía de las lenguas y carta etnográfica de México. Mexico.

Oviedo y Valdes, Gonzalo Fernandez de

1851–55   Historia general y natural de las Indias, islas y tierra-firme del Mar Oceano. 4 vols. Madrid.

Oxkutzcab, Crónica de

1557–1817   MS. in Peabody Museum. Reproduced by W. E. Gates and C. P. Bowditch, latter with introduction by A. C. Breton. (Also called Xiu Chronicle. Page 66 of Gates reproduction reproduced and translated in Morley, 1920.)

Pacheco Cruz, S.

1939   Léxico de la fauna yucateca. Merida.

Page, J. L.

1933   The climate of the Yucatan peninsula. In *Carnegie Inst. Wash.,* Pub. 431, pp. 409–22. Washington.

Parish records

MSS. Books recording baptisms, marriages and burials in churches at Oxkutzcab and Mama, Yucatan.

Peresianus, Codex

See Willard, 1933.

Perez, Juan Pio

1866–77   Diccionario de la lengua Maya. Merida.

1898   Coordinación alfabética. . . . Merida.

Perez, Codex

ca. 1837   MS. owned in Yucatan. Photograph made for Carnegie Inst. Wash.

Perez Martinez, Hector

1936   Ah Nakuk Pech, historia y crónica de Chac-xulub-chen. Mexico.

Peto, Plano del Departamento de

1930   MS. Merida.

POLLOCK, H. E. D.

    1936   Round structures of aboriginal Middle America. *Carnegie Inst. Wash.*, Pub. 471. Washington.

POMAR, JUAN BAUTISTA

    1891   Relación de Tezcoco. *In* Nueva col. doc. para la hist. de México, vol. 3. Mexico.

POPOL VUH

    1927   *See* Villacorta C. and Rodas N., 1927.

PRIEGO DE ARJONA, MIREYA

    1937   Notas acerca de bibliografía yucateca. *Ediciones del Museo Arqueológico e Histórico de Yucatán*, Pub. 4. Merida.

PRIESTLEY, H. I.

    1916   José de Gálvez, visitor-general of New Spain (1765-1771). . . . Berkeley.

RADIN, P.

    1920   The sources and authenticity of the history of the ancient Mexicans. *Univ. Calif. Pub. Amer. Arch. and Ethnol.*, vol. 17, no. 1. Berkeley.

RAMIREZ, CODEX

    See Radin, 1920.

RECOPILACIÓN DE LEYES DE LOS REYNOS DE LAS INDIAS

    1774   3d ed., 4 vols. Madrid.

REDFIELD, R.

    1934   Culture changes in Yucatan. *Amer. Anthropol.*, n.s., 36: 57–69. Menasha.

    1938   Race and class in Yucatan. In *Carnegie Inst. Wash.*, Pub. 501, pp. 511–32. Washington.

    1941   The folk culture of Yucatan. *Univ. Chicago Pub. Anthropol.*, Social Anthropol. Ser. Chicago.

——, AND A. VILLA R.

    1934   Chan Kom, a Maya village. *Carnegie Inst. Wash.*, Pub. 448. Washington.

RELACIÓN DE LA GENEALOGÍA Y LINAJE DE LOS SEÑORES QUE HAN SEÑOREADO ESTA TIERRA DE LA NUEVA ESPAÑA

    1891   *In* Nueva col. doc. para la hist. de México, 3: 263–81. Mexico.

RELACIONES DE YUCATÁN

    1898–1900   *In* Colección de documentos inéditos relativos al descubrimiento, conquista y organización de las antiguas posesiones españolas de ultramar. 2a ser., vols. 11 and 13. Madrid.

REMESAL, ANTONIO DE

    1932   Historia general de las Indias Occidentales y particular de la Gobernación de Chiapa y Guatemala. 2 vols. Guatemala.

RICKETSON, O. G., AND A. V. KIDDER

    1930   An archaeological reconnaissance by air in Central America. *Geog. Rev.*, 20: 177–206. New York.

ROSNY, LÉON DE

    1883   Codex Cortesianus. . . . Paris.

ROYS, L.

    1935   Maya planetary observations. In *Carnegie Inst. Wash.*, Pub. 456, Contrib. 14. Washington.

Roys, R. L.

1931   The ethno-botany of the Maya. *Middle Amer. Research Ser.*, Pub. 2. New Orleans.

1933   The Book of Chilam Balam of Chumayel. *Carnegie Inst. Wash.*, Pub. 438. Washington.

1935   Place names of Yucatan. *Maya Research*, 2: 1–10. New Orleans.

1935a Study of Maya colonial documents. *Carnegie Inst. Wash.*, Year Book 34, pp. 148–50. Washington.

1937   Study of Maya colonial documents. *Carnegie Inst. Wash.*, Year Book 36, pp. 157–58. Washington.

1938   History of Yucatan. *Carnegie Inst. Wash.*, Year Book 37, pp. 168–69. Washington.

1939   The titles of Ebtun. *Carnegie Inst. Wash.*, Pub. 505. Washington.

1939a History of Yucatan. *Carnegie Inst. Wash.*, Year Book 38, pp. 252–53. Washington.

1940   Personal names of the Maya of Yucatan. *Carnegie Inst. Wash.*, Pub. 523, Contrib. 31. Washington.

[1941] The Xiu chronicle. Part II: The Xiu chronicle. MS. in Peabody Museum, Harvard University.

——, F. V. Scholes, and E. B. Adams

1940   Report and census of the Indians of Cozumel, 1570. *Carnegie Inst. Wash.*, Pub. 523, Contrib. 30. Washington.

Sahagun, Bernardino de

1938   Historia general de las cosas de Nueva España. 5 vols. Mexico.

Salazar, Francisco Cervantes de

See Cervantes de Salazar.

San Buenaventura, Gabriel de

1888   Arte de la lengua Maya. J. G. Icazbalceta, ed. Mexico. (Originally published in 1684, Mexico.)

Sanchez de Aguilar, Pedro

1937   Informe contra idolorum cultores del obispado de Yucatán. . . . Merida.

San Francisco, Diccionario de

MS. 17th century; original missing. Copy by Juan Pio Perez. Gates reproduction. Copy by Hermann Berendt. Berendt Ling. Col., no. 3, *Univ. Mus.*, Philadelphia.

Sapper, K.

1897   Das nördliche Mittel-Amerika nebst einem Ausflug nach dem Hochland von Anahuac. Reisen und Studien aus den Jahren 1888–1895. Braunschweig.

1902   Mittelamerikanische Reisen und Studien aus den Jahren 1888 bis 1900. Braunschweig.

Saville, M. H.

1918   The discovery of Yucatan in 1517 by Francisco Hernández de Córdoba. *Geog. Rev.*, 6: 436–48. New York.

1921 Reports on the Maya Indians of Yucatan by Santiago Mendez, Antonio García y Cubas, Pedro Sanchez de Aguilar and Francisco Hernandez. *Mus. Amer. Ind.*, Notes and Monogr., 9: 133–226. New York.

SCHOLES, F. V.
1939 History of Yucatan. *Carnegie Inst. Wash.*, Year Book 38, pp. 248–52. Washington.

1941 History of Yucatan. *Carnegie Inst. Wash.*, Year Book 40, pp. 309–10. Washington.

——, AND E. B. ADAMS
1936 Documents relating to the Mirones expedition to the interior of Yucatan. *Maya Research*, 3: 153–76, 251–76. New Orleans.

1938 Don Diego Quijada, Alcalde Mayor de Yucatán. 2 vols. (Biblioteca Histórica Mexicana, vols. 14, 15.) Mexico.

——, C. R. MENENDEZ, J. I. RUBIO MAÑÉ, AND E. B. ADAMS
1936 Documentos para la historia de Yucatán. Vol. 1: Primera serie, 1550–1561. Merida.

1938 *Ibid.* Vol. 2: La Iglesia en Yucatán, 1560–1610. Merida.

1938a *Ibid.* Vol. 3: Discurso sobre la constitución de las provincias de Yucatán y Campeche, 1766. Merida.

——, AND R. L. ROYS
1938 Fray Diego de Landa and the problem of idolatry in Yucatan. In *Carnegie Inst. Wash.*, Pub. 501, pp. 585–620. Washington.

SCHWEDE, R.
1912 Über das Papier der Maya-Codices u. einiger altmexicanischer Bilderhandschriften. Dresden.

SELER, E.
1902–23 Gesammelte Abhandlungen zur Amerikanischen Sprach- und Altertumskunde. 5 vols. Berlin.

SHATTUCK, G. C.
1933 The peninsula of Yucatan. *Carnegie Inst. Wash.*, Pub. 431. Washington.

SIMPSON, L. B.
1934 Studies in the administration of the Indians in New Spain. *Ibero-Americana*, 7. Berkeley.

SOLORZANO PEREIRA, JUAN DE
1776 Política Indiana. . . . Madrid. (Originally published in Latin, 1629–39, Madrid.)

SOTUTA, DOCUMENTOS DE TIERRAS DE
In Roys, 1939, pp. 421–33.

SOTUTA, MAP OF
In Roys, 1939, p. 9.

SOTUTA, PLANO DEL DEPARTAMENTO DE
1929 MS. Merida.

SPINDEN, H. J.
1924 The reduction of Mayan dates. *Papers Peabody Mus. Harvard Univ.*, vol. 6, no. 4. Cambridge.

STANDLEY, P. C.

 1930 Flora of Yucatan. *Field Mus. Nat. Hist.,* Pub. 279, Bot. Ser., vol. 3, no. 3. Chicago.

STARR, F.

 1900–02 Notes upon the ethnography of southern Mexico. . . . 2 vols. Davenport.

STEGGERDA, M.

 1938 The Maya Indians of Yucatan. In *Carnegie Inst. Wash.,* Pub. 501, pp. 567–84. Washington.

 1941 Maya Indians of Yucatan. *Carnegie Inst. Wash.,* Pub. 531. Washington.

STEPHENS, J. L.

 1843 Incidents of travel in Yucatan. 2 vols. New York.

STOLL, O.

 1884 Zur Ethnographie der Republik Guatemala. Zürich.

STONE, D. Z.

 1932 Some Spanish entradas, 1524–1695. *Middle Amer. Research Ser.,* Pub. 4, pp. 209–96. New Orleans.

 1940 The Ulua Valley and Lake Yojoa. *In* The Maya and their Neighbors, pp. 386–94. New York.

 1941 Archaeology of the north coast of Honduras. *Mem. Peabody Mus. Harvard Univ.,* vol. 9, no. 1. Cambridge.

STRÖMSVIK, G.

 1931 Notes on the metates of Chichen Itza, Yucatan. *Carnegie Inst. Wash.,* Pub. 403, Contrib. 4. Washington.

STRONG, W. D.

 1940 Anthropological problems in Central America. *In* The Maya and their Neighbors, pp. 377–85. New York.

——, A. KIDDER II, AND A. J. D. PAUL, JR.

 1938 Preliminary report on the Smithsonian Institution–Harvard University archaeological expedition to northeastern Honduras, 1936. *Smithsonian Misc. Coll.,* vol. 92, no. 14. Washington.

TABI, DOCUMENTOS DE

 Documentos de tierras de la hacienda Sn. Juan Bautista Tavi en idioma Maya o Yucateca. MS. in Tulane Univ. New Orleans.

TAPIA, ANDRES DE

 1939 Relación de Andrés de Tapia. *Crónicas de la conquista de México.* Biblioteca del estudiante universitario, 2: 41–96. Mexico.

TEEPLE, J. E.

 1931 Maya astronomy. *Carnegie Inst. Wash.,* Pub. 403, Contrib. 2. Washington.

TEKAX, PLANO DEL DEPARTAMENTO DE

 1929 MS. Merida.

THOMPSON, J. E. S.

 1930 Ethnology of the Mayas of southern and central British Honduras. *Field Mus. Nat. Hist.,* Anthropol. Ser., vol. 17, no. 1. Chicago.

 1931 Archaeological investigations in the southern Cayo district, British Honduras. *Field Mus. Nat. Hist.,* Anthropol. Ser., vol. 17, no. 3. Chicago.

1932   The humming bird and the flower. *Maya Soc. Quarterly*, 1: 120–22. Baltimore.

1934   Sky bearers, colors and directions in Maya and Mexican religion. *Carnegie Inst. Wash.*, Pub. 436, Contrib. 10. Washington.

1934a Maya chronology: the fifteen tun glyph. *Carnegie Inst. Wash.*, Pub. 436, Contrib. 11. Washington.

1935   Maya chronology: the correlation question. *Carnegie Inst. Wash.*, Pub. 456, Contrib. 14. Washington.

1936   The civilization of the Mayas. *Field Mus. Nat. Hist.*, Anthropol. leaflet 25, 3d ed. Chicago.

1936a Exploration in Campeche and Quintana Roo and excavations at San Jose, British Honduras. *Carnegie Inst. Wash.*, Year Book 35, pp. 125–28. Washington.

1937   Mexico before Cortez. 2d ed. New York.

1938   Sixteenth and seventeeth century reports on the Chol Mayas. *Amer. Anthropologist*, n.s., 9: 584–604. Menasha.

1939   Excavations at San Jose, British Honduras. *Carnegie Inst. Wash.*, Pub. 506. Washington.

1939a The moon goddess in Middle America: with notes on related deities. *Carnegie Inst. Wash.*, Pub. 509, Contrib. 29. Washington.

1941   Dating of certain inscriptions of non-Maya origin. *Carnegie Inst. Wash.*, *Div. Hist. Research*, Theoretical Approaches to Problems, No. 1. Washington.

1941a Maya arithmetic. *Carnegie Inst. Wash.*, Pub. 528, Contrib. 36. Washington.

——, H. E. D. POLLOCK, AND J. CHARLOT

1932   A preliminary study of the ruins of Cobá, Quintana Roo, Mexico. *Carnegie Inst. Wash.*, Pub. 424. Washington.

TICUL, PLANO DEL DEPARTAMENTO DE

       MS. Merida.

TIZIMIN, BOOK OF CHILAM BALAM OF

       MS. Mexico. Gates reproduction; photostat made for S. G. Morley.

TORQUEMADA, JUAN DE

1723   . . . Los veinte i un libros rituales i monarchia indiana, con el origen y guerras, de los indios occidentales, . . . Madrid.

TOZZER, A. M.

1907   A comparative study of the Mayas and the Lacandones. New York.

1913   A Spanish manuscript letter on the Lacandones in the Archives of the Indies at Seville. *Proc. 18th Int. Cong. Amer.*, 2: 497–509. London.

1921   A Maya grammar with bibliography and appraisement of the works noted. *Papers Peabody Mus. Harvard Univ.*, vol. 9. Cambridge.

1933   Introduction. *In* Whorf, The phonetic value of certain characters in Maya writing. *Papers Peabody Mus. Harvard Univ.*, vol. 13, no. 2. Cambridge.

1941   *See* Landa, 1941.

——, AND G. M. ALLEN

1910   Animal figures in the Maya codices. *Papers Peabody Mus. Harvard Univ.*, 14: 273–372. Cambridge.

TROANO, CODEX

       See J. A. Villacorta C. and C. A. Villacorta, 1930.

VAILLANT, G. C.

1935   Chronology and stratigraphy in the Maya area. *Maya Research*, 2: 119–43. New Orleans.

VALDES ACOSTA, JOSE MARIA

1923–31   A través de las centurias. 3 vols. Merida.

VIENNA DICTIONARY

Bocabulario de mayathan por su abeceario (Spanish-Maya). MS. National Bibliothek. Vienna.

VILLA R., A.

1934   The Yaxuna-Cobá causeway. *Carnegie Inst. Wash.*, Pub. 436, Contrib. 9. Washington.

VILLACORTA C., J. A., AND F. RODAS N.

1927   Manuscrito de Chichicastenango (Popol Buj). Estudio sobre las antiguas tradiciones del pueblo quiché. Guatemala.

——, AND C. A. VILLACORTA

1930   Codices Mayas: Dresdensis, Peresianus, Tro-Cortesianus. Guatemala.

VILLAGUTIERRE SOTO-MAYOR, JUAN DE

1701   Historia de la conquista de la Provincia de el Itza, . . . Madrid.

WATERMAN, T. T.

1917   Bandelier's contribution to the study of ancient Mexican social organization. *Univ. Calif. Pub. Amer. Arch. and Ethnol.*, 12: 249–82. Berkeley.

WAUCHOPE, R.

1938   Modern Maya houses: a study of their archaeological significance. *Carnegie Inst. Wash.*, Pub. 502. Washington.

1940   Domestic architecture of the Maya. *In* The Maya and their Neighbors, pp. 232–41. New York.

WEITZEL, R. B.

1931   The Books of Chilam Balam as tradition. *Amer. Jour. Arch.*, 35: 319–23. Concord.

WILLARD, T. A.

1926   The city of the sacred well. New York.

1933   The Codex Perez: an ancient Mayan hieroglyphic book. Glendale.

WINSOR, J.

1884–89   Narrative and critical history of America. 8 vols. Boston and New York.

XIMENEZ, FRANCISCO

1929–31   Historia de la Provincia de San Vicente de Chiapa y Guatemala de la Orden de Predicadores. 3 vols. Guatemala.

YAXKUKUL, CRONICA DE

See Martinez H., 1926.

ZAVALA, SILVIO, AND MARIA CASTELO

1939   Fuentes para la historia del trabajo en Nueva España. Vol. 1, 1575–1576. Mexico.

ZURITA, ALONSO DE

1891   Breve y sumaria relación de los señores y maneras y diferencias que había de ellos en la Nueva España. . . . *In* Nueva col. de doc. para la historia de México, 3: 71–227. Mexico.

Index

Acacia, 6
Acala, people, 111
Acalan, people, settled at Tixchel, 70
Acalan, province, 112
  capital of, 63, 109
  Chontal-speaking, 102
  history of, 126
  merchandise shipped through, 52
  merchants of, 107, 114
  River of, 102
Ac ek, defined, 96
Acanbaro, town, 155
Acanceh, town, 181, 185, 186
Acansip, or Acanzip, border site, 180, 187
Acasaguastlan, town, 116, 117
Achiote in Honduras, 121
  See also Annatto
Acknowledgments, iii-iv
Acosta, Jose de, 95
Acrocomia mexicana, 40
Adams, E. B., 124
Administrative policy, developed in New Spain, 134
Administrative unit, independent states transformed
  into an, iii
Adultery, penalties for, 32
Advocate general of the natives, 162
Advocates in suits, 31
Adzes, 50
Agave
  associated with wine, 43
  fabrics of, 47
  hedge around town, 68
Agouti, 41, 44
Agriculture
  culture founded on, 74
  deities of, 81
  in Honduras, 121
  in Tabasco, 104
  mentioned, 9, 38, 39
  methods of, 178
  system of, 38
    affected by environment, 45
    relation of warfare to, 65
Agua del Venado, town, 156
Aguacate, 40, 105
Aguada, defined, 6
  See also Ponds
Aguan River, 113
Aguilar, Geronimo de, 35, 56
Ah, *see* name following for titles and personal
  names beginning thus
Ah Balam Chay, landholding organization, 37
Ah Canul, province, 11, 12, 34
  chiefs friendly to Spaniards, 77
  confederacy of towns in, 62
  founded by Canul family, 58
  governors of towns in, 185
  letter from caciques of, 138
  named for Canul family, 181
  people of, 187
  settled after fall of Mayapan, 59
Ah chibal, defined, 33

Ah Chuy-kak, war god, 78
Ah cuch cabs, 129, 132
  defined, 62
  functions of, 63
Ah cunyah, defined, 95
Ah dzacyah, defined, 95
Ah holpop, see Holpop
Ah kayom, defined, 112
Ah Kin Chan Tacu, landholding organization, 37
Ah Kin Chel, province, 11, 12, 43
  consumption of cacao in, 56
  enemies of, 53
  government of, 59
  salt beds in, 69
  wars of, 68
Ah kin chilam, defined, 90
Ah kulel
  assistant of priest at Nohaa, 112
  became principal cacique, 136
Ah kulels
  assistants of batab, 62, 129
  at Mani land convention, 186, 192
  served as advocates, 31
Ah men, defined, 95
Ah Puch, death god, 76
Ah pul, defined, 94
Ahau
  day name, 86
  defined, 107
Akal, defined, 6
Akalches, defined, 6
Ake
  ruins near Dzonotake, wall and ditch at, 68
  ruins near Tixkokob, 177
Al, defined, 33
Alau, defined, 86
Alcalde
  Indian
    of Ticul, 190
    office of, 149, 150
    See also Alcaldes
  Spanish, 156
Alcalde mayor of Yucatan, 153
Alcaldes, Indian, 140, 144
  of Calotmul, 194
  celebrations given by, 29
  discussed, 132, 134
  drunkenness of, 143
Alfaro Santa Cruz, Melchor de
  map by, 98, 100, 184
  report by, 56, 99, 126
Alguacil
  compared with *tupil,* 64
  defined, 134
Alliances, military, 67, 70
Allspice, 7, 8
Almanac
  colonial native, 88
  modern Yucatecan, 9
  religious and astrological, in Dresden Codex, 88
  Spanish, 89, 96
Almehen, 33, 129, 158, 159

213

Almehenil, defined, 33
Almehenob, controlled commoners, 136
Altars, 71
 among Itza, 71
 at Campeche, 15
Alum, 107
Alvarado, Pedro de, 157
Am, divining stones called, 95
Amatique, Bay of, 113, 114, 115
Amber, stone called, 24, 55, 107, 110
Anahtes, or *analtes,* defined and discussed, 91, 92
Anahuac Xicalanco, province, 57, 98
 Aztec merchants met by lords of, 107
Ancestors, deified, 35
Ancestry of caciques, 164
  See also Genealogy
Andrade, M. J., viii
Anghiera, Pietro Martire d'(Peter Martyr), 103, 109, 122
Animals
 figures of, 19
 knowledge of, 95
 medicinal use of, 93
  See also individual names of
Annals, 91
Annatto, 39, 56
  See also Achiote
Annonas, 40
Anthurium tetragonum, 10, 40
Antidotes for poison, 93
Antiquities, a Maya science, 88
Antler used as a musical instrument, 30
Apianus, Petrus, map by, 13
Apiculture, 42
Apoplanesia paniculata, 65
Apostates, fugitive, 155, 167
Apozonalli, discussed, 55
Araceae, 39
Arboledas, defined, 20
Archbishop of Mexico, 157, 163
Archers
 in colonial times, 167, 168
 shot at sacrificial victim, 82
Architecture
 decadence of, 22, 84
 in interior of Yucatan, 19
 religious, 71
Archives
 at Mani, 178
 Mexican, 146, 150
 public, 161
Archivo General de la Nación, Mexico, iii, 141
Aristocracy
 caste, 65
 hereditary, 129
  See also Nobility; **Nobles**
Arithmetic, knowledge of, 86
Armadillo, 41, 105
Armlet, jawbone used as, 67
Armor, *see* Cotton, armor
Aroça, Gonzalo, *see* Guerrero, Gonzalo
Arrow
 among Jicaque, 119
 among Lacandon, 110
 among Olmeca, 110
 described, 65
 fish shot with, 47
 in Tabasco, 108

Arrow—*continued*
 sacrificial victim struck with, 82
 shot from barricades, 68
Arrowhead, flint, 49
Arrowroot, 119
Arson, penalty for, 32
Ascension Bay, 56, 116
Aspergill of snakes' tails, 81
Astapa, town, 100
Astrology
 almanac in Dresden Codex, 88
 European, 96
Astronomy
 calculations in, 84
 knowledge of, 84
 material for, in Codex Peresianus, 88
 Maya, 96
 observations in, 84
 phenomena of, 97
 symbols of, 73
 tables of, 85
 treatises on, 97
Atasta, town, 101
Atitlan, town, 157
Atole, gruel, 43
Attacks, surprise, 67
Attorney for the natives, 130
Audiencia
 at Mani, 186
 defined, 132
 of Guatemala, 134
Auto, 191
Avendaño y Loyola, Andres de, 8
 account of Cehache and Itza by, 27
 account of swamps in Peten by, 6
 familiar with books of prophecy, 91
 visited Itza, 90, 125
Avenues, 17, 102
Axayacatl, doubtful parentage of, 166
Axe heads, 50
Axes
 copper, 38, 66
 in Honduras, 121
 stone, 38
Ayikal, defined, 34
Azadon, discussed, 121
Azoteas, defined, 18
Aztec
 merchants, 55, 99, 107
 name for Tabasco, 98
 rulers, 166
 slave dealers, 53

Baatun
 defined, 10
 eaten in time of famine, 40
Bacabs, gods, 74, 75
 Ritual of the, 94, 95
Bacalar, Lake, 7
Bacalar, town
 road to, 179, 183, 193
 women's costume at, 24
Bah tok, defined, 49
Bak, defined, 86
Bak, Pedro, witness, 194
Baktun, defined, 85
Balam, Chilam, prophet, 15, 79, 92
  See also Chilam Balam

Lordship, 132
Lore, secret, of ruling class, 33
Lorencillo, *see* Graff, Laurent de
Los Chenes, district of Yucatan, 5
Lots cast by sorcerers, 95
Lovers, gods of, 78
Lucuma campechiana, 40
Lunario, defined, 88
   See also Almanac
Lunations, 84
Lundell, C. L., 5, 6, 7, 10, 122

Maat, defined, 55
Macal, discussed, 39
Macana, defined, 66
Macaw, 55, 78
Macehual
   became governor, 152
   defined, 149
   Indians, 150, 151
Macuahuitl, 66
Macuspana, town, 101
Magistrate, *batab* acted as, 62
Mahogany, 7, 8
Maize, 8, 9, 20
   among Chol Lacandon, 104, 111
   among Zoque, 110
   cakes served at banquets, 29
   commerce in, 52
   cooked in pit oven, 43
   culture based on, 118
   fields in Motagua basin, 115
   god, 45, 82, 104, 109
   in the Antilles, 3
   in Honduras, 119
   in Sula valley, 116
   in Tabasco, 104, 105, 106
   offerings of, 25, 80
   on Polochic River, 115
   paste placed with dead, 27
   planting of, 38
   preparation of, 43
   sacred character of plant, 45
   tribute of, 61
Malanga, defined, 39
Malaria, 177
Mam, defined, 193
Mama, town
   schoolteachers at, iv
   represented at Mani land conference, 185, 188,
     191, 192
Mamey, 105
Manatees, 48, 105
Manche Chol, people, 111
Mandon, defined, 63
Manebal, defined, 187
Mangrove swamp, 5
Mani, Book of Chilam Balam of, 177
Mani, Chronicle of, 98, 175
Mani, Crónica de, 185
Mani, province, 11, 12, 123, 175, 180, 183
   batabs in, 62
   described, 176, 182
   founded by Xiu, 58
   government of, 59, 60
   governors of, 192
   halach uinic of, 133, 187
   holpops in, 64

Mani, province—*continued*
   map of, 179
   separated from Campeche by forests, 184
   tribute of, 61
   wars of, 69
Mani, town, 37, 135, 192, 194
   archives at, 178
   audiencia at, 186
   convention at, 178
   governors assembled at, 191, 192
   land treaty made at, iii, 37, 60, 129, 130, 137,
     138, 163, 175, 176, 179, 185, 190, 192
   ruling family of, 57
   temple of Kukulcan at, 77
   Xiu established at, 176
Manrique, Felipe, judge, 179, 187
Mantle, 24, 154
   described, 23
   presented to guest at banquet, 29
Manuscript
   colonial Maya, 84, 85, 125, 152
   hieroglyphic, *see* Codices
Map
   native, 56, 184
     obtained by Cortez, 101
     of Province of Mani, 179, 180, 189
   of Mani, 180
   of Sotuta, 181
   of Tabasco, 98, 99, 100
"Marido y conjunta persona," legal term, 166
Marina, Cortez' interpreter, 115
Market, 52
   Aztec, 55
   court, 17, 51
   in Chikincheel, 56
   places, 109
   square, 17
Marriage
   account of, 26
   affected by kinship, 28
   books of, 161, 164
   ceremony, 26
Marshes southeast of Chunhuhub, 184
Martyr, Peter, *see* Anghiera, Pietro Martire d'
Masks
   of calabash shells, 50
   of comedians, 30
   ceremonial, 106
   encrusted with turquoises, 55
   plated with gold leaf, 54
   set in stone column, 91
   wooden, 50
Mason, J. A., 46
Masons at Cozumel, 49
Mat
   bones of rulers wrapped in, 71
   symbol of authority, 44, 64
   woven from bulrushes, 47
Matchmaker, 26
Mathematics, 84
Matrilineal reckoning of descent, 36
Matun, defined, 55
Maudslay, A. P., 115
Maxcanu, town, 180, 181, 185, 186
   batab of, 137, 138, 185, 191
   governor of, 144, 150, 162
   lands of, 167
   native militia of, 187

Trade
  on Usumacinta River, 101
  route, Tabasco to Yucatan, 101
    See also Commerce
Trails, 51
  battles on, 67
  described, 5
Travelers entertained gratis, 31, 52
Treaty of Mani, *see* Mani, land treaty made at
Tree gourd, 49
Trees
  planted, 19, 20
  sacred, 71, 72, 75
    See also Fruit trees
Trespass due to agricultural system, 65
Tribute
  exemption from, 148, 165
  gun carried while collecting, 155, 156
  of Indians, 131
  mantles, 170
  to *batab,* 62
  to *halach uinic,* 62
Tributos reales, 148
Tro-Cortesianus, Codex, 96
Troughs, stone, 49
Trujillo, 113, 116, 117, 118, 119, 120
Trumpets, 15, 30
Tuchumite, defined, 54
Tuk, defined, 40
Tula, town, 152, 175
Tulane University, iii, 52, 179, 184
Tulapan, legendary place name, 175
Tulum, ruins
  city wall at, 68
  flat roofs at, 18
Tulum che, defined, 20
Tulumqui, town, 68
Tumbala, town, 111
Tun, Don Diego Jacinto, of Cuncunul, 141, 143
Tun, Don Gaspar, of Homun, 191, 192
Tun, Don Lucas, of Cuncunul, 141, 159
Tun, Napuc, prophet, 90
Tun, precious stone, 54
Tun, time period, 85
  real basis of chronological system, 87
Tupil, defined, 64
Tupilco, Laguna de, 98
Tupiles, discussed, 134
Turkeys
  cold food, 93
  in Tabasco, 105
  raised for food, 40
  sacrifices of, 81, 112
Turquoise mosaic, 106
Turquoises, 55
Turtle
  eggs, 48
  stars, a constellation, 96
Tut, Diego, forest guard, 188
Tut, Pedro, forest guard, 188
Tutelage of minor heirs, 28
Tutepec, town, 145
Tutul Xiu, province of, 11
    See also Xiu, Tutul
Tuuayin, border site, 189
Tuyu, Don Gonzalo, of Tixcacaltuyu, 137, 186, 189, 191, 192
Typha angustifolia, 47

Tzab, constellation, 96
Tzekel, defined, 7
Tzimezakal, or Tzemezakal, pond and border site, 180, 187
Tzitzila, border site, 193
Tziuek, border site, 189
Tzompantli, defined, 19
Tzotzceh, defined, 86
Tzuc, Don Juan, 194
Tzuccacab, town, 176, 179, 180, 182, 183, 185, 192, 193, 194
  lands of, 189
Tzuccehche, border site, 193
Tzucila, town, hidalgos of, 159
Tzucox, border site, 190

Uac-mitun-ahau, god, 73, 75
Uaymil, province, 70
Uc, Andres, of Tzuccacab, 194
Uc, Bonifacio, nephew of Don Juan Xiu
  baptized at Ppencuyut, 161
  confirmed in rights of Xiu family, 164, 165
  exempted from tribute, 148
Ucan, Pedro, messenger to Mani conference, 186
Uci, ruins near Motul, 177
Ucum, town, cacao brought from, 52
Uinal, 85
Uitz, defined, 177
Ulapa, town, 100
Ulua River, 66, 113, 116, 117, 118
Uman, town, 181, 185
Uprising
  at Cisteil, 168
  at Sacalum, 167
Upstarts in official hierarchy, 34
Urns, burial, 28
Ursa Minor, 96
Utila Island, 120
Uxmal, ruins, 22, 187, 190
  deserted, 19
  history of, 12
  lands in region of, 179
  remains at, 59
  temples at, 21
  Xiu family at, 9, 175, 177
Uz, Don Diego, of Tekax, 185, 191, 192, 194

Valiente, Alonso, secretary of Cortez, 164
Valladolid, town, 22, 66, 123
    See also Saci
Vaults, burial, 28
Vecino, defined, 21
Vegetation of northern Yucatan, 7
Velasco, Governor, *see* Fernandez de Velasco
Velasco, Viceroy Luis de, 137
Venison, 41, 44
Venus, planet, 76, 84, 96
Veracruz, state of, 110, 117
  gold mined in, 54
  Nahuatl spoken in, 57
  pottery from, 55
Veragua, 14
Verapaz, 55, 115
Vice prevented by governor, 170
Viceroy
  appeals to, 144, 153
  declared cacique exempt from tribute, 149